THE CONSTITUTION OF ARBITRATION

This work is the first systematic discussion of arbitration from a constitutional perspective, covering the most important types of arbitration, including domestic arbitration in private law, international commercial arbitration, investment treaty arbitration, and state-to-state arbitration. Victor Ferreres Comella argues for the recognition of a constitutional right to arbitration in the private sphere and discusses the constraints that the state is entitled to place on this right. He also explores the conditions under which investment treaty arbitration is constitutionally legitimate, and highlights the shortcomings of international adjudication from a constitutional perspective. The rich landscape of arbitration is explained in clear language, avoiding unnecessary technical jargon. Using examples drawn from a wide variety of domains, Ferreres Comella bridges the gap between constitutional and arbitral theory.

Victor Ferreres Comella is Professor of Constitutional Law at Pompeu Fabra University School of Law. He is widely known for his scholarship on constitutional theory and comparative constitutional law and works as counsel at the law firm Uría-Menéndez. He has taught at both New York University and the University of Texas at Austin and has lectured at many institutions across Europe and the Americas. He is the author of many books and articles, including *Constitutional Courts and Democratic Values: A European Perspective*, and *The Constitution of Spain: A Contextual Analysis*. In 1996, he was awarded the "Francisco Tomás y Valiente" Prize, instituted by the Spanish Constitutional Court and the Centro de Estudios Políticos y Constitucionales. He obtained his JSD at the Yale Law School.

COMPARATIVE CONSTITUTIONAL LAW AND POLICY

Series Editors

Tom Ginsburg
University of Chicago

Zachary Elkins
University of Texas at Austin

Ran Hirschl
University of Toronto

Comparative constitutional law is an intellectually vibrant field that encompasses an increasingly broad array of approaches and methodologies. This series collects analytically innovative and empirically grounded work from scholars of comparative constitutionalism across academic disciplines. Books in the series include theoretically informed studies of single constitutional jurisdictions, comparative studies of constitutional law and institutions, and edited collections of original essays that respond to challenging theoretical and empirical questions in the field.

Books in the Series

Redrafting Constitutions in Democratic Orders: Theoretical and Comparative Perspectives
Edited by Gabriel L. Negretto

From Parchment to Practice: Implementing New Constitutions
Edited by Tom Ginsburg and Aziz Z. Huq

The Failure of Popular Constitution Making in Turkey: Regressing Towards Constitutional Autocracy
Edited by Felix Petersen and Zeynep Yanaşmayan

A Qualified Hope: The Indian Supreme Court and Progressive Social Change
Edited by Gerald N. Rosenberg, Sudhir Krishnaswamy and Shishir Bail

Constitutions in Times of Financial Crisis
Edited by Tom Ginsburg, Mark D. Rosen and Georg Vanberg

Reconstructing Rights: Courts, Parties, and Equality Rights in India, South Africa, and the United States
Stephan Stohler

Constitution-Making and Transnational Legal Order
Edited by Tom Ginsburg, Terence C. Halliday and Gregory Shaffer

Hybrid Constitutionalism: The Politics of Constitutional Review in the Chinese Special Administrative Regions
Eric C. Ip

The Politico-Legal Dynamics of Judicial Review: A Comparative Analysis
Theunis Roux

The Invisible Constitution in Comparative Perspective
Edited by Rosalind Dixon and Adrienne Stone

Constitutional Courts in Asia: A Comparative Perspective
Edited by Albert H. Y. Chen and Andrew Harding

Judicial Review in Norway: A Bicentennial Debate
Anine Kierulf

Constituent Assemblies
Edited by Jon Elster, Roberto Gargarella, Vatsal Naresh, and Bjorn Erik Rasch

The DNA of Constitutional Justice in Latin America: Politics, Governance, and Judicial Design
Daniel M. Brinks and Abby Blass

The Adventures of the Constituent Power: Beyond Revolutions?
Andrew Arato

Constitutions, Religion and Politics in Asia: Indonesia, Malaysia and Sri Lanka
Dian A. H. Shah

Canada in the World: Comparative Perspectives on the Canadian Constitution
Edited by Richard Albert and David R. Cameron

Courts and Democracies in Asia
Po Jen Yap

Proportionality: New Frontiers, New Challenges
Edited by Vicki C. Jackson and Mark Tushnet

Constituents before Assembly: Participation, Deliberation, and Representation in the Crafting of New Constitutions
Todd A. Eisenstadt, A. Carl LeVan, and Tofigh Maboudi

Assessing Constitutional Performance
Edited by Tom Ginsburg and Aziz Huq

Buddhism, Politics and the Limits of Law: The Pyrrhic Constitutionalism of Sri Lanka
Benjamin Schonthal

Engaging with Social Rights: Procedure, Participation and Democracy in South Africa's Second Wave
Brian Ray

Constitutional Courts As Mediators: Armed Conflict, Civil-Military Relations, and the Rule of Law in Latin America
Julio Ríos-Figueroa

Perils of Judicial Self-Government in Transitional Societies
David Kosař

Making We the People: Democratic Constitutional Founding in Postwar Japan and South Korea
Chaihark Hahm and Sung Ho Kim

Radical Deprivation on Trial: The Impact of Judicial Activism on Socioeconomic Rights in the Global South
César Rodríguez-Garavito and Diana Rodríguez-Franco

Unstable Constitutionalism: Law and Politics in South Asia
Edited by Mark Tushnet and Madhav Khosla

Magna Carta and Its Modern Legacy
Edited by Robert Hazell and James Melton

Constitutions and Religious Freedom
Frank B. Cross

International Courts and the Performance of International Agreements: A General Theory with Evidence from the European Union
Clifford J. Carrubba and Matthew J. Gabel

Reputation and Judicial Tactics: A Theory of National and International Courts
Shai Dothan

Social Difference and Constitutionalism in Pan-Asia
Edited by Susan H. Williams

Constitutionalism in Asia in the Early Twenty-First Century
Edited by Albert H. Y. Chen

Constitutions in Authoritarian Regimes
Edited by Tom Ginsburg and Alberto Simpser

Presidential Legislation in India: The Law and Practice of Ordinances
Shubhankar Dam

Social and Political Foundations of Constitutions
Edited by Denis J. Galligan and Mila Versteeg

Consequential Courts: Judicial Roles in Global Perspective
Edited by Diana Kapiszewski, Gordon Silverstein, and Robert A. Kagan

Comparative Constitutional Design
Edited by Tom Ginsburg

Towering Judges
Edited by Rehan Abeyratne and Iddo Porat

The Constitution of Arbitration
Victor Ferreres Comella

The Constitution of Arbitration

VICTOR FERRERES COMELLA
Universitat Pompeu Fabra

CAMBRIDGE
UNIVERSITY PRESS

CAMBRIDGE
UNIVERSITY PRESS

University Printing House, Cambridge CB2 8BS, United Kingdom

One Liberty Plaza, 20th Floor, New York, NY 10006, USA

477 Williamstown Road, Port Melbourne, VIC 3207, Australia

314–321, 3rd Floor, Plot 3, Splendor Forum, Jasola District Centre, New Delhi – 110025, India

79 Anson Road, #06–04/06, Singapore 079906

Cambridge University Press is part of the University of Cambridge.

It furthers the University's mission by disseminating knowledge in the pursuit of education, learning, and research at the highest international levels of excellence.

www.cambridge.org
Information on this title: www.cambridge.org/9781108842839
DOI: 10.1017/9781108906395

First published 2021

A catalogue record for this publication is available from the British Library.

Library of Congress Cataloging-in-Publication Data
NAMES: Ferreres Comella, Victor, author.
TITLE: The Constitution of Arbitration / Victor Ferreres Comella, Universitat Pompeu Fabra (Barcelona).
DESCRIPTION: Cambridge, United Kingdom; New York, NY : Cambridge University Press, 2021. | Series: Comparative constitutional law and policy | Includes bibliographical references and index.
IDENTIFIERS: LCCN 2020039518 (print) | LCCN 2020039519 (ebook) | ISBN 9781108842839 (hardback) | ISBN 9781108822824 (paperback) | ISBN 9781108906395 (ebook)
SUBJECTS: LCSH: Arbitration (International law) | International commercial arbitration.
CLASSIFICATION: LCC KZ6115 .F47 2021 (print) | LCC KZ6115 (ebook) | DDC 347/.09–dc23
LC record available at https://lccn.loc.gov/2020039518
LC ebook record available at https://lccn.loc.gov/2020039519

ISBN 978-1-108-84283-9 Hardback

For Carla

Contents

Acknowledgments

In the course of writing this book, I have incurred many intellectual debts. I am deeply grateful to several colleagues at the University of Texas at Austin School of Law, who made it possible for me to start a research project on arbitration. About a decade ago, in the spring of 2010, I had an interesting conversation with Larry Sager – at that time the Dean of the Law School – on the practical importance of arbitration and the need to study it from a constitutional perspective. He convinced me to offer a course on that subject and suggested that I should coteach it with Robert Bone, a distinguished expert on civil procedure. And so we did. We started in the spring of 2011 and have repeated the experience almost every year. It has been a great honor to coteach with Bob, whose intellectual rigor and pedagogical skills are superb. I have learned a lot. Many of the ideas I advance in the book are the upshot of long conversations with him. I am also in great debt to Alan Rau, one of the leading arbitration scholars in the world, who offered all kinds of help as soon as he learned that I was interested in this field. We have spent lots of hours talking about arbitration, which is our common passion. His knowledge of the theory and practice of arbitration is so vast that he never ceases to impress me every time we talk about any issue that is related to arbitration – which means almost every time we talk. I have already mentioned Larry Sager, but I need to add that Larry and I have cotaught a seminar on globalization for several years, and we have discussed extensively the constitutional issues surrounding investment treaty arbitration when running that seminar, which has been a source of great insights for me. Larry has an enormous capacity to imagine new ways of thinking about problems and to find the right institutional and doctrinal solutions to them. I am very thankful to him for sharing so much intellectually rewarding time. Another person whose help I must acknowledge is Andrés Jana. It has been a pleasure to interact with him during his visits to the University of Texas. Students have always loved his participation in the courses and seminars. They have appreciated his professional stature as a prominent international lawyer, as well as his academic sensitivity. Andrés has been extremely supportive of my project since the very beginning, and I have to thank him warmly for that.

So Larry, Bob, Alan, and Andrés have created the intellectual and human environment at the University of Texas without which I would have been unable to start thinking about arbitration in any serious way. They all read earlier drafts of my work and provided excellent comments and suggestions. I tend to view them as an "arbitral quartet," each playing a different instrument, altogether producing an interesting musical outcome. My gratitude extends to Dean Ward Farnsworth, who has always been supportive of my collaboration with the University of Texas as a visiting professor over the years.

I should mention that my legal scholarship has been strongly influenced by the teachings and writings of Owen Fiss. Although Fiss has not centered on arbitration in his work, his powerful ideas on the law and the role of courts in the legal process can be fruitfully made to bear on discussions about arbitration. I hope that my qualified defense of arbitration in this book is in keeping with the basic pillars of the Fissian edifice. In any event, I wholeheartedly thank Owen for his sharp comments on earlier versions of this book, and for his enduring friendship.

I am much obliged to Pau Bossacoma, Ramón Casas, Rosalind Dixon, Bardo Fassbender, Alex Ferreres, Mattias Kumm, Cristian Gual, Fernando Pantaleón, and Miguel Virgós, who generously read earlier versions of the book manuscript and supplied excellent criticisms and suggestions. They saved me from many mistakes. They are not responsible, of course, for the remaining errors and flaws.

I also want to express my thanks to the various audiences that provided useful feedback when I gave presentations of my work at different universities, including Universitat Pompeu Fabra (Spain), Instituto de Empresa (Spain), Università degli Studi di Roma Tre (Italy), ITAM (Mexico), Wissenschaftszentrum Berlin Für Sozialforschung (Germany), as well as at conferences organized by SELA (Seminario en Latinoamérica de Teoría Constitucional y Política) in Lima (Perú), and by the Energy Center of the University of Texas at Austin, in Santiago de Chile (Chile).

At Pompeu Fabra University in Barcelona I have been blessed for more than two decades now with the friendship of admirable colleagues. They have made my academic life delightful in so many ways. I want to thank, in particular, the head of the department of constitutional law, Alejandro Saiz Arnaiz, for his constant encouragement and advice, and for his wonderful capacity to make all the members of the department act as a united team.

While writing this book I have had the opportunity to participate as a consultant at Uría Menéndez law firm in Spain. I thank Luis de Carlos, José María Segovia, Salvador Sánchez-Terán, Antonio Herrera, Jesús Remón, Miguel Virgós, Fernando Pantaleón, Gabriel Bottini, Cristian Gual, Daniel Sarmiento, Óscar Morales, Manuel Álvarez, and many other lawyers at the firm for having me on board and giving me the chance to work on interesting and complex cases. It is a source of intellectual challenges to interact with the formidable teams of lawyers at the firm.

I am also very grateful to Zach Elkins, Ran Hirschl, and Tom Ginsburg, the editors of the Cambridge University Press series on Comparative Constitutional Law and Policy, as well as Matt Gallaway, Senior Editor with the Press, for their endorsement of my book proposal and their excellent suggestions to improve the manuscript. During the production stages of the book, it was a pleasure to work with Daddis Cameron, James Baker, Akash Datchinamurthy, and Helen Kitto, whose performance was outstanding.

Finally, let me say that I would have been unable to carry out this project without the love and support of my family, all the members of which have been looking forward to the date when the book would finally be out. They have been extremely patient with me during all these years of time-consuming work. Many thanks!

Introduction

The Varieties of Arbitration

"War is too important to be left to the generals," George Clemenceau famously said. Likewise, we can contend, arbitration is too important to be left to arbitrators and experts in arbitration. Legal scholars and practitioners, as well as ordinary citizens, should be aware of the significant part this institution plays in our world. They should join the conversation over its normative foundation and the specific shape it ought to take.

Of course many people have a rough idea what arbitration is about. They know it's a way of resolving disputes without going to court. By way of arbitration, the contending parties select someone they trust to adjudicate their difference. The public is probably less cognizant of the fact that the decision made by the arbitrator (the "award") is conferred great force by the law: it binds the parties as if it were a court judgment. Few people, in any event, are familiar with the mechanics of arbitration.

Arbitration has traditionally attracted critics, who have pointed out that the use of arbitral procedures may jeopardize core legal rights of the parties and under-enforce public law. Critical voices have been heard in the media, thus contributing to a general alertness to the potential drawbacks of arbitration.

It is striking, in this context, that most constitutional scholars have neglected arbitration in their studies. They have tended to treat arbitration as a marginal institution, a small piece in the grand scheme of things constitutional. Experts in arbitration, in turn, have failed to link their analyses to a broader constitutional discourse. In spite of the brilliance and sophistication they have often displayed in their academic work, such experts have generally forgotten about the constitution.

My ambition in writing this book has been to help establish bridges between these two epistemic communities. Constitutional theory, I believe, can shed interesting light on arbitration. What the constitution says regarding fundamental rights, democracy, the rule of law, checks and balances, and the role of the judiciary, for example, cannot be ignored when we reflect upon the place of arbitration in a modern legal order. We live in a constitutional age, after all, and constitutions have an enormous impact on the structure and evolution of legal systems. On the other hand, constitutional theory will benefit greatly from the discussions experts in arbitration have engaged in. Their writings offer profound insights on adjudication, which can help constitutional lawyers enlarge and refine their own intellectual constructions.

The book I have finally come up with is quite broad in scope. There is, indeed, a large variety of settings where arbitration has flourished. The parties to a contract, for example, may stipulate that any future controversy concerning the performance of the contract will be resolved by arbitrators. This form of arbitration is particularly prominent when private actors engage in international legal transactions. A large number of arbitral institutions have been created around the world to facilitate this kind of arbitration. Although the parties may decide to select arbitrators and design arbitral procedures by themselves, they are often inclined to use the administrative services provided by specialized centers, which play a critical part in the evolution of arbitral practices through the distinct rules they craft.

But arbitration transcends the boundaries of private law. Consider investment treaty arbitration. Many countries have entered into international agreements according substantive protections to foreign investors. States commit themselves to treat investors fairly, for example, and to pay compensation if property needs to be expropriated. Such treaties typically include clauses enabling investors to initiate arbitral proceedings to vindicate their rights against the host state. These rights are of a public law nature.

Also in the international arena, states have traditionally brought their differences to arbitral tribunals for an effective settlement. Before permanent courts were set up in the twentieth century, arbitration was the only mechanism states could use if they wished a neutral institution to adjust their controversies. For a long historical period, indeed, the development of public international law was placed in the hands of arbitrators.

So arbitration operates in many different regions of the legal landscape, involving both private and public law, and both domestic and international law. If we wish to acquire an informed understanding of the world of arbitration, we need to cast a wide net that will capture the most important modalities of arbitration.

The book is thus structured in three parts, dealing with arbitration in the sphere of private law, investment treaty arbitration, and state-to-state arbitration, respectively. Here is a brief summary of the central topics we will be exploring.

Part I focuses on arbitration in private law. Any constitutional inquiry into arbitration must begin at the national level. It is there that the central debates about the role of arbitration in a modern legal system have traditionally been entertained. We will ask ourselves, first, why is it normatively important for individuals to be empowered to resolve their disputes through arbitration? As I will argue, there is a liberal case in favor of arbitration. A legal order that respects private autonomy should grant private parties the right to arbitrate their disagreements. There are good arguments, moreover, sponsoring the constitutionalization of such a right. Whether the right to arbitration should ultimately figure in the constitution, however, depends on certain assumptions concerning the scope of the constitutional realm and the conditions under which rights may be restricted. As we will discuss, anchoring the right to arbitration in the constitution is easier in some countries than it is in others, depending on specific features of their distinctive constitutional traditions.

The right to arbitration cannot be absolute, of course. The state is authorized to establish constraints. The law typically spells out certain requirements that arbitral agreements and awards must meet before courts can enforce them. Which requirements are warranted and which ones are not? We will consider, in particular, norms concerning impartiality, fairness, nondiscrimination, and reason-giving.

And what happens when mandatory law is at stake in a given dispute? That is, when the state does not allow private parties to contract away from certain norms that protect basic interests and values, is it nevertheless possible for such norms to be arbitrated? And how should the law respond to the unequal bargaining position of the parties, as is the case in consumer and employment contracts, for example? When discussing mandatory law, it is important to bear in mind that part of that law is embodied in the constitution. What should arbitrators do when they confront a piece of legislation they deem unconstitutional?

A further question concerns the role of arbitration in the lawmaking process. Courts contribute to this process through the production of case law. What part should arbitrators play in this regard? Are they well-equipped to generate a body of consistent rulings? Should they be expected to do so? Once we have a picture of the space that arbitration is entitled to occupy in the legal order, we will address the issue of arbitral independence. Is the degree of independence that arbitrators possess the right one? Maybe they are too detached from the state? Regular courts are linked to the democratic branches in various ways, and we generally think there are good reasons for this. Should we be worried that arbitrators are not so linked?

Part I closes with a specific chapter on international commercial arbitration. In private law transactions potentially involving the jurisdiction of more than one state, it is common for the contending parties to turn to arbitration. Local courts are usually avoided. There are two main reasons for this preference. One has to do with the legal infrastructure that has been erected at the international level, which is very favorable to arbitration. The New York Convention of 1958 on the Recognition and Enforcement of Foreign Arbitral Awards, in particular, is a powerful instrument to protect and enforce arbitral agreements and awards. There is no equivalent instrument that effectively secures the execution of choice-of-court agreements and court judgments on a global stage, as we will see. The other reason that explains arbitration's bloom in this field is connected to the need to construct a neutral forum where local prejudices or biases are excluded. Domestic courts are distrusted, for they may favor the local party to the controversy. The neutral forum argument in support of arbitration raises interesting issues about the best strategies we should pursue to achieve objectivity in a world where nationality seems to matter. In the international commercial setting, moreover, the question needs to be posed concerning the role of arbitrators in the lawmaking process. Do international arbitrators produce a body of transnational law that is autonomous from democratically enacted domestic law? Are there reasons to be concerned about this?

We then move, in Part II of the book, to investor-state arbitration. As already mentioned, many international treaties enable foreign investors to start arbitration proceedings against the host state, if the latter violates certain substantive protections. The main arbitral facility in the investment field is ICSID (the International Centre for Settlement of Investment Disputes), which is housed within the World Bank.

A central question to take up is whether it is constitutionally acceptable for the existing legal regime to grant foreign investors this distinctive form of protection. Is the protection they get excessive? Are local investors discriminated against, to the extent that they do not benefit from the rules and structures that apply to foreigners? The issue has constitutional implications, of course. Constitutions typically guarantee the right not to be discriminated against on grounds of nationality or origin. What reasons can be adduced to justify the special regime that has been set up to safeguard the interests of foreign investors? Under what conditions is that regime in conformity with constitutional standards? Critics of investment arbitration have argued that arbitrators are biased in favor of foreign investors. As a result, local investors suffer unequal treatment and the state's power to regulate matters in the public interest is unduly curtailed. Is this criticism warranted? How should arbitrators go about deciding cases in a manner that meets constitutional standards of equality and respects the regulatory powers of the state?

In the investment arena, arbitrators are expected to play a prominent role in the development of the law. How effective are the existing arbitral arrangements, however, in securing adjudicative consistency? Questions emerge, moreover, about the political checks arbitrators should be subject to, in order to inject a degree of democratic legitimacy into the arbitral regime. At this juncture, an important issue concerns the desirability of designing permanent tribunals, which might supersede classical forms of arbitration.

Investor-state arbitration also poses intricate questions regarding the coherence of public international law. The treaties that protect foreign investors need to be accommodated within supranational organizations, such as the European Union. They are to be harmonized, too, with international instruments that safeguard human rights, including workers' rights, indigenous rights, public health, the environment, and other public goods and values. So we need interpretive tools and institutional mechanisms to ensure that investment arbitration fits with other pieces of the international legal order, both vertically and horizontally.

Finally, Part III of the book looks at state-to-state arbitration. When it comes to the adjudication of disputes among states, public international law exhibits certain features that are absent in domestic law. In contrast to what is true of adjudication by domestic courts, international courts need the consent of the contending parties to gain the authority to settle a controversy through a binding decision. No international tribunal has been vested with compulsory jurisdiction to adjust differences between states. If we contemplate this aspect of the international order from the platform set up by national constitutions, we can perceive its rudimentary character. As I will be arguing, we should not validate or normalize this shortcoming of international law in the name of state sovereignty. We should instead be critical of the arbitral foundations of international adjudication.

As we will see, the contrast between international courts and arbitral tribunals is a nuanced one. We will discuss various questions regarding state-to-state disputes. What potential advantages does arbitration offer? What are its downsides? Should certain types of norms, such as "peremptory" rules of international law, be excluded from the arbitral forum? What is the task of arbitration in the development of the law? And when is arbitration likely to be used to settle controversies between members of an international organization?

So these are the main themes of the book. Although the scope of the inquiry will be broad, I will center on issues that are particularly salient from a constitutional perspective. At some junctures during this *tour d'horizon*, moreover, I will leave questions open. My hope is that by offering a general picture of the arbitral landscape, and by using constitutional principles and concepts to interpret what we see in that landscape, we can attain a better understanding of this fascinating part of modern law.

I should note that the book is written in a comparative spirit. As just explained, it compares distinct types of arbitration that have developed in different domains: domestic arbitration in private law, international commercial arbitration, investor-state arbitration, and state-to-state arbitration. The arbitral experience exhibits a rich variety of forms, even if common characteristics can be observed. The book is also comparative in that it uses examples drawn from different countries and international organizations to illustrate the basic ideas.

It also bears emphasizing that my discussion takes place at a normative theoretical level. Since I want to subject arbitration to constitutional scrutiny, I need to presuppose certain moral principles and values. Only in light of such standards is it possible to endorse or criticize existing laws and practices and suggest potential reforms. The principles and values I will assume throughout the book are those that flow from the liberal democratic tradition. I rely on this tradition to elaborate a normative constitutional discourse on arbitration. The discourse, therefore, cannot have a universal reach, for it only makes sense in the context of constitutional orders that are committed to liberal and democratic political conceptions. On the other hand, the theory I want to develop is not confined to the law of any particular jurisdiction. It seeks to be general. Each constitutional legal order has its own specific traits, of course, which need to be taken into account when constructing legal doctrines to operationalize abstract principles and values. It is nevertheless possible, I submit, to enter a constitutional conversation that transcends those specific features. This book should thus be taken to be a contribution to liberal-democratic constitutional theory regarding arbitration. The examples gathered from several jurisdictions are brought to the discussion for illustrative purposes, to better understand major problems that are of common concern in liberal democracies.

PART I

Arbitration and Private Law

1

The Liberal Case for Arbitration

1.1 WHAT IS ARBITRATION?

To start our discussion, we need to have a preliminary idea of how arbitration works. As already noted in the Introduction, arbitration is a dispute-resolution mechanism that makes it possible for the parties to settle their controversies without ending up in court. The most salient feature of arbitration is that it rests on consent. It is only because the parties agree to submit their differences to the judgment of arbitrators that the latter get the authority to decide. The law does not confer on arbitrators an adjudicative authority that is detached from the will of the parties. An agreement to arbitrate is normally signed in advance, before the controversy arises. It is also possible, though less common, for parties to choose to arbitrate their dispute after it has crystallized.[1]

Courts, in contrast, exercise a governmental power over litigants. Being part of the machinery of the state, courts wield legal "power" (*potestas*). Thus, when a plaintiff brings a suit to the competent court, the consent of the defendant is irrelevant to establish the foundation of that court's authority to render a binding decision. In the same way that the state exercises other powers (to tax, to impose sanctions, to expropriate, to regulate, for example), without the consent of the person that is subject to those powers, the state is also vested with the power to adjudicate controversies brought by plaintiffs, without the consent of defendants.

Another notable characteristic of arbitration is that the adjudicators are typically chosen by the disputants. The parties can directly agree on the name of the arbitrators, or they can request an arbitral center to designate them. The parties can also determine the number of arbitrators: they can appoint a single arbitrator, or they can set up an arbitral tribunal instead, usually comprising three members. Courts, in contrast, are formed and run by the state. Litigants cannot freely pick the judges. It is

[1] As we will see later in the book, the laws in some countries have established compulsory forms of arbitration for certain types of controversies, in which case the foundations of arbitral authority are disconnected from the consent of the parties. Throughout the book, however, we will study the standard modality of arbitration, which is grounded in the agreement of the disputants.

true that the parties can sometimes choose a particular judicial forum among several alternatives that the law offers. But the leeway parties enjoy in this regard is nothing compared to the broad range of possibilities they can avail themselves of when they resort to arbitration.

Most commonly, the parties will pay the arbitrators for their services. In the past, it was not rare for arbitrators to charge nothing for their performance. In some settings, arbitration was an honorific activity gratuitously undertaken. Nowadays, however, arbitrators are generally remunerated. If the parties use an arbitration center, moreover, they will have to pay for the administrative services it delivers. Courts, on the other hand, are funded by the state. Litigants may be required to pay some fees, but such fees defray a small fraction of the administrative expenses associated with adjudicating a controversy in court. The expenses are covered by the state with taxpayer money. And judges, of course, are public officials whose salary is paid by the government.[2]

Another difference between arbitration and litigation in court is that the jurisdiction of arbitrators dissolves after they have settled the controversy they have been charged with. An arbitral tribunal is a one-shot institution. Courts, in contrast, are permanent bodies. Their existence transcends the specific disputes they resolve.

The procedures in arbitration also depart, sometimes significantly, from those typically unfolding in a courtroom. There is lots of flexibility in arbitration in this connection. The law empowers the parties to specify the procedures arbitrators must employ. The parties can design the procedures themselves, on an ad hoc basis, or they can select the rules that an arbitral center or some other institution has already laid down. The same degree of liberty is not offered to the parties that litigate in court.[3]

One of the remarkable things about arbitration is the wide variety of forms it exhibits. What rules must arbitrators consider when deciding the merits of a dispute, for example? As we will discuss later in the book, arbitrators are often instructed to apply the relevant law produced by public authorities. Sometimes, however, the parties direct the arbitrators to decide in light of their own sense of justice, taking into account the particular circumstances of the case, without being bound by the existing body of law. This is called *ex aequo et bono* arbitration. The disputants may even stipulate that arbitrators must decide in accordance with the moral principles

2 It should be noted, however, that fixed judicial salaries are typical of modern states that have attained a high level of bureaucratization. In earlier periods, judges in many countries received fees from the contending parties. Interestingly, it has sometimes been argued that one of the reasons for the traditional hostility of English judges toward arbitration had to do with competition for fees. At a time when judges received no fixed salaries, they were not interested in facilitating arbitration, since arbitration would diminish their revenues. This thesis about the sources of judicial hostility to arbitration has been contested, however. On this controversy, see Derek Roebuck, "The Myth of Judicial Jealousy," 10 *Arbitration International* 395 (1994).

3 There is certainly some room for parties to make procedural rules when they go to court. The range of choices when they use arbitration, however, is much wider. On this issue, see Robert G. Bone, "Party Rulemaking: Making Procedural Rules Through Party Choice," 90 *Texas Law Review* 1329 (2012).

of a particular religion. In some instances, the parties go so far as to limit the range of solutions that arbitrators can choose from. In "final offer arbitration," for example, each party submits its "final offer" to the arbitrator after making the relevant arguments to support its position. The arbitrator then decides which is the most reasonable offer, without being allowed to construct an intermediate solution.

There is also rich variety with regard to the professional background of arbitrators. Quite often, arbitrators are trained in the law, but they may also be experts in technical or scientific matters, or businesspeople with experience in a specific commercial or industrial sector, or respected members of a religious community.

Do lawyers participate in arbitral proceedings as counsel for the contending parties? Sometimes they do, sometimes they don't. The level of "legalization" of the arbitral process differs from place to place and over time. It depends, among other things, on whether arbitrators are required to apply the law and whether they must themselves be lawyers.

There is also room for flexibility in terms of the degree of "symmetry" arbitral arrangements display. Normally, both parties to the arbitration agreement have the right to use arbitration if a dispute breaks out. Sometimes, however, only one of the parties is given such a right. Likewise, arbitration is typically symmetric in that the arbitral award binds the two parties exactly in the same way. Sometimes, however, the arbitration agreement specifies that only one of the parties will be bound by the arbitral award, so that the other can bring suit in court if he or she disagrees with the decision. Other times, the binding force of the arbitral decision is conditioned on the damages award not exceeding a certain limit.

So arbitration has many faces. There is a large array of institutional and procedural schemes that are offered to the parties who resort to it.

Arbitration, of course, has a long history. Underdeveloped forms of arbitration must have existed in most parts of the world before courts were set up. After all, it takes a relatively developed state to create a judicial machinery. What is striking is how arbitration has grown around the globe in the past decades, after a long historical period during which the law in many countries treated arbitration with a certain degree of hostility.

For a long time, indeed, arbitration agreements were not specifically enforceable. In many jurisdictions, courts would not stay judicial proceedings and send the case to arbitration if one of the parties invoked an arbitration clause contained in a contract. This meant that, in practice, arbitral agreements had no legal bite. The kinds of controversies to which arbitration could apply, moreover, were very limited: while purely contractual claims were amenable to arbitration, claims based on mandatory norms embodied in legislation were not. The idea that arbitration could be used to adjudicate rights that the parties were not allowed to give up by way of contracts, or to enforce norms that safeguard public interests, was completely rejected.

At present, in contrast, the laws in many nations promote arbitration. They facilitate the judicial enforcement of arbitral agreements and awards, and they espouse an expansive conception of the matters that are susceptible to arbitral decision-making. In part, this policy in favor of arbitration has been influenced by the international commercial community. In this connection, the United Nations Commission on International Trade Law (UNCITRAL) adopted in 1985 a Model Law on International Commercial Arbitration that many countries in the world have followed. The Model Law, which was later amended in 2006, was designed to assist states in modernizing their laws on arbitral procedure. The pro-arbitration spirit of that document has penetrated many domestic legal systems.[4]

After this introductory overview of arbitration, we now turn to the following normative question: Why should arbitration be granted public backing by the state? What are the normative moral grounds on which this protection rests?

1.2 ARBITRATION AND PRIVATE AUTONOMY

A liberal case can be made, I want to argue, for the law to enable private parties to use an arbitral forum to resolve their controversies. The argument in support of arbitration appeals to the value of private autonomy.

In a liberal political regime, individuals are assumed to be the best judges of their own interests in most contexts, under appropriate conditions of rationality. It is therefore justified for them to be accorded the freedom to arrange their own affairs.[5] Individuals are recognized the moral capacity to form and pursue a conception of the good life. The state must therefore respect the choices they make in their private sphere.[6]

Of course individuals may have limited information, or may suffer from cognitive biases, or may experience weakness of the will, causing them to do things that prove to be contrary to their true interests. The government through its laws may sometimes have to "nudge" individuals in a particular direction to prevent them from making wrong decisions.[7] Individuals, moreover, need to be protected when they are

[4] For a comparative view of modern arbitration laws, see Gary Born, *International Commercial Arbitration* (Alphen aan den Rijn: Kluwer Law International, 2014); and Stephan Balthasar (ed.), *International Commercial Arbitration. International Conventions, Country Reports and Comparative Analysis* (Munich: C.H. Beck; Oxford: Hart; Baden-Baden: Nomos, 2016). For earlier comparative studies, see Julian D. M. Lew, Loukas A. Mistelis, and Stefan Michael Kröll, *Comparative International Commercial Arbitration* (The Hague: Kluwer Law International, 2003); and Jean-François Poudret and Sébastien Besson, *Comparative Law of International Arbitration* (London: Sweet & Maxwell, 2007). Although all these books focus on international commercial arbitration, they also provide a wealth of information regarding domestic arbitration.

[5] The classical exposition of this idea is John Stuart Mill, *On Liberty* (1859).

[6] See Ronald Dworkin, *Sovereign Virtue. The Theory and Practice of Equality* (Cambridge, Massachusetts: Harvard University Press, 2002).

[7] For a comprehensive treatment of this governmental strategy, see Richard H. Thaler and Cass R. Sunstein, *Nudge. Improving Decisions About Health, Wealth, and Happiness* (New York: Penguin, 2009).

subject to structures of social or economic subordination. We cannot be oblivious to the material constraints affecting individual choice. Furthermore, considerations related to human dignity may justify the establishment of rules that entrench certain individual interests against alienation in the market. The value of individual liberty, therefore, is part of a larger normative whole that includes norms of equality and dignity. It remains the case, however, that in a liberal political order a wide space must be opened up for the exercise of individual judgment and choice. Individuals must be able to lead their own lives, even if the choices they make turn out to be wrong.

In a liberal state, individuals are accordingly granted a basic right to private autonomy that enables them to engender legal relationships with other individuals and to shape the content of such relationships, in the form of specific rights and obligations. Freedom of contract, the right to association, and the right to marry, for example, flow from this basic right to private autonomy.

In many areas, the right to private autonomy extends to the legal persons that are created by the agreement of private individuals, such as corporations, foundations, and associations. (In this book, I will often use the expression "individuals" or "private individuals" in a broad sense, to cover different forms of private persons.)

One of the implications of the recognition of private autonomy is that the law must make it possible for individuals to resolve their disagreements through arbitration. The basic right to private autonomy supports the more specific "right to arbitration." The contending parties should be entitled to choose the method they believe will work best to settle a current or future dispute affecting their interests. The nature of the relationships private persons develop depends, in part, on the procedures they decide to employ to resolve controversies. Moreover, private persons often have good reasons to prefer arbitration to litigation in court. Arbitration presents some important advantages, as we will see later. The state should therefore channel this preference for arbitration through the appropriate set of laws.

Individuals cannot, of course, decide how controversies are to be settled that affect third parties. Nor is it permissible for them to impinge upon the basic principles and values animating the legal order. As we will discuss, the law can subject arbitration to significant constraints to protect the public good. But with regard to the interests that individuals can freely dispose of, the contending parties should be understood to have a prima facie right to elect arbitration as a dispute-resolution mechanism.

The right to arbitration coheres with other aspects of private autonomy that liberal states typically recognize in their laws, regarding the resolution of controversies. Importantly, individuals are generally empowered to negotiate settlements to bring their disputes to an end. To the extent that individuals can freely dispose of their rights and interests, the law recognizes the legal force of settlements. This being so, it would be inconsistent for the law not to enable the contending parties to resort to arbitration.

Actually, the arbitral process is designed to be an impartial adjudicative mechanism, since a neutral third party is charged with the task of finding the facts and applying the law (or the pertinent substantive standards) to the dispute. As we will study, arbitration is governed by rules that seek to secure its reliability in terms of enforcing the relevant norms. Settlements, in contrast, are more problematic. The imbalances in bargaining power may lead the parties to agree to settlements that greatly deviate from the decision that a neutral adjudicator would have reached.[8] It would be paradoxical, therefore, if a legal order based on private autonomy were to allow settlements but not arbitration, given that the latter is a more objective way of resolving controversies than the former.

It is important to understand that the right to arbitration that is being advanced here cannot generally be exercised without the help of the state. A purely private ordering for arbitration is only feasible in special settings, such as in closely knit communities, or in markets where a small number of businesses are engaged in ongoing relationships. Private institutions can sometimes threaten their members with expulsion from the group or with the imposition of reputational costs if they fail to comply with arbitral agreements and awards.[9] Most often, however, the intervention of public authorities is indispensable to guarantee arbitration's viability. A legal framework must be built defining the conditions under which arbitration agreements can be brought to legal existence and become enforceable. Arbitration agreements are thus anchored in a legal system. As we will see, moreover, courts are needed to back up the arbitral process. As a general rule, arbitration cannot succeed as an effective mechanism for resolving disputes without the assistance of courts. Furthermore, arbitral awards need to be treated as court judgments in many respects, if they are to have significant legal bite. Arbitration is thus a legal institution constructed and shaped by the state, as well as an expression of the autonomy of the parties. It exhibits a mixed public–private quality.

In this context, it may be useful to compare arbitration to marriage, in spite of the many differences between the two. Marriage as a legal institution cannot exist effectively without the state. Indeed, we need laws that specify the properties that a particular arrangement between two individuals must possess before it can be publicly regarded as marital. Certain governmental organs, moreover, are typically in charge of registering marriages for them to generate legal effects. At the same time, marriage is an institutional structure that individuals are entitled to opt for. Individual liberty encompasses a "right to marry." Marriage thus displays a mixed public–private nature.

[8] For a criticism of settlements, on the grounds that they are often tainted by the disparities in resources between the parties, see Owen Fiss, "Against Settlement," in Owen Fiss, *The Law As It Could Be* (New York: New York University Press, 2003), pp. 90–104.

[9] For a general discussion of the conditions under which a purely private form of arbitration may be viable, drawing from historical examples involving international commerce, see Thomas Hale, *Between Interests and the Law. The Politics of Transnational Commercial Disputes* (Cambridge: Cambridge University Press, 2015).

Note that, in many jurisdictions, the right to marry does not simply mean that persons should be free to elect marriage, if marriage happens to be one of the institutions that the law incorporates. The right to marry entails a further requirement: the legal system must include marriage among the institutions it designs. The International Covenant on Civil and Political Rights, adopted by the General Assembly of the United Nations in 1966, seems to mirror this understanding when it enshrines the right to marry in article 23. After providing that the family "is entitled to protection by society and the State," article 23 announces the right to marry, and requires public institutions to regulate marriage in accordance with the principle of equality: "States Parties to the present Covenant shall take appropriate steps to ensure equality of rights and responsibilities of spouses as to marriage, during marriage and at its dissolution." The Covenant thus presupposes that the state must make the matrimonial institution available to individuals. If a state eliminated marriage as a legal institution, it would frustrate the right to marry.

Similarly, we can say, the right to arbitration is not reducible to the right of individuals to choose arbitration, in the event that the state elects to include the latter in the dispute-resolution menu. The right to arbitration goes further: it requires the state to make arbitration a component of the legal system, so that individuals can decide whether or not to employ arbitration to bring their disputes to an end. The interaction that takes place in the ordinary contractual domain is not, of course, as deep as that of marriage, nor is a special legal status conferred on the contracting parties. Still, the arbitral legal framework facilitates a valuable type of relationship.

Now, the fact that we need public institutions to sponsor arbitration does not mean that the state has free rein to regulate arbitration in any direction it wants. There are limits to the state's legislative discretion. Because arbitration is tied to private autonomy, a conceptual space is opened up for the articulation of arguments that criticize a given law on the grounds that it does not respect the individual right to arbitration. Not all the conditions that the state may wish to impose on arbitration pass the justificatory tests that such a right generates, as we will discuss later in the book. The same reasoning applies to marriage, to go back to the earlier analogy. The fact that marriage is a legal institution constructed by the state does not entail the consequence that the state is totally free when shaping its contours. An argument can be convincingly made, for example, that requiring the spouses to be a man and a woman is an unacceptable condition from a liberal and egalitarian perspective.

It bears emphasizing, on the other hand, that the right to arbitration is not absolute. The state is entitled to fix the legal boundaries of this right and the constraints that arbitration must observe. The state can exclude certain matters from the arbitral forum, for example. Or it may lay down procedural principles that parties cannot contract around. Or it may enact special rules to protect parties with a weaker bargaining position, such as consumers and employees. We will explore these and other related topics in Chapter 3.

1.3 THE STRENGTHS OF ARBITRATION

The value of private autonomy, I have claimed so far, is at the heart of arbitration. There are good reasons, moreover, why individuals may prefer arbitration to litigation in court in various contexts. Such preference is not an irrational one that the state may have to tolerate out of respect for individual choice – as might be the case if the parties asked someone to settle a dispute by flipping a coin. Their decision to opt for arbitration is often grounded in good reasons, which the state should be sympathetic with. Actually, if arbitration did not present significant potential advantages, it would be hard to understand why contending parties would ever resort to it. Since courts are subsidized by the state while arbitration is not, the rational course of action for individuals would always be to litigate. Why pay for services that can be obtained free of charge (or paying relatively low fees) in court?[10]

The advantages most commonly associated with arbitration are linked to the specialized expertise and competence of the arbitrators, the relative economy and speed of the proceedings, and the protection of privacy and confidentiality.

1.3.1 *Specialized Expertise and Competence*

When parties litigate in court, the judges in charge of deciding cases tend to be generalists. They possess a broad knowledge of the law, but they are not experts in very specialized fields. When parties resort to arbitration, in contrast, they can hire specialists. In areas governed by highly complex laws, or where scientific and technical expertise is particularly relevant, arbitration emerges as an attractive alternative to litigation. There is good reason for the law to facilitate arbitration on this account.

Of course, once a controversy arises, the party with a very weak case will be hurt by having the matter entrusted to an expert who can easily see through his claims. That party would have better chances to prevail in a nonspecialized forum. A generalist adjudicator would probably have a harder time trying to understand the issues and figuring out what the right answer was. Before the dispute breaks out, however, both parties may be inclined to prefer adjudicative expertise, to the extent they don't know *ex ante* who is most likely to have the stronger case.

The degree to which arbitration offers this comparative advantage over courts depends, of course, on how the judiciary is structured. If the judiciary does not exhibit any kind of internal specialization, the pressures in favor of choosing arbitration may be stronger than if a certain degree of judicial specialization has been established. Different nations have designed their judicial systems differently in this regard. Civil law countries have traditionally leaned toward a high level of specialization. The division of labor runs all the way up to the supreme courts, which

10 On this point, see Christopher R. Drahozal and Stephen J. Ware, "Why Do Businesses Use (or Not Use) Arbitration Clauses?," 25 *Ohio State Journal on Dispute Resolution*, 433 (2010), pp. 446–449.

typically consist of specialized chambers.[11] The common law world, in contrast, has been less eager to embrace judicial specialization. The supreme courts are normally granted general jurisdiction over all kinds of matters. We nevertheless find specialized tribunals in common law countries, involving family law, patents, bankruptcy, taxation, commercial law, corporate law, among other matters. The London Commercial Court and the New York Commercial Division are two prominent examples in the commercial sphere, while the Delaware Court of Chancery stands out in corporate law. In recent decades, many specialized business tribunals have been formed in the United States.[12] To a significant extent, the reason for their establishment has to do with the need for courts to compete more effectively with arbitration. Litigants are likely to appreciate the value of specialized legal knowledge. If arbitration offers specialized expertise, so should courts. This trend toward judicial specialization is an example of litigation becoming more like arbitration in some respects, a process that Christopher Drahozal suggests might be called the "arbitralization" of litigation.[13]

It is interesting to note that the state has also transformed its administrative structures in the direction of specialization as society has evolved and become more complex. Arbitration is tied to larger trends toward a deep intellectual division of labor. In the United States, for example, the campaign in favor of modern arbitration laws in the commercial arena was part of the Progressive movement that arose at the end of the nineteenth century, which insisted, among other things, on the importance of expertise in a modern, industrialized society. Both specialized arbitrators in commercial dealings and specialized administrative agencies were embodiments of a profound faith in experts.[14]

It is true that a high degree of specialization has its downsides. Experts in a particular field may lose sight of the broader legal and social context in which a given problem needs to be located. Specialists may be prey to "cognitive loafing": out of inertia or overconfidence, they may be reluctant to think critically about their narrow professional understandings. Administrative agencies, for example, have been said to suffer from this cognitive bias.[15] A balance needs to be struck somewhere between specialized knowledge, on the one hand, and the ability to see things through systematic and critical lenses, on the other. As we will note at a later

[11] See John Henry Merryman and Rogelio Pérez-Perdomo, *The Civil Law Tradition: An Introduction to the Legal Systems of Europe and Latin America* (Stanford: Stanford University Press, 2007), pp. 86–90; and Lawrence Baum, *Specializing the Courts* (Chicago: The University of Chicago Press, 2011), pp. 22–24.

[12] See Christopher R. Drahozal, "Business Courts and the Future of Arbitration," 10 *Cardozo Journal of Conflict Resolution*, 491 (2009).

[13] Ibid., p. 492.

[14] On the connection between modern arbitration laws regarding commerce and the Progressive movement in the United States, see Imre Szalai, *Outsourcing Justice. The Rise of Modern Arbitration Laws in America* (Durham, North Carolina: Carolina Academic Press, 2013), pp. 173–179.

[15] See Mark Seidenfeld, "Cognitive Loafing, Social Conformity, and Judicial Review of Agency Rulemaking," 87 *Cornell Law Review*, 486 (2002).

stage, parties may be better served if the arbitral tribunal they set up combines specialized experts with more generalist jurists.

In addition to the potential benefits of specialization, there is a related strength that arbitration exhibits: the parties can select capable jurists (even if they are not specialists) equipped with the necessary skills to decide a case in a competent manner. Indeed, the parties may fear that if their dispute is litigated in court, they run the risk that the judge randomly assigned to the case will turn out to be a bad judge – not knowledgeable enough or lacking the moral character that is required to adjudicate a controversy properly. Again, the weight to be accorded to this potential advantage of arbitration depends on the quality of the judiciary, as well as on the relative difficulty of the issues that a given case poses. Other things being equal, countries boasting a first-rate judicial system are less likely to push individuals to embrace arbitration than countries whose judiciary performs rather poorly.

A modality of arbitration worthy of note in this context consists of hiring judges to provide arbitral services. In Sweden, for example, it has been a traditional practice for judges sitting on the highest courts to be appointed to chair arbitral tribunals handling commercial cases.[16] Only the most prestigious judges are commonly nominated to play this role. The business community appears to be satisfied with this system. A similar practice exists in Denmark.[17] Active judges can also be designated as arbitrators in Germany, with governmental approval.[18]

A different version of arbitration connected to judges was implemented in Delaware some years ago.[19] Delaware is well-known for its mature and refined corporate law, which has proven to be attractive to many companies. That law is adjudicated by capable, specialized judges sitting in the Court of Chancery. In 2009, in response to perceived threats to Delaware's position stemming from private arbitration, the legislature decided to grant the Court of Chancery the power to arbitrate particular kinds of business disputes. To qualify for arbitration, at least one party had to be a business entity formed or organized under Delaware law, and neither party could be a consumer. The dispute had to involve an amount-in-controversy of at least one million dollars. If the parties agreed to avail themselves of this modality of arbitration, the Chancellor would select a Chancery Court judge to hear the case. The proceeding would be conducted in a Delaware courthouse during normal business hours. Arbitration costs were six thousand dollars per day.

16 For a description and evaluation of the Swedish arbitral system, see Yves Dezalay & Bryant G. Garth, *Dealing in Virtue. International Commercial Arbitration and the Construction of a Transnational Legal Order* (Chicago: The University of Chicago Press, 1996), pp. 182–196.

17 Steffen Pihlblad, Christian Lundblad, and Claus Søgaard-Christensen, *Arbitration in Denmark* (Copenhagen: DJØF Publishing, 2014), pp. 45–46.

18 Richard Kreindler, Reinmar Wolff, and Markus S. Rieder, *Commercial Arbitration in Germany* (Oxford: Oxford University Press, 2016), p. 125.

19 For a discussion of Delaware's arbitration program, see Brian J. M. Quinn, "Arbitration and the Future of Delaware's Corporate Law Franchise," 14 *Cardozo Journal of Conflict Resolution*, 829 (2013).

The arbitral decision finally rendered could be challenged before the Delaware Supreme Court, but the grounds for reversal were limited.

One of the most controversial aspects of Delaware's state-sponsored arbitral system was the confidentiality rule. Arbitration petitions were considered confidential and were not included as part of the public docketing system. Attendance at the proceeding was limited to the parties and their representatives, and all materials and communications produced during the arbitration were protected from disclosure. This triggered a citizens' challenge. Delaware Coalition for Open Government went to court to argue that Delaware's program was unconstitutional, since it infringed upon the public's First Amendment right to access judicial trials. The challenge was successful, putting an end to Delaware's experiment.[20] Indeed, both the federal district court and the Court of Appeals that adjudicated the case stressed the differences between Delaware's state-sponsored arbitral proceedings and the traditional forms of private arbitration. The fact that the contested proceedings were conducted before active judges in a courthouse was a relevant factor to take into account, they reasoned. The arrangements under review, moreover, derived a great deal of legitimacy and authority from the state. So the interests in openness outweighed the private interests of the parties in confidentiality.[21]

This interesting case illustrates the difficulty of devising hybrid adjudicative mechanisms that blend principles derived from distinct arbitral and judicial practices. It also highlights the importance of specialization and expertise. If Delaware has been an appealing forum for decades, this is due to a significant extent to the quality of its specialized judiciary.

In sum, the parties' preference for arbitration on account of specialization and competence is a very reasonable one. It is actually congruent with other institutional arrangements that the state has developed or supported to better deal with complex issues in modern society.

1.3.2 *Relative Speed and Economy*

A second advantage associated with arbitration has to do with speed and economy of resources. By means of the arbitral process, the contending parties don't have to wait in line for their case to be decided by courts, which may be overcrowded. When parties choose arbitration, they can hire someone who is ready to handle the dispute soon. It is true that selecting the arbitrators takes time. There may be delays if the parties do not agree on the appointments. Courts have an advantage in this respect, since they are already established when litigation starts. Arbitration is nevertheless

20 A subsequent statute regulated arbitration in innovative ways to make it faster, but it no longer enlisted Court of Chancery judges to arbitrate disputes. On these later developments, see Christopher R. Drahozal, "Innovation in Arbitration Law: The Case of Delaware," 43 *Pepperdine Law Review*, 493 (2016).

21 See *Delaware Coalition for Open Government, Inc.* v. *Strine*, 733 F.3d 510 (3rd Cir. 2013).

likely to adjust the difference earlier than litigation in court. Again, this preference for a prompt resolution of controversies is perfectly legitimate, and the state should be sensitive to it.

The advantage of arbitration as far as time is concerned can be reinforced if the law establishes that the grounds upon which courts are authorized to set aside arbitral awards are rather limited. The disputes will be settled earlier if the law makes it difficult for judges to quash the awards. Indeed, the tendency in many jurisdictions is for the law to specify very narrow grounds for judicial reversal of awards. Courts are commonly authorized to police excesses of arbitral power and breaches of due process. Judicial review of the merits of the case is generally not available, or is only allowed under rather strict conditions. Of course, if the stakes are very high, the parties may think it too risky to preclude the opportunity to appeal the merits of the decision. They may prefer litigation in court, which offers broad avenues of appeal. Arbitration is therefore more likely to be attractive when the stakes are not too large.[22]

Another factor that can help expedite the resolution of disputes is this: the parties may opt for arbitration in order to limit the amount of time and resources they will devote to future legal fights. They may fear that, if a conflict arises, they will be tempted to overspend on legal strategies in order to prevail. To tie their hands in advance, they may agree to choose an arbitral procedure that sets some limitations on discovery of documents, for example, or on the length of the hearings. Note that before a dispute arises, parties usually act under a veil of ignorance. In many cases (though not in all of them), the parties cannot easily predict who will benefit from those limitations and who will be harmed by them. To the extent that this is so, the parties are in a good position to decide in a fair way the maximum amount of resources they will allocate to the disposition of a future controversy.

This strategy to reduce the costs of litigation is similar in spirit to other strategies that parties may deploy in the contractual sphere. It has been suggested, for example, that risk-neutral business parties commonly prefer adjudicators to adopt a relatively simple "textualist" approach to the interpretation of their contracts, to a more complicated "contextualist" approach that requires the assessment of a wider evidentiary base. Although the latter approach would permit the adjudicators to reach a more accurate interpretation of the contracts, the parties may prefer to sacrifice accuracy to a certain degree, in order to lower adjudication costs. Strict enforcement of the parties' contractual precommitment can thus increase their joint welfare.[23]

All this does not mean, however, that speed is the overriding goal that parties seek through arbitration. If the parties simply wanted a quick resolution of their controversy, no matter how inaccurately the arbitrators determined the facts and the

22 For some evidence of this, see Drahozal and Ware, "Why Do Businesses Use (or Not Use) Arbitration Clauses?," pp. 453–467.

23 See Alan Schwartz & Robert E. Scott, "Contract Interpretation Redux," 119 *The Yale Law Journal*, 926 (2010).

applicable law, the parties might just as well let the arbitrators decide the case by flipping a coin or by rendering a judgment that "splits the baby." But the parties actually vindicate their legal rights when a dispute emerges, and they expect the arbitrators to hand down an award that is correct both as to the facts and the relevant law. As William Park explains, "an arbitrator's main duty lies not in dictating a peace treaty, but in delivery of an accurate award that rests on a reasonable view of what happened and what the law says."[24] So even if the parties may go for arbitration because the resolution of the dispute will be more expeditious and economical than if they went to court, they are still primarily interested in obtaining a correct decision. Some amount of time and resources will consequently have to be spent to adjudicate the case. An ancient adage, Park reminds us, holds that truth is the daughter of time: *veritas filia temporis*.

Indeed, if accuracy did not matter at all, it would be hard to understand why the expertise of arbitrators is widely regarded as a significant strength of arbitration. If parties hire experts in particular fields to perform arbitration services, this must be because they expect such experts to get things right. Furthermore, as we will see in Chapter 5, arbitration is very popular in the domain of international transactions, since it provides parties with a neutral forum to adjudicate disputes. Domestic courts are distrusted, for they may be inclined to favor the local party, whereas arbitrators are comparatively reliable, to the extent that they are detached from the local judiciaries. This virtue of arbitration in terms of objectivity would make no sense if reaching the right legal outcome were not a key consideration motivating the parties' decision to choose arbitration.

Actually, the parties may sometimes decide to organize an arbitral procedure that absorbs a larger amount of time than a judicial procedure would. The parties and the arbitrators may end up spending more time working on a complex case, for example, than the parties and judges would spend if that case were litigated in court. But because the parties can find arbitrators that are ready to devote all their available time to the dispute for which they have been hired, the decision may be rendered earlier than if the case were handled by courts. Arbitration can thus be faster, not necessarily because less amount of time is allocated to the dispute, but because the relevant actors can agree to concentrate all their efforts on a single case and start working on it sooner.

1.3.3 *Privacy and Confidentiality*

A third reason why parties may be inclined to select arbitration instead of litigation is tied to their desire to keep the dispute private and confidential. Arbitration serves this goal, since the public can be excluded from arbitral proceedings (privacy), and the

24 William W. Park, "Arbitrators and Accuracy," 1 *Journal of International Dispute Settlement*, 25 (2010), p. 27.

parties, lawyers, arbitrators and other persons who participate in the proceedings can be required to keep confidential the information they have access to (confidentiality).

Privacy and confidentiality are legitimate considerations, which are consistent with the general protection of privacy liberal constitutions typically guarantee. If arbitration is conducted in closed proceedings, the dispute can be adjudicated in a less confrontational manner, avoiding the tension that litigation in court is prone to generate (especially when trials are covered by the media). Actually, the social meaning of commencing arbitration may be different from the social meaning of filing a lawsuit. If the parties wish to preserve their long-term relationship, arbitration is likely to be better than a judicial process.

Arbitration, moreover, can strongly protect sensitive information, which may be a significant concern in some cases, involving trade secrets, for example. To be sure, courts can safeguard sensitive information through protective orders, but the parties may deem arbitration to be superior in this regard. There is always the risk that judges will not issue a protective order, or will issue one that is too narrow in scope.

An interesting question to address at this juncture is why constitutions in liberal democracies generally do not permit the contending parties to jointly require the judge to conduct a trial in secret, while they do permit the parties to agree to arbitrate their dispute in a private and confidential manner. The general understanding, indeed, is that the parties to a controversy cannot dispose of the public's right to access judicial proceedings, yet they are entitled to keep the proceedings closed if they choose an arbitral forum. What can be said in justification of this contrast? Here is a plausible answer: as already noted, judges are part of the machinery of the state and thus wield an adjudicative power that can be exercised over any member of the political community. The public is interested in watching how judges perform their functions, for these judges will be deciding future cases involving other litigants. Publicity is a necessary check over any governmental authority, including courts. Judges will be more careful if they know they are being scrutinized by the public. Because society is affected in this way, litigants cannot decide to run a trial in secret. They cannot dispose of the interests of others, who need to have the ability to inspect how state institutions are operating. In contrast, arbitrators chosen by the contending parties hold no power at all over the rest of people. If the parties have trust in the particular arbitrator they have chosen, and they don't think that publicity is necessary for purposes of enhancing the quality of arbitral performance, society need not interfere with that choice. The arbitrator, moreover, has an important incentive to act properly: he will not be hired in future disputes if he does a poor job. Arbitrators need to build a good reputation among participants in the relevant economic and professional sectors if they want to ensure demand for their services.

There is another consideration to bear in mind in this connection, which will be discussed in more detail in Chapter 4: we need courts to produce a consistent body of case law that interprets and refines the existing sources of law. The task of judges is not simply the resolution of disputes. They must also formulate rules through a system of precedents. Without publicity, of course, this function cannot be carried out. Arbitration, in contrast, is not expected to contribute much by way of rule formulation, for its central mission is dispute resolution. Lack of publicity in arbitration is thus not a problem from this perspective.

For these reasons, the parties' wish to ensure privacy and confidentiality in arbitration can be squared with constitutional principles requiring publicity in adjudication, while their preference for running judicial trials in secret would be plainly inconsistent with those principles.

All this is not to say that arbitration is necessarily incompatible with publicity. In actual practice, some arbitral regimes are relatively open. Publicity has its own advantages. For example, it can help secure voluntary compliance with arbitral decisions. The reputational costs of disregarding an award that gets published may be too high, particularly in small communities where people interact for an extended period of time. Historically, merchant guilds often relied on this strategy to construct private systems of arbitration. The same is true today in some settings. Consider, for instance, the Federation of Oils, Seeds, and Fats Association, a private organization based in London representing companies that are engaged in trading particular commodities. Members of the industry are appointed to arbitrate disputes among such companies. One of the factors that explains the success of this arbitral regime is publicity: the organization posts a list of companies that fail to comply with the awards rendered against them, a list that is shared by the members of the association.[25]

Transparency, moreover, is of great help to private actors interested in using arbitral services. The best way for contending parties to learn about the competence and skills of potential arbitrators is for the awards issued by the latter to be available to the public. This benefit, of course, can be made compatible with confidentiality if arbitral awards are published in a redacted form, so that the identity of the parties and other personal details are not revealed.[26] This solution, however, is not so easy to implement in practice: the published form has to reveal sufficient facts to enable public scrutiny, but disclosure of facts can allow others to infer the identities of the parties. In spite of this difficulty, the publication of awards in redacted form is practiced in certain domains. The American Arbitration Association (AAA), for example, provides for this type of publication in consumer and employment arbitration.[27] In the sphere of international commercial

[25] See Hale, *Between Interests and Law: The Politics of Transnational Commercial Disputes*, pp. 286–287.

[26] See Alberto Malatesta and Rinaldo Sali (eds.), *The Rise of Transparency in International Arbitration. The Case for the Anonymous Publication of Arbitral Awards* (Huntington: Juris, 2013).

[27] Rule 43(c) of the AAA's Consumer Arbitration Rules (Rules amended and effective September 1, 2014) establishes that "the AAA may choose to publish an award rendered under these Rules; however, the names of the parties and witnesses will be removed from awards that are published, unless a party agrees in writing to have its name included in the award." In turn, Rule 39(b) of the AAA's

arbitration, there is also a clear trend in many quarters toward inserting arbitral decisions in public reports.[28]

Furthermore, the state may be justified in some arbitral contexts in imposing a measure of transparency for deterrence purposes. With regard to consumer contracts, for example, the state may want to ensure that companies engaging in abusive behavior will pay reputational costs. In California, for instance, the law requires arbitral centers to publish information about the consumer cases they handle, including the nature of the dispute, the name of the non-consumer party, the name of the arbitrators, the total fees charged by the arbitrators, the mode of disposition, and the outcome.[29]

So privacy and confidentiality are usually legitimate reasons why parties may prefer arbitration to litigation in court, but these reasons get defeated in some cases by more weighty considerations that speak in favor of transparency.

1.4 THE NON-UTILITARIAN CHARACTER OF THE LIBERAL CASE

I have been arguing that individuals should have the freedom to resort to arbitration, not only out of respect for their general liberty to pursue their interests in the private sphere as they deem appropriate, but also because in many instances there are indeed good reasons to prefer arbitration over litigation in court. These reasons are related to the expertise and competence of arbitrators, the relative speed and economy with which the dispute can be disposed of, and privacy and confidentiality.

It is important to realize that this liberal case in favor of arbitration does not rest on a utilitarian argument that points to the advantages of arbitration for the community as a whole. The defense of arbitration does not depend on a utilitarian calculus of this sort. In particular, it does not turn on whether arbitration increases social welfare through the reduction of judicial dockets.

It is certainly reasonable to assume that arbitration can help decrease the amount of resources that society spends on dispute resolution. As already noted, the arbitral procedures the parties design or choose are often less complex than judicial procedures. More importantly, ordinary mechanisms of appeal are excluded when arbitration is employed. As a result, when controversies are arbitrated, society as a whole

Employment Arbitration Rules and Mediation Procedures (Rules amended and effective November 1, 2009) provides that "an award issued under these rules shall be publicly available, on a cost basis. The names of the parties and witnesses will not be publicly available, unless a party expressly agrees to have its name made public in the award."

28 For the historical evolution of publicity in international commercial arbitration, see Alec Stone Sweet and Florian Grisel, *The Evolution of International Arbitration. Judicialization, Governance, Legitimacy* (Oxford: Oxford University Press, 2017), pp. 121–125.

29 On this trend toward transparency, see Judith Resnik, "Diffusing Disputes: The Public in the Private of Arbitration, the Private in Courts, and the Erasure of Rights," 124 *The Yale Law Journal*, 2804 (2015), pp. 2894–2900.

normally devotes fewer resources to their resolution than would be the case if those controversies were handled by courts.

This utilitarian advantage of arbitration, however, is not the key consideration for purposes of justifying why individuals should be empowered to submit their differences to arbitration. Even if the utilitarian considerations sponsoring arbitration turned out to be weaker than they are often thought to be, the case for arbitration would maintain its force. Imagine, for instance, that an empirical study conducted in a particular country or social sector revealed that, because litigation costs are very high, parties tend to settle early, whereas the lower costs of arbitration relieve the parties of such pressures. As a result of this dynamic, the widespread use of arbitration in that country or sector would produce negative effects from a utilitarian point of view, since a larger amount of resources would be spent on dispute resolution procedures, all things considered. In that situation, however, arbitration would not be deprived of its rationale. The right to private autonomy would do its normative work to ground arbitration.

The case for arbitration is thus not utilitarian. Furthermore, the right to arbitration needs to be hedged against purely utilitarian calculations. It may have to yield, ultimately, if the countervailing public interests are weighty enough, but it should not be defeated easily.

Suppose, for example, that arbitration is used to resolve a particular dispute that raises relatively novel legal issues, as to which no judicial precedents are clearly in point. If the case went to the courts instead of being referred to arbitrators, a judicial opinion with precedential value for future controversies would be delivered. As already mentioned, one of the most significant differences between arbitrators and courts is that only the latter are expected to produce a consistent body of rulings to clarify the relevant sources of law and fill in legal gaps. A body of case law is indeed an important "public good" that the judiciary produces. This being so, it is socially detrimental for a dispute that presents novel issues to be arbitrated: the judiciary is thereby deprived of the opportunity to rule on those issues. The law will remain uncertain until a similar controversy arises in the future and is placed in the hands of courts.

In spite of the social costs such legal uncertainty produces, however, individuals have a right to opt for arbitration. Arguably, the right to arbitration trumps in this case the utilitarian considerations that speak in favor of sending the case to the judiciary. It would be wrong for the law to disregard the arbitral forum the parties have freely selected, and force them to refer their difference to the courtroom, in order to produce a judicial ruling that will have precedential value.

If it turned out, however, that arbitration attracted such a large portion of the disputes arising in a given field that courts were no longer in a position to refine and update the relevant case law, the state might be justified in placing restrictions on arbitration. As we will note in Chapter 4, in those circumstances the legislature would have good reason to exclude certain types of disputes from arbitration, to make sure only courts would adjudicate them. Alternatively, the legislature could allow for fuller judicial review of the legal merits of awards, in order to make it possible for the judicial voice to be heard with regard to the interpretation of the law. These would be relatively exceptional measures, however, uniquely warranted by the gravity of the systemic consequences that would follow from arbitration replacing courts to such a large extent.

Another example: suppose that the courts in a given country are extremely overcrowded, or the judges are not very competent, or the procedures are too cumbersome. The judiciary in that country exhibits some structural defects that need to be remedied through a radical program of legislative reforms. Until the appropriate changes are made, arbitration becomes especially appealing as a way out of the flawed judicial system. Suppose, however, that the consequence of permitting a significant number of people to bypass courts in this way reduces the incentives for the government to introduce the much needed reforms. If all citizens, in all types of disputes, were subject to the courts, the pressures on the political branches to improve the judiciary would be stronger. But once the arbitral door is opened, the pressures become weaker. As Albert Hirschman explained in his classic study, if it is easy for people to "exit" an organization that is failing them, it is less likely that they will resort to the "voice" option as a mechanism of recuperation to improve the performance of the organization.[30] A utilitarian argument could thus be made that society is worse off if arbitration is permitted in this context.

Despite such negative consequences, however, individuals can insist on their right to choose arbitration. This right is part of their basic liberty to decide how to organize their private affairs, and it should be taken seriously. Whether this right should be sacrificed to the public interests involved in this case depends on the gravity of the problem. Arguably, it is unlikely that arbitration will have the side effect of reducing the political pressures to improve the judiciary to such an extent that it is justified for the state to block arbitration. In the first place, arbitration only provides a partial exit from the judicial system, for it basically applies to private law, and only in part. The rest of the law, including criminal law, administrative law, tax law, gets litigated. So everybody is subject to the power of courts. In addition, arbitration cannot succeed in practice without the support of a well-functioning judiciary, so parties do not exit the judicial system altogether when they end up in arbitration. Courts, indeed, may be needed to compel arbitration, to assist arbitrators with the production of evidence, or to review and enforce the awards. Furthermore, the fact that some people, in some cases, can eschew courts in a limited way will probably make the rest of the people more indignant about the poor quality of the judiciary and will accordingly intensify their pressures on the government to rectify the problem. The trial bar may effectively channel those pressures. So the negative

[30] Albert O. Hirschman, *Exit, Voice, and Loyalty. Responses to Decline in Firms, Organizations, and States* (Cambridge, Massachusetts: Harvard University Press, 1970).

impact arbitration may have on the public good in the scenario we are contemplating is likely to be too modest to warrant the severe curtailment of the basic right to arbitration.

In other cases, on the other hand, the right to arbitration should clearly give way to overriding public interests. Consider consumer contracts. Suppose that a particular legal system primarily relies on class actions to ensure that businesses are deterred from engaging in behavior that violates the legal rights of consumers. The space for arbitration may then have to be narrowed down. If businesses insert arbitration clauses in their contracts of adhesion with individual consumers, and such clauses ban class-wide arbitration, the practical result is that the collective kind of redress that the legal system assumes to be necessary to protect consumers is eliminated. As a response to this problem, the state may provide in its laws that consumer arbitration is only valid if class-wide arbitral proceedings are available for consumers, or it may bar consumer arbitration altogether, if class-wide arbitration is not workable. There are weighty reasons here for the collective interest to prevail over the individual right to arbitration, as we will discuss in Chapter 3.

It is important to stress that utilitarian considerations cannot easily justify going in the opposite direction either. Imagine that a utilitarian calculus reveals that in a number of settings arbitration is great from the point of view of social welfare: if people use arbitration, courts will not be overcrowded and the community as a whole will be better off. As a general principle, however, the law should not force individuals to arbitrate. Arbitration should normally be based on consent. Laws that make arbitration compulsory for some types of disputes are thus problematic. Such laws are at odds with the liberal foundation of arbitration. In addition, they compromise the right of individuals to have access to court. The state must accordingly come up with persuasive reasons to justify the enactment of laws that force private parties to arbitrate their differences. As we will see in Chapter 2, courts in different countries have supplied contrasting rulings when reviewing the validity of such laws.

Likewise, utilitarian considerations should not drive courts overwhelmed with heavy caseloads to shape aggressive pro-arbitration doctrines in order to remit part of their cases to arbitrators. If such doctrines undermine the liberal grounding of arbitration, which is connected to freedom of choice, they are questionable. Individuals have a right to resist arbitration procedures they have not consented to, no matter how convenient it may be for public courts to get rid of a significant portion of their work.[31]

[31] Some commentators are worried about the attitude of United States' courts in this regard. Thus, Ian R. Macneil, *American Arbitration Law. Reformation-Nationalization-Internationalization* (New York: Oxford University Press, 1992), p. 172, referring to the Supreme Court of the United States, writes that "one cannot immerse oneself in the arbitration cases without coming to the conclusion that a major force driving the Court is docket-clearing pure and simple." Similarly, Resnik, "Diffusing Disputes: The Public in the Private of Arbitration, the Private in Courts, and the Erasure of Rights," p. 2849, notes that what was once described as old judicial hostility to arbitration "has been replaced by

1.5 THE CONJUNCTION OF TWO BASIC RIGHTS: THE RIGHT TO ARBITRATION AND THE RIGHT TO JUDICIAL PROTECTION

If we postulate the existence of the right to arbitration, we have at our disposal better intellectual resources to address certain legal issues. It is often contended, for example, that a person who enters an arbitration agreement is thereby giving up his right to go to court. In some countries, such as the United States, he is also said to be waiving a more specific right to trial by jury. If so, the argument goes, that waiver should be expressed in a very clear and explicit manner.

If we acknowledge the operating force of the right to arbitration, however, there are then two basic rights in play. Individuals can decide to go to court (in which case they exercise their basic right to judicial protection, including a right to trial by jury, if applicable), or they can instead go for arbitration (in which case they also exercise a basic right). They have a basic liberty to choose which of the two forms of dispute resolution to resort to.

There is still an asymmetry, of course: a party does not need the consent of the other party in order to institute an action in court, whereas it does need the consent of the other party in order to settle the dispute by means of an arbitral procedure. But if we consider the shared will of the two parties, arbitration is an option within the dispute resolution menu. The parties exercise a basic right when they select arbitration.

When things are seen in this light, the criteria to determine the existence of consent to arbitrate must be less strict than if only the right to go to court were brought to the picture. In order to show that the parties have consented to arbitration it should not be necessary for them to overcome a *strong legal presumption* against it. Such a strong presumption would be at odds with the recognition of a right to arbitration. Of course, if A asserts that B consented to arbitration, A must shoulder the burden of proof of this claim. As Alan Rau points out, however, "a heavy thumb is not to be placed on the *other* pan of the scale so as to unduly handicap the proponent" of arbitration.[32] The recognition of a basic right to arbitration helps support this central idea.

There should be no need, for example, for the consent to be expressed in a special form. In many jurisdictions, the arbitration agreement must be in writing, but there is a trend in modern legislation toward relaxing this formal requirement, or even eliminating it altogether, especially in the sphere of international commercial arbitration. The 2006 version of the UNCITRAL Model Law, for instance, includes Option 2 for article 7, under which no writing requirement is established. The Swedish Arbitration Act, for example, does not impose it.[33]

hesitancy about, if not hostility towards, adjudication." She cites a page of the federal judiciary's website advising disputants to avoid the expense and delay of having a trial whenever possible.

32 Alan Scott Rau, *The Allocation of Power between Arbitral Tribunals and State Courts* (Leiden: Brill Nijhoff, 2018), p. 59 (emphasis in the original).

33 Finn Madsen, *Commercial Arbitration in Sweden* (Stockholm: Jure Förlag AB, 2016), p. 42.

Similarly, if the right to arbitration is part of the legal background against which contracts have to be interpreted, courts should not rely on a strong presumption that the parties do not wish to give up their right to go to court, when dealing with defects in the writing of an arbitration agreement. If the agreement exhibits inconsistencies, judges should attempt to resolve them in the best manner, in order to implement the will of the parties. Judges should not engage in a restrictive interpretation of the agreement.[34]

Consent can actually be implicit: it can sometimes be based on default rules established by the law. Contract law often relies on such rules to facilitate contractual transactions. The law presumes that, if the parties are silent about a particular matter, they want it to be governed by the clause that most people normally agree upon when they enter the same type of contract, or that most people would agree upon if they acted in a rational manner. If the parties have reason to be aware of the existence of the default rule, and if contracting around it is not costly, we can conclude that the parties have actually consented to it.[35]

With respect to domestic transactions, however, it is not generally warranted for the law to lay down a default rule in favor of arbitration in contractual agreements. Arbitration has its own strengths and weaknesses when compared to adjudication by courts. There is no evidence that most parties select an arbitral forum to settle contractual disputes, nor is there any ground to believe that most parties would do so if they acted rationally. With regard to international commercial transactions, on the other hand, the advantages of arbitration are so strong, for reasons we will explore in Chapter 5, that the case for the establishment of default arbitration is more powerful.[36]

34 As Jean-Louis Delvolvé argues, "if one is prepared to recognise the existence of a right to arbitration as a freedom which is constitutionally guaranteed," it is no longer possible to regard arbitration as an exception "always to be applied and interpreted restrictively." See Jean-Louis Delvolvé, "The Fundamental Right to Arbitration," in Martin Hunter, Arthur Marriott, and V. V. Veeder (eds.), *The Internationalisation of International Arbitration. The LCIA Centenary Conference* (London/Dordrecht/Boston: Graham&Trotman/Martinus Nijhoff, 1995), p. 149.

35 See Randy E. Barnett, "The Sound of Silence: Default Rules and Contractual Consent," 78 *Virginia Law Review*, 821 (1992), p. 866.

36 See Gilles Cuniberti, "Beyond Contract – The Case for Default Arbitration in International Commercial Disputes," 32 *Fordham International Law Journal*, 417 (2008). Cuniberti has later developed the argument in his book, *Rethinking International Commercial Arbitration. Towards Default Arbitration* (Cheltenham: Edward Elgar Publishing, 2017). See, also, Jack Graves, "Court Litigation over Arbitration Agreements: Is It Time for a New Default Rule?," 23 *The American Review of International Arbitration*, 113 (2012); and Gary Born, "BITS, BATS and Buts: Reflections on International Dispute Resolution," available at www.wilmerhale.com. For a critical view, see Scott Rau, *The Allocation of Power between Arbitral Tribunal and State Courts*, pp. 62–64. Rau argues that sophisticated players engaged in international contracting are already aware of the potential advantages of arbitration, so they need no help from the state through the adoption of default rules in favor of arbitration. For the other players, such rules are "more likely to operate as a trap for the unwary, who may be surprised to learn that their alternatives have been foreclosed before a dispute has even arisen" (p. 63, footnote 91). Rau also doubts that international arbitration is always a blessing, for much depends on the individual party's circumstances.

It bears emphasizing that the relaxation of the forms of consent cannot be extended to all domains. In consumer contracts, for example, the quality of consent is generally very low, given the complexity of the terms that are often included in them, and given the fact that such contracts are take-it-or-leave-it deals, technically known as "contracts of adhesion."[37] The question arises whether the law should bar or restrict arbitration clauses in consumer contracts, as we'll discuss later in the book. If arbitration is permitted, certain formalities may need to be established to preserve the rights of consumers.

1.6 CONCLUSION

All things considered, there is a persuasive argument that a liberal polity should enable individuals to arbitrate private law disputes implicating interests they can freely dispose of. The right to arbitrate flows from the basic guarantee of private autonomy. Arbitration, moreover, exhibits certain features that make it attractive as a dispute resolution mechanism. It offers potential advantages that individuals have good reason to secure, for some of their disputes at least. The state must accordingly support arbitration through the enactment of the pertinent laws. It must also put the judicial machinery at the service of the arbitral process. Arbitration would scarcely have legal bite if arbitral awards were not recognized significant legal authority.

With all this background in mind, we now proceed to explore the basic constitutional question: Given the liberal foundation on which arbitration can be understood to rest, should the right to arbitration be enshrined in the constitution of a liberal democratic polity? If individuals have the right to arbitrate their private affairs, should the constitution incorporate such a right?

[37] For a thoughtful critique of the abuses perpetrated through contracts of adhesion, see Margaret Jane Radin, *Boilerplate: The Fine Print, Vanishing Rights, and the Rule of Law* (Princeton: Princeton University Press, 2013).

2

Constitutionalizing the Right to Arbitration

The case for arbitration presented in Chapter 1 offers a plausible reason for liberal constitutions to enshrine the right to arbitration. The argument developed in the chapter suggests in effect that arbitration is an important piece of the constitutional framework protecting liberty in the private domain. If the constitution does not explicitly mention the right to arbitration, judges could ascribe this right to the more abstract constitutional clauses guaranteeing privacy, for example, or the right to the free development of one's personality, or freedom of contract.

The idea of conferring constitutional status on arbitration is not unprecedented.[1] The French Constitutions of 1791 and 1795 explicitly recognized the fundamental right of citizens to submit their disputes to arbitration.[2] The Spanish Constitution of 1812 did the same.[3] The framers of this constitutional charter, which was the first one in Spanish history, had conducted their deliberations in Cádiz, a liberal and cosmopolitan city in the south of the country with an important harbor channeling commerce with the Americas. In the minds of the political representatives of the emerging bourgeoisie, arbitration was connected to freedom of commerce.[4] Under Spanish influence, many Latin America countries followed suit: the Constitutions of Costa Rica, El Salvador, Guatemala, Honduras, Mexico, Nicaragua, Panama, Peru, and Venezuela explicitly protected the right to arbitration as "inherent to every person," or as a liberty or right no citizen "could be deprived of."[5] A similar provision guaranteeing arbitration could be found in the Greek Constitution of 1827.[6]

1 For references, see Julian D. M. Lew, Loukas A. Mistelis, and Stefan M. Kröll, *Comparative International Commercial Arbitration* (The Hague: Kluwer Law International, 2003), p. 85.

2 See title III, chapter V, article 5, of the French Constitution of 1791; and articles 210 and 211 of the Constitution of 1795.

3 See articles 280 and 281 of the Spanish Constitution of 1812.

4 See José Fernando Merino Merchán, "La Constitución de 1812 y el arbitraje," 85 *Revista de las Cortes Generales*, 29 (2012).

5 See article 158 of the Constitution of Costa Rica of 1844; article 58 of the Constitution of El Salvador of 1824; article 179 of the Constitution of Guatemala of 1825; article 67 of the Constitution of Honduras of 1825; article 156 of the Constitution of Mexico of 1824; article 120 of the Constitution of Nicaragua of 1826; article 156 of the Constitution of Panama of 1841; article 164 of the Constitution of Peru of 1839; and article 190 of the Constitution of Venezuela of 1830.

6 See article 139 of the Greek Constitution of 1827.

Whether the right to arbitration ultimately belongs in a constitution, however, depends on certain elements of the relevant constitutional culture. In this regard, comparing the United States, Europe, and Latin America is instructive, as we will see next.

2.1 ARBITRATION AND THE DIVERSITY OF CONSTITUTIONAL CULTURES

2.1.1 *The United States*

In spite of the important role of the market in the United States, American constitutional doctrine is apt to be reluctant to embrace the idea that arbitration is constitutionally guaranteed as a right at the federal level. The prevailing understanding that emerged after the New Deal is that the federal Constitution does not protect freedom of contract as a fundamental right. This was a reaction against the excessive pro-market activism the Supreme Court had engaged in during the *Lochner* era. In this context, it is difficult to argue that arbitration enjoys constitutional protection, since arbitration is too closely linked to freedom of contract.

Moreover, there is a tendency in American jurisprudence to hold the view that constitutional rights must trigger a high level of judicial scrutiny. It is quite hard for laws constraining rights to pass judicial muster. This strict conception gives rise to a relatively narrow list of rights that are regarded as fundamental for constitutional purposes.[7] The right to arbitration, which is in the same normative neighborhood as freedom of contract, does not seem to deserve such a high level of judicial scrutiny.

Actually, it would be dangerous to constitutionalize arbitration in the United States, in so far as the Constitution has not been read by the Supreme Court to embody norms enjoining the government to affirmatively protect the interests of consumers or employees, for example, or to satisfy social rights more generally. The Constitution is portrayed as a charter of negative liberties sheltering individuals against governmental interference. It does not incorporate norms forcing the government to promote the interests of weaker parties or to provide social goods and services to secure real equality.[8] The Court's "negative liberties" view is quite

7 The point I am making here is a rough generalization that needs to be qualified. American courts sometimes subject constitutionally protected liberties to a more relaxed type of scrutiny, and they engage in casuistic balancing in a number of fields. For a nuanced discussion, see Stephen Gardbaum, "The Myth and the Reality of American Constitutionalism," 107 *Michigan Law Review*, 391 (2008), pp. 416–461; and Vicki C. Jackson, "Constitutional Law in an Age of Proportionality," 124 *The Yale Law Journal*, 3094 (2015). Perhaps arbitration could be recognized as a right entitled to a low level of judicial review.

8 State Constitutions stand in contrast to the federal Constitution in this regard, since they often contain an array of social rights. See John J. Dinan, *The American State Constitutional Tradition* (Lawrence, Kansas: University Press of Kansas, 2006), pp. 184–221.

entrenched, in spite of the criticism it has elicited.[9] In this context, it would be normatively dysfunctional to grant constitutional status to the right to arbitration. The constitutional silence on consumers, employees, and social rights would make it tough for the government to defend laws that place restrictions on arbitration in the name of public interests. To be sure, the government does not need to root in the Constitution the goals it seeks to promote. But when the interests it pursues must be "compelling" for the limitations it imposes on rights to survive judicial scrutiny, the absence of a constitutional anchor for those interests puts the government in a more difficult position. If arbitration were elevated to the category of a constitutional right, legislative constraints on arbitration would be rather hard to uphold.

Courts in the United States, moreover, have generally held that constitutional rights (to due process and equality, for example) do not apply in the arbitral context. No state action is regarded to be present here. Although some scholars have suggested that the judiciary is sufficiently entangled with private arbitration to trigger the application of constitutional rights, courts have refused to follow this path.[10] The upshot is that constitutional principles that govern litigation have no bearing on arbitral processes. The legislature, therefore, could not invoke constitutional principles of due process when justifying restrictions on a hypothetical right to arbitration.

Importantly, arbitration in the United States is already fully safeguarded by ordinary statutes. The passage of the Federal Arbitration Act in 1925, in particular, meant a strong protection for arbitration. The Act enacted into law the arbitration program advanced by the business community under the leadership of the New York Chamber of Commerce. The new legislation was approved without dissent by both houses of Congress.[11] Over the years, the Supreme Court has read this Act to incorporate a liberal policy in favor of arbitration. This federal piece of legislation

9 Critics have contended that the Court neglects an important political tradition that has understood the Constitution to presuppose the existence of a certain type of economic and social order without which political equality cannot be realized, a tradition that was particularly vibrant during the age of Jacksonian democracy, the Progressive Era, and the New Deal. For this argument, see Joseph Fishkin & William E. Forbath, "The Anti-Oligarchy Constitution," 94 *Boston University Law Review*, 671 (2014). In the same vein, some scholars have argued that the Constitution is better read to implicitly protect social rights. The fact that the judiciary cannot fully enforce them, due to institutional limitations, should not be taken to mean that social rights are not part of the constitutional domain. See, for example, Lawrence Sager, *Justice in Plainclothes. A Theory of American Constitutional Practice* (New Haven: Yale University Press, 2006), pp. 84–128. Mark Tushnet, in turn, has drawn from comparative law to show how creating weak forms of judicial review might allow for stronger welfare rights under American constitutional law. See Mark Tushnet, *Weak Courts, Strong Rights. Judicial Review and Social Welfare Rights in Comparative Constitutional Law* (Princeton: Princeton University Press, 2009).

10 For a discussion of the issue, see Sarah Rudolph Cole, "Arbitration and State Action," 1 *Brigham Young University Law Review*, 1 (2005).

11 For an account of the economic interests and legal conceptions that drove the enactment of the Act, see Tomas Hale, *Between Interests and Law* (Cambridge: Cambridge University Press, 2015), pp. 183–195.

is a source of limitations on state legislatures, since federal law preempts state law in the event of a conflict. In addition, the Act has a special relationship with other federal statutes: it operates as a "super-statute" guarding arbitration through some set of presumptions.[12] The Supreme Court, for example, has read the field of arbitrable matters to extend beyond the realm of purely contractual law to cover mandatory law enacted by Congress. The Court has held that claims based on federal statutes are presumed to be arbitrable unless Congress commands otherwise. Arbitration benefits from this presumption, since Congress has to shoulder the burden of indicating somehow or other that a particular statutory right is not open to arbitration.[13]

The Federal Arbitration Act does not have the same authority as the federal Constitution, however. Nor does the Act belong to the "constitutional canon" as other super-statutes do. The Civil Rights Act of 1964, for example, was the product of an intense process of popular mobilization, which justifies the central place it occupies in the current constitutional order.[14] This is not true of the Federal Arbitration Act, in spite of the wide congressional consensus it rested upon when it was enacted.

So assigning constitutional status to arbitration in the United States is quite problematic. It would actually be very undesirable to do so. A constitutional theory in support of arbitration could be abusively enlisted to further expand the objectionable rulings on arbitration that the Supreme Court has developed in recent years, which have seriously undercut the effectiveness of many laws aimed at protecting consumers and employees, as we will see in Chapter 3.

It is worthy of note that the idea of constitutionalizing arbitration was not unheard of in the past, at the state level. In 1915, for example, the state of New York held a Constitutional Convention to revise its fundamental charter of government. The leaders of the movement to modernize arbitration law lobbied for the introduction of a provision in the Constitution to guarantee the enforceability of arbitration agreements. They failed, in part because doubts arose among members of the Convention as to whether such a provision properly belonged in a constitution. Instead, a modern arbitration statute was enacted in 1920 to shield arbitration against the traditional hostility of courts. The statute's conformity with the New York Constitution was later challenged in a case before the Court of Appeals of New York. In an opinion authored by Judge Benjamin Cardozo, the Court finally rejected the constitutional objections.[15]

[12] On the category of "super-statutes" in American law, see William N. Eskridge Jr. and John Ferejohn, *A Republic of Statutes: The New American Constitution* (New Haven: Yale University Press, 2010).

[13] It is controversial how Congress is supposed to express its will for these purposes, and how clear that expression of will must be in order for it to rebut the presumption in favor of the arbitrability of statutory claims. A case that illustrates this uncertainty is *Compucredit Corp.* v. *Greenwood*, 132 S.Ct. 665 (2012).

[14] On the constitutional nature of the Civil Rights Act of 1964 and other federal laws that are connected with it, see Bruce Ackerman, *We the People, Volume 3: The Civil Rights Revolution* (Cambridge, Massachusetts: Harvard University Press, 2014).

[15] See Imre Szalai, *Outsourcing Justice. The Rise of Modern Arbitration Laws in America* (Durham, North Carolina: Carolina Academic Press, 2013), pp. 63–65, 105–106.

In Texas, on the other hand, the efforts to embody arbitration in the Constitution succeeded. Every Constitution since 1845 provided that it was "the duty of the Legislature to pass such laws as may be necessary and proper to decide differences by arbitration, when the parties shall elect that method of trial."[16] This provision was repealed by the voters in 1969 as one of the "obsolete, superfluous and unnecessary sections of the Constitution," but a House Joint Resolution stated that the repeal was not intended to make any substantive changes. The Supreme Court of Texas has referred to this constitutional tradition to emphasize the fundamental importance of arbitration as a manifestation of freedom of contract.[17]

2.1.2 *Europe*

The European constitutional context differs from that of the United States. In Europe, the constitutional domain is deemed to be quite broad. It is usually understood to encompass freedom of enterprise and freedom of contract, which naturally extend to corporations and other legal persons. This protection of a liberal economic order coexists with a deep commitment to principles of social justice, which are also enshrined in the constitutional texts. All these different rights and principles have to be balanced in a harmonic way. In general, restrictions on rights are accepted by courts, if they are suitable, necessary, and proportional to achieve legitimate goals.[18] When assessing the limitations that the legislature has placed on rights, the judiciary is inclined to reject strict scrutiny. It tends to be relatively deferential in many areas.

The Charter of Fundamental Rights of the European Union is a good example of this European conception. The Charter includes, among others, the "freedom to conduct a business" (article 16) and the "right to property" (article 17), together with rights and principles on "solidarity" (articles 27–38), which cover matters relating to working conditions, social security, health care, environmental protection, and consumer rights. As far as limitations of fundamental rights and freedoms are concerned, article 52(1) provides that "subject to the principle of proportionality, limitations may be made only if they are necessary and genuinely meet objectives of general interest recognized by the Union or the need to protect the rights and freedoms of others." A broad understanding of the rights and principles that are to be safeguarded under the Charter is thus combined with the principle of proportionality as the main adjudicative tool to resolve normative tensions.

16 See article VII, section 15, of the Constitutions of 1845, 1861, and 1866; article XII, section 11, of the Constitution of 1869; and article XVI, section 13, of the Constitution of 1876.

17 See, for instance, *Nafta Traders, Inc.*, v. *Quinn*, 339 S.W.3d 84 (2011). Footnote 57 of the opinion contains the references to the various Texas Constitutions, as well as the House Joint Resolution mentioned in the text.

18 On the origins and evolution of the principle of proportionality in Europe, see Nicholas Emiliou, *The Principle of Proportionality in European Law. A Comparative Study* (London: Kluwer Law International, 1996).

In this context, awarding a constitutional rank to the right to arbitration becomes plausible. The extensive conception of the constitutional realm invites the recognition of the right to arbitration as an implicit right connected to the general principle of private autonomy. The Constitutional Courts of Italy and Spain, for example, have held that arbitration is covered by the constitutional clauses that protect liberty in the sphere of private law.[19] Courts in Germany have also tied arbitration to constitutionally guaranteed private autonomy.[20]

There is no general reluctance in Europe, moreover, to embrace the notion that constitutional rights display effects in the private sphere ("horizontal effects"). There is certainly discussion as to whether constitutional rights bind private actors directly, or whether they do so only indirectly, by way of the ordinary legislation that the state must enact to ensure that rights are observed in private relations.[21] Whatever the answer to this technical question is, the key point is that it is generally accepted by scholars and judges in Europe that constitutional rights can enter the private realm. The jurisprudence of the German Constitutional Court has been particularly influential in this regard.[22] The Court of Justice of the European Union, in turn, has held that the Charter of Fundamental Rights of the European Union confers on private individuals certain rights that they can rely upon in a dispute with another individual.[23]

The European Court of Human Rights has also had a wide impact regarding the issue of the horizontal effect of rights. It has held that the European Convention on Human Rights requires states to adopt and implement measures aimed at protecting human rights against violations perpetrated by private persons. Whether this means that rights have a direct horizontal force is an intricate issue.[24] But there is no doubt that Convention rights can be relevant in private relationships.

All this has implications for arbitration, of course, given the fact that arbitration is conducted by private persons and not by public authorities. Thus, in the *Mutu and Pechstein* case, the European Court of Human Rights saw no conceptual problem in holding that the Court of Arbitration for Sport (CAS), which is a private arbitral tribunal seated in Switzerland, had breached one of the parties' fundamental rights guaranteed by article 6 of the Convention, which provides that "in the

19 See *sentenza* 127/1977, July 4, 1977; and STC 176/1996, November 11, 1996.

20 For references, see Stephan Balthasar, "International Arbitration in Germany," in Stephan Balthasar (ed.), *International Commercial Arbitration. International Conventions, Country Reports and Comparative Analysis* (Munich: C.H. Beck; Oxford: Hart; Baden-Baden: Nomos, 2016), p. 381.

21 For a comparative view on this issue, see András Sajó and Renáta Uitz (eds.), *The Constitution in Private Relations: Expanding Constitutionalism* (AJ Utrecht: Eleven International Publishing, 2005).

22 For a recent discussion of the German constitutional doctrine on the horizontal effects of fundamental rights, in the context of a comparative study that includes Canada and the United States, see Jud Mathews, *Extending Rights' Reach. Constitutions, Private Law, and Judicial Power* (New York: Oxford University Press, 2018).

23 See Judgment of 6 November 2018, C-569/16, *Bauer* case, para. 89.

24 On this question, see Pieter van Dijk, Fried van Hoof, Arjen van Rijn, and Leo Zwaak (eds.), *Theory and Practice of the European Convention on Human Rights* (Cambridge: Intersentia, 2018), pp. 26–30.

determination of his civil rights and obligations . . . everyone is entitled to a fair and public hearing within a reasonable time by an independent and impartial tribunal established by law."[25] The European Court of Human Rights considered that in the circumstances of the case one of the athletes who brought complaints was entitled to a public hearing during the arbitral proceedings, as she had requested. Even if Switzerland was technically the defendant in the case before the Court, which is an international tribunal, the violation of the right resulted directly from the decision of the arbitral tribunal denying a public hearing (a decision which the Swiss judiciary later failed to correct). The Court was very explicit when it concluded that there had been an infringement of Article 6 of the Convention "on account of the non-public nature of the proceedings before the CAS."[26] It is thus plain that the rights guaranteed by the Convention can bind a private body like the CAS.

It is interesting to note that the Swiss Code of Civil Procedure stipulates that an arbitral award may be reviewed by Swiss courts if the European Court of Human Rights has determined in a final judgment that the European Convention or its protocols have been violated, if compensation is not an appropriate remedy for the effects of the violation, and the review is necessary to remedy the violation.[27] Notice how the assumption here is that a fundamental right enshrined in the European Convention has been breached by the arbitral tribunal, which is a private body. If the arbitral award needs to be overturned to properly execute the European Court of Human Right's judgment, this is because the award itself is the source of the breach of the fundamental right involved.

In this European context, in sum, the idea that there is a basic right to arbitration strikes a constitutional chord. The right can be easily connected to a more general right to private autonomy that is part of the constitutional grammar. At the same time, arbitration can be upgraded to the constitutional rank without unduly upsetting reasonable normative frameworks. The justifiable restrictions the legislature may decide to place on the arbitral process can be easily rooted in constitutional norms, many of which are applicable in the private arena and can thus extend to arbitration.

2.1.3 *Latin America*

The constitutionalization of the right to arbitration finds an especially friendly environment in Latin America. Actually, a number of Latin American countries explicitly mention arbitration in their constitutional documents.[28] The Constitution of Costa Rica, for instance, contains the right of every person to terminate his

[25] See *Mutu and Pechstein* v. *Switzerland*, nos. 40575/10 and 67474/10, Judgment of 2 October 2018.

[26] Ibid., para. 183.

[27] See article 396(2) of the Swiss Code of Civil Procedure.

[28] For references, see José Carlos Fernández Rozas, *Tratado del Arbitraje Comercial en América Latina* (Madrid: Iustel, 2008), pp. 300–301.

patrimonial disputes through arbitration.[29] Similarly, the Constitution of Honduras establishes that no person who can freely administer his interests can be deprived of the right to terminate his private law disputes through arbitration.[30] A similar provision is included in the Constitution of El Salvador, which recognizes such a right as a specific manifestation of the more general right to liberty of contract in accordance with the laws.[31] In other countries, such as Colombia, Ecuador, Paraguay, and Panama, arbitration is mentioned in the constitutional text, though not in the form of a right.[32] Interestingly, the Constitutional Court of Colombia has connected the availability of alternative forms of dispute resolution to article 1 of the Constitution, which proclaims, among other things, the "democratic and participatory" character of the Colombian state.[33] The Constitution of Venezuela provides that the law shall promote arbitration as an alternative dispute resolution mechanism.[34] The Constitution of Peru, in turn, makes reference to arbitration by way of an exception to the general principle that reserves the jurisdictional function to regular courts. Arbitration also figures in the constitutional provision that guarantees freedom of contract.[35]

All this is in keeping with the historical Latin American precedents mentioned earlier, which emerged under the influence of the Spanish Constitution of 1812. It is interesting to point out that, in spite of the traditional recognition of the constitutional status of arbitration in Latin America, for the greater part of the nineteenth and twentieth centuries no domestic arbitration culture developed in most countries in the region. According to Andrés Jana, part of the explanation lies in the fact that the nascent states tended to jealously safeguard their sovereignty and thus distrusted private endeavors in the area of dispute resolution.[36] Indeed, as Horacio Grigera Naón notes, the "initial flourishing of arbitration in the region originated in the commercial and trade sectors, and not in government circles."[37] So the constitutionalization of arbitration at an early historical stage did not mean much in terms of actual legislative and judicial support.

One of the reasons why anchoring arbitration in the Constitution has not encountered great obstacles in Latin America has to do with the expansive conception of the constitutional domain generally embraced in the region, a conception that is even

[29] See article 43 of the Constitution of Costa Rica of 1949.

[30] See article 110 of the Constitution of Honduras of 1982.

[31] See article 23 of the Constitution of El Salvador of 1983.

[32] See article 116 of the Constitution of Colombia of 1991; article 190 of the Constitution of Ecuador of 2008; article 248(2) of the Constitution of Paraguay of 1992; and article 202 of the Constitution of Panama of 1972.

[33] See *Sentencia* C-163/99, March 17, 1999.

[34] See article 258(2) of the Constitution of Venezuela of 1999.

[35] See articles 139(1) and 62 of the Constitution of Peru of 1993.

[36] Andrés Jana L., "International Commercial Arbitration in Latin America: Myths and Realities," 32 *Journal of International Arbitration*, 413 (2015), pp. 418–421.

[37] Horacio A. Grigera Naón, "Arbitration and Latin America: Progress and Setbacks," 21 *Arbitration International*, 127 (2005), p. 141.

more comprehensive than that of Europe. Latin American Constitutions tend to include very long and detailed lists of rights, encompassing many civil and political rights, as well as economic, social, and cultural rights. As Carlos Bernal observes, "since the 1917 Mexican Constitution of Queretaro, numerous international instruments and national constitutions have entrenched human and constitutional rights with economic and social content." Latin America is particularly committed to their protection: "All Latin American constitutions entrench economic and social rights, and guarantee a higher average number of them in comparison to other regions in the world."[38] Whether the political arrangements laid down in the Constitutions are properly designed to secure the satisfaction of such rights is, of course, another matter.[39]

The horizontal effect of rights is also widely acknowledged in the region. The Inter-American Court of Human Rights has reflected this understanding when it has held that states may be found to be in breach of the American Convention on Human Rights if they fail to guarantee respect for human rights by private persons.[40] Medical malpractice in a private hospital causing death or injuries, for example, amounts to a violation of the Convention human right to life and physical integrity. Public authorities may be held responsible for this result, if the applicable laws and enforcement machineries prove to be defective.[41]

So Latin American constitutions offer judges the normative resources they may need to justify reasonable restrictions on the right to arbitration. Even if arbitration may be regarded, at least in part, to be a creature of contract, constitutional principles bear on it. The Constitutional Court of Peru, for example, has held that the private character of the contractual agreement setting up an arbitral tribunal does not imply the consequence that arbitrators can disregard constitutional principles (such as those protecting fundamental rights). The Court has stated that the Constitution applies to private relations, and has thus concluded that arbitrators must observe constitutional precepts in accordance with the case law produced by the Court.[42] In Brazil, likewise, due process principles contained in the federal Constitution are understood to apply to both judicial and arbitral forums.[43]

38 Carlos Bernal, "The Constitutional Protection of Economic and Social Rights in Latin America," in Rosalind Dixon and Tom Ginsburg (eds.), *Comparative Constitutional Law in Latin America* (Cheltenham: Edward Elgar Publishing, 2017), pp. 326–327.

39 For an account of the history of Latin American constitutionalism criticizing the mismatch between the very ambitious catalogues of constitutional rights, on the one hand, and the deficiency of the political structures that have been built, on the other, see Roberto Gargarella, *Latin American Constitutionalism, 1810–2010. The Engine Room of the Constitution* (Oxford: Oxford University Press, 2013).

40 See Advisory Opinion OC-23/17 of November 15, 2017, Series A No. 23, para. 119.

41 See *Case of Albán Cornejo et al* v. *Ecuador*, Judgment of November 22, 2007, Series C No. 171, paras. 118–119.

42 See Exp. N01567-2006-PA/TC, *Compañía de Exploraciones Algamarca*, April 30, 2006.

43 Nuno Lousa and Raquel Galvão Silva, "International Arbitration in Brazil," in Balthasar (ed.), *International Commercial Arbitration*, p. 257.

In sum, each country has its own constitutional and legal traditions, which make it more or less feasible to constitutionalize the right to arbitration, as this brief comparative overview of the United States, Europe, and Latin America reveals.

Let us suppose, next, that the Bill of Rights of the Constitution of a given country contains clauses guaranteeing the right to arbitration, whether explicitly or implicitly, and that the Constitution underpins all the necessary countervailing norms that will do the constraining work on arbitration. What is the point, one may ask, of constitutionalizing the right to arbitration? What consequences follow from inserting such a right in the constitution? What difference does it make?

2.2 LEGITIMATING ARBITRATION AGAINST CONSTITUTIONAL CHARGES

One potential advantage of constitutionalizing the right to arbitration is this: in some countries, arbitration may be vulnerable to constitutional attacks, and the best way to shield arbitration against such attacks is to root it in the constitution. The explicit or implicit recognition of a constitutional right to arbitration can thus serve a defensive purpose.

The extent to which there is room for calling into question the constitutionality of arbitration depends, of course, on the content of the existing constitution. Arbitration may be more or less contestable, in accordance with the text of the constitution. There may be no need to elevate arbitration to constitutional status if there is nothing in the constitutional document that potentially casts doubts on its validity.

It is not rare, however, for constitutions to contain clauses that critics may invoke to challenge the validity of arbitration. In particular, many constitutions establish that the adjudicative power is vested in courts. Call this the "judicial exclusivity clause." The Spanish Constitution, for instance, provides in article 117 that the "jurisdictional power" pertains to courts exclusively. The same is true of article 102 of the Italian Constitution, which declares that the "jurisdictional function" is carried out by ordinary courts. Similarly, article III, section 1 of the Constitution of the United States vests the "judicial power" of the United States in federal courts. Critics of arbitration could point to constitutional provisions of this sort to question the legitimacy of arbitration or, less radically, to require the establishment of very serious obstacles to it. After all, enabling private arbitrators to adjudicate controversies seems to amount to a breach of the judicial exclusivity norm announced in the constitution.

To counter the objection that invokes the judicial exclusivity clause, it will not do to point to superficial differences between courts and arbitrators. It is sometimes argued, for example, that courts have the power to enforce their own decisions, while arbitrators cannot enforce the awards they issue: the parties seeking execution must resort to the judiciary. But this difference is not as important as it seems for purposes of our discussion here. At the international level, for example, the International Court of Justice has no power to enforce its own judgments, as we will see in Part III of the book. Yet, nobody seriously doubts on this account that the Court exercises a jurisdictional task. By the same token, the fact that domestic arbitrators cannot execute their own awards should not distract us from observing the larger picture: both courts and arbitrators deliver decisions that are binding on the contending parties. How are we going to justify the adjudicative authority that arbitrators exert, when the constitution proclaims that only courts can carry out the jurisdictional function?

In order to defend arbitration against constitutional censure, we must emphasize a major difference between courts and arbitrators. The key difference is this: as already noted, courts do not need the consent of both parties to earn the authority to resolve a dispute. Arbitrators, in contrast, do. This critical difference allows us to answer the objection that appeals to the judicial exclusivity clause. Indeed, what the constitution reserves to courts exclusively is a "power" (*potestas*), the power to adjudicate a dispute that one party brings against another. When the decision-maker does not need the consent of the defendant for purposes of issuing a binding decision that settles the difference, the decision-maker exercises a true "power." When, in contrast, the decision-maker needs the mutual consent of the parties in order to be authorized to make a binding decision, he or she does not really exercise a "power." One of the characteristics of modernity is that only the state wields the adjudicative power. When things are seen in this way, arbitration does not appear to be an exception to the judicial exclusivity rule, for the simple reason that arbitrators exercise no "power" when they resolve a controversy, their mandate to decide being conferred by the parties.

Now, this theory in defense of the constitutionality of arbitration gains strength if the right of individuals to arbitrate their disputes is assumed to be part of the constitutional order. The distinction between adjudicative power, on the one hand, and authority based on consent, on the other, is not a distinction without a difference, but one that carries great normative significance. It reflects the critical role that a liberal political order assigns to private autonomy.

The Italian Constitutional Court, for example, convincingly appealed to the "constitutional guarantee of private autonomy" to justify its conclusion that the availability of arbitral tribunals does not breach article 102 of the Constitution, which reserves the jurisdictional function to regular judges. The Constitutional Court reasoned that article 102 cannot be read in isolation. It needs to be interpreted in harmony with the rest of the constitutional document, which safeguards the private autonomy of citizens in a number of its provisions.[44]

On the other hand, if arbitration is not linked to the constitution through an explicit or implicit recognition of the right to arbitrate, things can get more

44 See *sentenza* 2/1963, February 5, 1963, para. 2; and *sentenza* 127/1977, July 4, 1977, para. 1.

complicated. In the United States, for example, some scholars have argued that arbitration is in tension with article III, section 1 of the Constitution, which vests the judicial power of the United States in federal courts. Peter Rutledge, for instance, maintains that the constitutionality of arbitration turns on the establishment of sufficient checks by article III courts on the decisions made by arbitral tribunals. Only if courts can supervise arbitral awards to a sufficient extent is arbitration in conformity with the exclusivity clause. In particular, Rutledge contends that the "manifest disregard of the law" doctrine, which permits courts to review awards on their merits, to verify that no clear legal error has been committed by the arbitrators, is a necessary piece of the arbitral framework, without which the constitutionality of arbitration would be doubtful. He concludes that the manifest disregard of the law doctrine "saves private commercial arbitration from constitutional defect."[45] The problem, however, is that there is controversy in the United States as to whether this traditional doctrine is still good law.[46] In many countries, moreover, no similar doctrine has developed: the task of judges when supervising arbitral awards is limited to jurisdictional and procedural issues (or to the protection of public policy). If, as Rutledge suggests, arbitration only passes the constitutional test if the law empowers the courts to review the substantive legal merits of arbitral decisions (even if courts are to do so deferentially), arbitration has shaky foundations.

Similarly, an implicit right to arbitration must be presupposed in order to make sense of the jurisprudence of the European Court of Human Rights. This Court has had the opportunity to rule on the issue of whether arbitration based on the agreement of the parties is compatible with article 6 of the European Convention on Human Rights, which proclaims the individual right to a public hearing by an independent and impartial tribunal established by law. An arbitral agreement, of course, operates as a barrier to such a hearing. Is arbitration at odds with the Convention, then? The Court's answer is no. Voluntary arbitration is legitimate, the Court has reasoned, since by choosing arbitration the parties waive their right to go to court. This does not mean, however, that all the guarantees mentioned in article 6 of the Convention can be surrendered by means of arbitration. The Court has held that while the right to a public hearing can be waived in advance, the independence and impartiality guarantee cannot.[47]

There is no easy way to justify this distinction between publicity, on the one hand, and independence/impartiality, on the other, unless we assume that the European Convention on Human Rights implicitly protects the right to arbitration (as

45 Peter B. Rutledge, *Arbitration and the Constitution* (Cambridge: Cambridge University Press, 2013), p. 49.

46 For a discussion on this matter, with a proposal to clarify the issue through legislative reform, see Chistopher R. Drahozal, "Codifying Manifest Disregard," 8 *Nevada Law Journal*, 234 (2007).

47 See *Suovaniemi* v. *Finland*, no. 31737/96, Decision of 23 February 1999.

a manifestation of the very broad right to "respect for private life" enshrined in article 8). Indeed, if we understand that private persons have a right to resort to arbitration to settle a controversy governed by private law, then we have some guidance as to which guarantees, of those that flow from article 6, can be given up, and which ones cannot. As we will explore in Chapter 3, it is a justified restriction of party autonomy for the law to require that arbitrators be independent and impartial. It is perfectly legitimate for the law to prescribe that the parties cannot contract around this norm. It is thus reasonable for the European Court to read the Convention to extend the independence/impartiality principle to arbitration. In contrast, it would not be plausible to interpret the Convention to require arbitral proceedings to be public. Such a rule would destroy a key feature of arbitration. It is true, as explained in Chapter 1, that a trend toward transparency can be observed in some arbitral quarters. Still, many arbitral procedures are conducted confidentially. And although confidentiality is not the only reason why arbitration is employed, it is a relevant consideration that parties take into account when they opt for arbitration. So it is the need to safeguard an implicit right to arbitration that best accounts for the European Court's otherwise arbitrary distinction between article 6 requirements that can be waived (publicity) and those that cannot (independence and impartiality).

In sum, constitutionalizing the right to arbitration protects arbitration against potential objections based on national constitutions or international human rights conventions.

Admittedly, there are other ways to grant constitutional status to arbitration, without using the specific legal technique of proclaiming a "right to arbitration." The constitution, for example, may explicitly include arbitral tribunals within the list of "courts" that can adjudicate disputes, as the Portuguese Constitution does.[48] Alternatively, the constitution may mention arbitration as a dispute resolution mechanism that the law must regulate, and even promote, as is true of some Latin American countries referred to earlier. It is worthy of note, in this regard, that the constitutionality of arbitration was a matter of controversy in Mexico until the Constitution was amended in 2008. A new clause was included in article 17 of the Constitution empowering the legislature to regulate alternative dispute resolution mechanisms.[49] It is better, however, if a constitutional link is formed through the recognition of the right to arbitration. From a normative point of view, this strategy makes transparent that the ultimate reason why arbitration is constitutionally safeguarded is that it is an expression of the autonomy of the parties, which is an important value in a liberal political order.

[48] See article 209 of the Constitution of Portugal of 1976.

[49] For a discussion of this issue, as it unfolded before the constitutional amendment was adopted in 2008, see José Carlos Fernández Rozas, "La Constitución mexicana y el arbitraje comercial," 16 *Cuestiones Constitucionales: Revista mexicana de Derecho constitucional*, 159 (2007), pp. 165–180.

2.3 PROTECTING ARBITRATION AGAINST LEGISLATIVE MEASURES

Another effect of constitutionalizing the right to arbitration is that arbitration gets hedged against the risk that the ordinary legislature might eliminate arbitration as a dispute resolution method. Admittedly, it is extremely unlikely that the democratic parliament in an advanced legal system will do any such thing in the future. It nevertheless makes sense to enshrine the right to arbitration, just in case.

Constitutional entrenchment also serves an expressive function. Entrenchment of a right sends a message to the political community that the state is not free to decide whether or not to respect that right. As Alon Harel argues, "its value is grounded in the fact that constitutional entrenchment of moral or political rights is in itself a form of public recognition that the protection of rights is the state's *duty* rather than merely a discretionary gesture on its part, or that it is contingent upon its own judgments concerning the public good."[50] The constitutional recognition of the right to arbitration can thus express the central idea that arbitration is not an institutional scheme the legislature has simply chosen to open up for private actors to resolve their differences. Arbitration is instead a dispute resolution mode whose availability the state must guarantee. Constitutional entrenchment of arbitration confirms the expectation that the legislature has no license to adopt measures that are obviously destructive of this component of private autonomy.

A related consequence of inserting the right to arbitration in the constitution is that the legislature bears the burden of justifying in court the restrictions it decides to place on arbitration. The legislature does not have free rein to decide what to do in this connection. In general, constitutions have become key instruments to buttress a public culture of justification in democratic political communities.[51] The constitutional text is a source of principles that citizens can invoke to contest governmental measures. The state is forced to explain itself before a court, when the measures it has adopted seem to breach those principles. The constitutional judges may be more or less skeptical when they listen to the arguments advanced by public authorities. They can be more or less deferential when they review the constitutionality of a law. Whatever the standard of scrutiny courts apply, the critical point of judicial review is to ensure that governmental institutions are sensitive to the relevant constitutional principles. So if the right to arbitration is made part of the constitutional canon, the legislature needs to be careful when it shapes the arbitral legal regime. Whenever it sets out restrictions that arguably affect that right, it bears the burden of justification.

[50] Alon Harel, *Why Law Matters* (Oxford: Oxford University Press, 2014), p. 149 (emphasis in the original).

[51] On the role of constitutions and courts in the development of a culture of justification, see Mattias Kumm, "The Idea of Socratic Contestation and the Right to Justification: The Point of Rights-Based Proportionality Review," 4 *Law & Ethics of Human Rights*, 142 (2010); and Moshe Cohen-Eliya and Iddo Porat, "Proportionality and the Culture of Justification," 59 *American Journal of Comparative Law*, 463 (2011).

In Chapter 3, we will explore some examples of legislative restrictions whose justification is questionable. The advantage of anchoring the right to arbitration in the constitution is that objections to such laws can be brought to the judicial forum.

When hearing constitutional challenges against arbitration laws, courts in various countries are likely to follow different approaches. Some courts will craft doctrines based on categorical rules, while others will be inclined to engage in a more flexible inquiry. In some jurisdictions, for example, the primary doctrine that courts have worked out to protect arbitration relies on general contract law. The doctrine holds that the ground for blocking the enforcement of an arbitration agreement must be a ground that also applies to any other contract. In other words, no special contractual rules can be established that single out arbitration agreements in an unfavorable way.[52] In other places, courts will favor a more flexible kind of scrutiny, on the assumption that the state may have good reasons to condition and restrict the enforceability of arbitral agreements, even if those reasons only apply to a limited set of contracts. Suppose, for example, that the legislature stipulates that certain types of standard clauses in consumer contracts must be properly highlighted to guarantee transparency. The fact that this requirement does not apply to all kinds of contract, but is instead confined to consumer agreements, does not necessarily mean that the state does not have sufficiently good grounds to prescribe it. Judges relying on notions of reasonableness may well reach the conclusion that such a law is constitutionally warranted.

Some courts, moreover, may be strongly sensitive to the particular configuration of facts in each case. The Constitutional Chamber of the Supreme Court of Costa Rica, for instance, once struck down a law that excluded from arbitration certain contractual disputes between foreign companies and their local representatives.[53] The legislature had justified the exclusion on account of the disparity in bargaining power between the contracting parties. The Court held that the law breached the fundamental right to arbitration enshrined in article 43 of the Constitution. It also asserted, however, that judges should scrutinize the arbitration agreements in each specific case, if one of the parties alleged that contractual consent was vitiated.

Whatever the mix of categorical rules, standards of reasonableness, and case-by-case analysis that judges resort to, the important point is that the constitutional

[52] This is the doctrine that the United States Supreme Court has developed, in light of the provision of the Federal Arbitration Act that establishes that arbitration agreements can be refused enforcement only on "grounds as exist at law or in equity for the revocation of any contract" (chapter 1, section 2). See, for example, *Doctor's Associates, Inc.* v. *Casarotto*, 517 U.S. 681 (1996). The legal context in the United States is complicated as a result of its federal structure. Courts must assess state laws against the Federal Arbitration Act. If there is a conflict, the federal statute preempts state law. To avoid preemption, the grounds that state laws stipulate to render arbitral agreements invalid or unenforceable must be rooted in general principles of contract law. Although the Constitution of the United States does not encompass a right to arbitration, the Federal Arbitration Act operates as a normative constraint on state legislatures.

[53] *Resolución* No 10352–2000, November 22, 2000.

entrenchment of the right to arbitration opens up a space for contesting in court the validity of legislative choices regarding arbitration.

It is interesting to observe that enshrining arbitration in the constitution as a liberty right can help reinforce the case against the passage of laws that compel individuals to arbitrate disputes they have not consented to arbitrate. Of course, there is already an argument against the constitutionality of such laws: individuals have a fundamental right to go to court to vindicate their legal interests. If individuals have not consented to arbitration, the judicial doors should be open to them. The recognition of arbitration as a liberty right is nevertheless useful to strengthen the constitutional charges that can be brought against the establishment of forms of compulsory arbitration. Whether the latter are ultimately constitutional will depend, of course, on the specific terms of each constitution. If the right of access to courts is subject to broad exceptions, for example, there is considerable room for the legislature to impose arbitration. If, in contrast, a categorical right of access to courts is constitutionally guaranteed, compulsory arbitration will be ruled out. There is lots of variation on this issue across countries. The Supreme Court of the United States, for instance, has sometimes upheld statutes forcing private parties to resort to arbitration.[54] The Italian Constitutional Court, in contrast, has declared compulsory arbitration to contravene the Constitution.[55] The same position has been adopted by the Spanish Constitutional Court,[56] as well as by the Constitutional Court of Colombia.[57] For its part, the Constitutional Chamber of the Supreme Court of Costa Rica once invalidated a statute that forced arbitration on the parties. But the Chamber later qualified its doctrine, allowing for the possibility of exceptions in some special cases.[58] The Constitutional Court of Malta has also evolved. In 2004, the Maltese legislature introduced mandatory arbitration for certain defined categories of disputes, in an attempt to reduce the heavy judicial caseload. The Constitutional Court first held mandatory arbitration to be unconstitutional, but it later reconsidered its position and confirmed the validity of the law.[59]

The European Court of Human Rights, in turn, has accepted compulsory arbitration, but with an important proviso. The Court has declared that if one of the contending parties subjected to compulsory arbitration asks arbitrators to hold a public hearing, the hearing must be granted (unless the denial can be justified in the particular circumstances of the case). In other words, arbitration

54 See *Hardware Dealers Mutual Fire Insurance Co.* v. *Glidden Co.*, 284 U.S. 151 (1931); and *Thomas* v. *Union Carbide Agricultural Products Co.*, 473 U.S. 568 (1985). For a discussion of the argumentative lines the Court has followed when upholding forms of compulsory arbitration, see Alan Scott Rau, "The Culture of American Arbitration and the Lessons of ADR," 40 *Texas International Law Journal*, 449 (2005), pp. 478–483.

55 See *sentenza* 127/1977, July 4, 1977.

56 See STC 1/2018, January 11, 2018.

57 See *Sentencia* C-242/97, May 20, 1997; and *Sentencia* C-060/01, January 24, 2001.

58 See *Resolución* No 2307–1995, May 9, 1995; and *Resolución* No 10352–2000, November 22, 2000.

59 See *Untours Insurance Agency Ltd and Emanuel Gauci* v. *Victor Micallef, Saviour Micallef, Anthony Theuma and Kevin Bartolo*, January 25, 2013, Constitutional Court (App. No.81/2011/1).

that is not based on consent can only be accepted if the principle of publicity that typically applies to courts is observed – if one of the contending parties requests a public hearing. If the right to a public hearing is not satisfied, the Convention is thereby breached.[60]

2.4 PROTECTING ARBITRATION AGAINST JUDICIAL RULINGS

There is a third potential advantage of constitutionalizing the right to arbitration that deserves brief comment. The advantage is confined to legal systems of a particular kind. A significant number of countries in the world have created specialized constitutional tribunals whose primary function is to check the validity of legislation against the constitution. Such tribunals are detached from the rest of courts – which form the so-called "ordinary judiciary." In Europe, for example, most nations have established this arrangement.[61]

In some jurisdictions that follow this model, it is possible for constitutional tribunals to review the decisions of ordinary courts, if the latter are challenged on the grounds that they are not in conformity with fundamental rights. This is so in Germany and Spain, for instance. In an institutional setting of this kind, a modest benefit can be reaped if arbitration is rooted in the constitution as a right. The benefit is this: it has sometimes been claimed that ordinary judges are not in a good position to decide foundational issues about arbitration, for they are institutionally biased.[62] In the past, for example, courts in many countries were hostile to arbitration, either because judicial fees depended on the number of cases that were litigated, or because courts did not want to lose power. Nowadays, a different concern is often mentioned, one that goes in the opposite direction: judges may be too willing to send cases to arbitration in order to unclutter their dockets. To the extent that there is something to be said for this theory that questions the institutional neutrality of the judiciary when it comes to arbitration, countries that have created special constitutional tribunals can more easily escape the problem. Since the constitutional tribunal is detached from the ordinary judiciary, it is in a comparatively neutral position to deal with foundational questions about the role of arbitration in our society.

60 Thus, in *Scarth* v. *the United Kingdom*, no. 33745/96, Judgment of 22 July 1999, the Court maintained that the arbitration procedure conducted in that case was not in conformity with article 6 of the Convention. Since the arbitration was not voluntary, the public hearing that one of the parties requested should have been granted. The Court has confirmed this jurisprudence in the case of *Mutu and Pechstein* v. *Switzerland*, nos. 40575/10 and 67474/10, Judgment of 2 October 2018.

61 On this "centralized" model of constitutional review in Europe, see Alec Stone Sweet, *Governing with Judges. Constitutional Politics in Europe* (Oxford: Oxford University Press, 2000); Victor Ferreres Comella, *Constitutional Courts and Democratic Values. A European Perspective* (New Haven: Yale University Press, 2009); and Maartje de Visser, *Constitutional Review in Europe. A Comparative Analysis* (Oxford: Hart Publishing, 2013).

62 See, for instance, Richard C. Reuben, "Democracy and Dispute Resolution: The Problem of Arbitration," 67 *Law and Contemporary Problems*, 279 (2004), pp. 307–308.

Now, in order for the constitutional tribunal to be able to intervene in these matters, it is necessary to grant arbitration a constitutional status, and to do so through the recognition of a right to arbitration, since the jurisdiction of the constitutional tribunal when reviewing decisions of ordinary courts is limited to issues involving constitutional rights. So, if the right to arbitration is constitutionalized, a neutral institution can then control moves by ordinary judges that may be undermining arbitration in unacceptable ways or forcing arbitration on unwilling parties.

2.5 CONCLUSION

In this chapter, I have sought to show that there are good normative and institutional reasons favoring the incorporation of the right to arbitration in the constitution. The recognition of this right can be achieved through the introduction of an explicit constitutional clause or by way of judicial construction. The right to arbitration coheres with the fundamental values that a liberal political order seeks to honor. Different constitutional traditions are more or less likely to embrace this right, however, depending on how broadly they take the constitutional domain to be, how strictly they expect judges to assess governmental restrictions on rights, and how they deal with the issue of the horizontal effect of rights.

Having explored so far the configuration of arbitration as a right, it is now time to discuss the boundaries and constraints that arbitration ought to observe against the background of constitutional norms. This is the task of the next chapter.

3

Boundaries and Constraints

In this chapter we will explore the limits of arbitration. The state, as we will see, defines the boundaries of arbitration – the kinds of matters that are amenable to arbitration. It also lays down some norms the parties cannot contract around when designing the arbitral process. These two aspects are intertwined: the constraints it is reasonable for the law to impose on the procedural structure of arbitration may depend on the types of controversies that are legally amenable to arbitration.

Before we proceed, it is important to introduce a key distinction we need to keep in mind throughout our discussion.

3.1 AN IMPORTANT DISTINCTION

In the earlier chapters we have assumed that arbitration is being used to terminate a conflict that only affects the interests of the parties. Insofar as individuals are free to dispose of their own interests as they see fit, arbitration should be a protected option in a liberal political regime, I have argued. What happens, however, when the state adopts certain substantive rules that are mandatory – that cannot be derogated from by agreement of the parties?

Such rules may be mandatory in order to safeguard public goods. Antitrust law, for example, protects the efficient functioning of a competitive market. Two private companies are not entitled to contract around antitrust law, since the latter serves general interests that are different from, and broader than, the private interests of the parties. The state may also adopt mandatory rules to preserve the interests of the weaker party to a contract, who may be pressed by the stronger party to accept unfair terms. The state assumes that such terms would not have been agreed upon if the weak party had not been so weak. The law accordingly recognizes rights that individuals cannot waive through contract. In an employment agreement, for example, the parties are not authorized to insert a clause allowing the employer to discriminate against the employee on grounds of race, gender, or age, say. Similarly, consumer contracts are governed by statutes granting consumers certain rights that cannot be given up. The law may actually go further and establish constraints on freedom of contract even if there is no serious concern about disparity in bargaining power. The law may want to protect human dignity or personal integrity when doing so.[1]

Individuals, of course, may decide not to bring actions in court to enforce mandatory law. That is, they may choose not to exercise the rights such law confers on them. The state, in turn, may or may not put in motion other procedural mechanisms to compensate for this lack of individual vindication of rights. This does not affect, however, the basic operational principle regarding mandatory law: the parties to a contract cannot exclude in advance the applicability of such law. And the question arises: How should the state regulate the relationship between arbitration and mandatory norms? Should arbitrators be empowered to decide issues that attract mandatory law, or should their authority be confined to disputes that only implicate those rights the parties are free to waive in advance?

The basic right to arbitration we have discussed in Chapters 1 and 2 loses some of its force here, so that it becomes easier for the state to justify significant restrictions on arbitration. The core of the right to arbitration is linked to cases where the legal interests at stake can be freely disposed of by the parties antecedently. If the constitution grounds a right to arbitration, the legislature is prima facie required to open up the arbitral forum to such cases. The legislature is not constitutionally bound, however, to go further and extend arbitration to private disputes located in the realm of mandatory law. The Constitutional Court of Colombia, for example, correctly upheld the constitutionality of a statute that limited arbitration to disputes over matters private parties were legally entitled to dispose of. A citizen had challenged the statute through a "public action" (a form of *actio popularis*), with the argument that article 116 of the Colombian Constitution does not mention such limitation when it refers to arbitration. The Court rejected the argument, and circumscribed the constitutional protection of arbitration to disputes over rights of which the parties had full disposition.[2]

Even if the constitutional right to arbitration does not force the legislature to expand the domain of arbitration to cover differences governed by mandatory law, the legislature may nevertheless decide to take that step. In recent decades, the courts in many countries have construed the laws to permit arbitration of claims that are strongly tied to important public policies, such as those operating in the spheres of antitrust law and antidiscrimination law.[3] This evolution bears an important

[1] See Anthony T. Kronman, "Paternalism and the Law of Contracts," 92 *The Yale Law Journal*, 763 (1983), and Margaret Jane Radin, "Market-Inalienability," 100 *Harvard Law Review*, 1849 (1987).

[2] See *Sentencia* C-098/01, January 31, 2001.

[3] In the United States, the Supreme Court leading cases on this matter are *Mitsubishi* v. *Soler Chrysler-Plymouth*, 473 U.S. 614 (1985), and *Gilmer* v. *Interstate/Johnson Lane Corp.*, 500 U.S. 20 (1991). In the European Union, the most important decision on arbitrability rendered by the Court of Justice of the European Union is Judgment of 1 June 1999, C-126/97, *Eco Swiss* case.

consequence: the state is then licensed to set more stringent constraints on arbitration, to ensure that mandatory law is correctly interpreted and applied.

In what follows, we will first explore the requirements the legal system is authorized to lay down when no mandatory law applies to the substantive merits of the dispute. We will later extend our discussion to cases where mandatory law enters the picture.

It bears clarifying that some ingredients of mandatory law are always present in practice. The rules prescribing the conditions under which contracts are validly formed, for example, are rules the parties cannot disregard. The rules stipulating the conditions that must be fulfilled for someone to possess legal capacity to enter into a contract, for instance, cannot be derogated from by agreement of the parties, for obvious logical reasons. No case can thus be located in a sort of bubble, beyond the reach of mandatory law. In many instances, however, mandatory rules on the valid formation of contracts figure in the uncontested background of the dispute, since the contending parties have no quarrel about their interpretation and application.

So the distinction I have in mind for purposes of our discussion here relates to the terms of the specific controversy that arises in a given case. Does the controversy relate to rights that can be freely disposed of by the parties by way of contractual agreements, or does it relate instead to rights that cannot be given up because mandatory law covers them? Are the parties discussing, for example, whether the goods were delivered in accordance with the terms of the sales contract, or are they discussing whether the contract violates antitrust law, or whether one of the parties infringed upon the statutory (or constitutional) right of the other not to be discriminated against on grounds of race, gender, or age?

3.2 JUSTIFYING LEGAL CONSTRAINTS ON ARBITRATION: THE NEED FOR A FOCUSED ANALYSIS

The constraints that lawmakers and courts are justified in placing on the arbitral process need to be assessed on a case-by-case basis. Some constraints are warranted, while others are not. We must consider each of them separately. There is no convincing argument that can endorse the authority of the state to establish any limitations it wants.

It is sometimes contended that arbitration is strongly backed by the state and that, therefore, it should observe whatever limitations the law sets out. Indeed, without the legal framework that the state has built in favor of arbitration, and without the assistance that courts lend to the arbitral process, arbitration would rarely work as an effective dispute resolution mode. The state, it is argued, is accordingly empowered to establish any restrictions it deems appropriate.[4]

[4] This view is well captured by John Collier and Vaughan Lowe, *The Settlement of Disputes in International Law. Institutions and Procedures* (Oxford: Oxford University Press, 1999), p. 233, where they explain that powerful arguments have been made against delocalization of international

This argument is not convincing, however. Arbitration agreements certainly need the help of the state. But this is also true of contracts in general. Without the state's backing, the actual force of contracts is usually limited. It is true that people sometimes manage to create private orderings without top-down public intervention. Historically, for example, merchant guilds produced norms that its members had powerful incentives to abide by. Being excluded from the guild, or suffering the reputational costs associated with noncompliance, were too high a price for members to pay.[5] Generally speaking, however, private deals in a modern economy encompassing a large number of players can only be struck in the shadow of the state. Contracts to perform actions in the future cannot be operative without the legal structures and judicial support provided by the state. Classical economists and jurists in the nineteenth century tended to ignore the active involvement of governmental institutions to enable contractual liberty. As Patrick S. Atiyah explains, it came to be assumed in the classical era that "if parties are to have freedom to make a present exchange, then logically it follows that they must also have freedom to bind themselves to make a future exchange." The assumption was wrong, of course, since "a gulf separates these two freedoms." The first freedom "involves only the passive recognition by the State of what parties themselves choose to do, while the second involves the active intervention of the State to compel one party to do something which he no longer wants to do."[6]

Now, the fact that we need the state to empower individuals to enter into legally binding contracts does not mean that the state has unlimited authority to set out all kinds of restrictions on contracts. A piece of wisdom we should draw from constitutional doctrine is that when the government distributes funds, licenses, benefits, etc . . ., it does not enjoy unbounded discretion to fix the conditions the recipients must meet, since constitutional rights may be involved.[7] In the same vein, the state does not have free rein to lay down all sorts of limitations on the enforceability of contracts, even if it is true that we need the state to bring contracts into legal existence. As Stephen Smith observes in the context of his discussion about moralistic restrictions on enforceability, "if there are good reasons to enforce contracts in general, then good reasons are required before refusing to enforce particular kinds of contract."[8]

commercial arbitration: "The freedom to settle disputes by arbitration is a concession, a derogation from the monopoly claimed by the State in the administration of justice; and the concession is made subject to such conditions, including the supervision and regulation of arbitral proceedings by the local law, as the State may choose."

5 For an account of historical instances of successful private orderings, see Avner Greif, *Institutions and the Path to the Modern Economy: Lessons from Medieval Trade* (Cambridge: Cambridge University Press, 2006).

6 P. S. Atiyah, *The Rise and Fall of Freedom of Contract* (Oxford: Oxford University Press, 1979), p. 441.

7 For a general discussion of this issue, see Cass R. Sunstein, *The Partial Constitution* (Cambridge, Massachusetts: Harvard University Press, 1993), pp. 291–318.

8 Stephen A. Smith, *Contract Theory* (Oxford: Oxford University Press, 2004), p. 257.

It is sometimes argued that arbitration agreements are treated better than most other contracts. Thus, courts must stay the judicial proceedings and refer the parties to arbitration, if one of them invokes a valid arbitration agreement. This is a form of "specific" enforcement, a form of performance that many contracts do not enjoy.[9] In some jurisdictions, moreover, courts may issue orders compelling the recalcitrant party to arbitrate the dispute. Arbitration agreements thus enjoy a privileged position in the legal system, and any constraints the laws establish, the argument goes, must therefore be accepted.

This argument is not plausible, however. Given the very nature of an agreement to arbitrate a dispute, the state must enforce that agreement through a court decision that refers the parties to arbitration. If the only remedy for breach were a damages award for the party that wanted the case to be arbitrated, the agreement would scarcely have any legal bite.

A different theory to base the state's authority to stipulate restrictions on arbitration argues as follows. Arbitral awards are treated by the legal system in many respects as if they were the judgments of a court. This equivalent treatment is only justified if the arbitral award is the upshot of a process that is truly adjudicative. Parties are certainly free to choose any method they like to settle a dispute in a peaceful manner. But if they wish the decision of an arbitrator to be treated by the law as if it were the judgment of a court, then the arbitral process must be similar to the judicial process.

The problem with this theory, however, is that it can end up justifying so many requirements that the arbitral process must fulfill (in order to make it sufficiently similar to a lawsuit in court) that the difference between arbitration and litigation almost evaporates. It would be absurd, for example, to argue that arbitrators should not receive any fees from the parties, on the ground that judges are not paid by the parties. To justify reasonable constraints, the theory needs to discriminate between those judicial norms that must be transferred to the arbitral forum, and those others that need not be. As we will see, there are good reasons for the norm that requires adjudicative impartiality, for example, to apply to arbitration. But it is debatable whether other features of the judicial process should be transplanted to arbitration. What about the requirement that judges must be trained in the law, for example, or that their decision must come in the form of a reasoned opinion? The theory that says that arbitration must look like judicial adjudication in order for arbitral awards to be treated as if they were court judgments is too broad. We need to engage in a more focused and refined analysis of the arbitral process, in order to determine

9 This observation, however, is more relevant in common law countries, where specific performance of contracts has traditionally been regarded as a rather exceptional remedy, than in civil law countries, where specific performance tends to be viewed as normal. On this difference, which is nowadays less important in practice than it used to be, see Konrad Zweigert and Hein Kötz, *An Introduction to Comparative Law* (Oxford: Oxford University Press, 1998), pp. 470–485.

which particular judicial features must necessarily be present, and which ones need not be.

So we must follow a nuanced approach when assessing the various constraints that the law establishes on the architecture of the arbitral process. The analysis needs to distinguish between different kinds. We will here discuss some of them. We start with the impartiality and fairness requirement.

3.3 IMPARTIALITY AND FAIRNESS

According to the laws in all relevant jurisdictions, the arbitral process must be fair. The arbitrator must be impartial. He or she must proceed even-handedly, allowing both sides the opportunity to produce evidence and make legal arguments. And her final decision on the merits of the case must be based on an objective assessment of the factual and legal materials.

Arguably, the normative foundation of the impartiality and fairness requirement is connected to human dignity and personal integrity. The law cannot give its institutional support to an arbitral agreement that allows a party to be treated unfairly. The law cannot endorse a contractual clause, for example, that establishes that one of the parties, A, will unilaterally appoint the single arbitrator that will decide the case, while B renounces in advance his right to challenge the arbitrator on impartiality grounds. The impartiality of the arbitrator, as well as the general fairness of the proceedings, cannot be contracted out, even if the party who is apt to suffer the lack of even-handedness has received some economic benefit in exchange.[10]

Of course, if the arbitrators in charge of adjudicating a particular dispute are biased, or the procedure they conduct is not fair for other reasons, the disfavored party may still decide not to object during the arbitral proceedings and not challenge the award later in court. The state will typically not interfere with such choices. What the law cannot permit, however, is for a party to surrender in advance his right

[10] Section 1034(2) of the German Code of Civil Procedure, for example, provides that "if the arbitration agreement grants preponderant rights to one party with regard to the constitution of the arbitral tribunal which place the other party at a disadvantage, the other party may request the court to appoint the arbitrator or arbitrators in deviation from the nomination made, or from the agreed nomination procedure." See, however, in the United States, the case of *Westinghouse Electric Corporation v. New York City Transit Authority*, 735 F. Supp. 1205 (S.D.N.Y. 1990), April 13, 1990. The arbitrator that settled the dispute was not only paid by one of the parties, the New York Transit Authority, but was actually its Chief Electrical Officer. The judges nevertheless upheld the arbitral award, which had been challenged on impartiality grounds. They reasoned that the corporation had freely consented to submit the controversy to arbitration by that organ. This judicial opinion has been criticized, as inconsistent with the impartiality norm embodied in the Federal Arbitration Act. See, for example, Ian R. Macneil, Richard E. Speidel, and Thomas J. Stipanowich, *Federal Arbitration Law. Agreements, Awards, and Remedies under the Federal Arbitration Act* (Volume III) (Boston: Little, Brown, 1999), 28:56. For a different view, see Alan Scott Rau, Edward F. Sherman, and Scott R. Peppet, *Arbitration* (New York: Foundation Press, 2006), pp. 266–267.

to an impartial and fair adjudication of his claims. The other party should not be entitled to enlist the judicial machinery to enforce an arbitration agreement that contains such a waiver.[11]

Actually, in those legal systems where constitutional rights display horizontal force in the arbitral sphere, the requirement of arbitral impartiality may derive from the constitution itself, if the latter enshrines the general principle of impartiality in adjudication. In Germany, for instance, the principles of independence and impartiality "are considered indispensable constitutional requirements in order for arbitral proceedings to be equivalent to state court litigation."[12] The equal treatment of the parties in arbitral proceedings "is a statutory implementation of the constitutional equal treatment requirement contained in art 3 para 1 of the German Constitution."[13] The same is true in Switzerland: the Supreme Court has held that the guarantees of independence and impartiality recorded in the Constitution and the European Convention on Human Rights apply to arbitration.[14] Indeed, the European Court of Human Rights has preserved the independence/impartiality norm that figures in article 6 of the European Convention on Human Rights against erosion by arbitral practices. As already noted in Chapter 2, the Court has held that when individuals freely opt for arbitration, they can waive some components of the right to judicial protection enshrined in article 6 (such as the right to a public hearing), but they cannot renounce in advance their right to an independent and impartial adjudicator.

Given the centrality of the impartiality norm, the next question is how much flexibility should the parties enjoy when designing the procedures for selecting arbitrators?

When a single arbitrator is picked to handle a case, the general practice is for both parties to jointly agree on the appointment. If they do not reach an agreement, the arbitral center that manages the arbitration proceedings (if one has been chosen) will typically intervene. If that fails, courts will usually step in. There is no serious concern about this procedure, as far as impartiality goes, provided that the parties have the relevant information (regarding conflicts of interest, for example) and there is no fundamental imbalance in bargaining power. Arbitral institutions, moreover, ordinarily offer parties a roster of potential arbitrators to choose from. This makes it

[11] In Sweden, the parties may agree that a challenge to an arbitrator's impartiality "shall be conclusively determined by an arbitration institution," so that courts will not be authorized to intervene later (see section 11 of the Swedish Arbitration Act). But such an agreement can only be entered into after the concrete grounds of bias have become known to the parties, not in advance. See Finn Madsen, *Commercial Arbitration in Sweden* (Stockholm: Jure Förlag AB, 2016), p. 166.

[12] Richard Kreindler, Reinmar Wolff, and Markus S. Rieder, *Commercial Arbitration in Germany* (Oxford: Oxford University Press, 2016), p. 135.

[13] Ibid., p. 177.

[14] For references to the Supreme Court's case law, see Roman Richers and Melissa Magliana, "International Arbitration in Switzerland," in Stephan Balthasar (ed.), *International Commercial Arbitration. International Conventions, Country Reports and Comparative Analysis* (Munich: C.H. Beck; Oxford: Hart; Baden-Baden: Nomos, 2016), p. 641.

easier for the parties to find suitable arbitrators. In addition, the fact that the disputants negotiate the appointment of the arbitrator in the shadow of the courts or of an impartial nominating authority is a critical element to ensure a reasonable choice.

On the other hand, when tripartite arbitral tribunals are constituted, things get more complicated. Typically, each party unilaterally appoints an arbitrator, and then these two co-arbitrators (or the parties themselves) jointly select a presiding arbitrator or chairperson.

A question arises then: Should it be legally acceptable for the parties to specify that only the presiding arbitrator must be impartial, so that the co-arbitrators may be partial to the side that unilaterally appointed them?

There seems to be no powerful reason to deny the parties this option. The impartiality of the tribunal is ultimately guaranteed by the neutrality of the presiding arbitrator. It might be said that the disputants are wasting their money when, in addition to the counsel defending them during the proceedings, they are paying the services of co-arbitrators expected to act as partisan lawyers when the arbitral panel meets to deliberate and vote. But the parties may counter that they are willing to pay this extra money, to make sure that their respective positions and arguments will not be ignored during the arbitral deliberations. They expect the co-arbitrators to play the role of the "devil's advocate." This kind of intervention may be necessary to reduce the cognitive biases often associated with groups. Indeed, if the arbitration panel were a cohesive group eager to reach consensus, it might overlook important counterarguments.[15]

In the United States, for example, this arrangement is legally permitted. It is perfectly possible for the parties to stipulate that only the chair of the arbitral tribunal must be impartial. The American Arbitration Association, a leading arbitration house in the United States, explicitly contemplates this type of clause for domestic arbitration.[16]

In most jurisdictions in the world, however, the impartiality requirement is mandatory for all the members of the arbitral tribunal. The problem, then, is this: does it make sense for the law to allow the parties to unilaterally appoint the co-arbitrators, *if it insists that the latter must be impartial*? Isn't there a mismatch between the impartiality norm and the practice of unilateral appointments? Shouldn't all the arbitrators be jointly nominated by the parties?

In defense of the practice of unilateral appointments, it is sometimes said that if a party designates an arbitrator that is clearly biased, its chances of victory are small,

15 See Catherine A. Rogers, *Ethics in International Arbitration* (Oxford: Oxford University Press, 2014), pp. 327–334.

16 The Commercial Arbitration Rules and Mediation Procedures of the American Arbitration Association (amended and effective October 1, 2003) include Rule 18(b), which provides that "the parties may agree in writing" that the unilaterally appointed arbitrators "shall be non-neutral, in which case such arbitrators need not be impartial or independent and shall not be subject to disqualification for partiality or lack of independence."

since the chairperson will be skeptical of that party's case. It is doubtful, however, that this safeguard is sufficient. If party A believes that party B will choose a biased arbitrator, her best strategy may be to do the same, unless he or she is very confident that the chairperson will infer from B's choice that B's case must be very weak. Relying on the chairperson's response is too risky. In any event, even if there are incentives for parties and arbitrators to avoid extreme partisanship, the degree of objectivity of the unilaterally-nominated co-arbitrators will be lower than if they were jointly nominated.

Also by way of defense, a distinction is sometimes drawn between partiality and sympathy. The co-arbitrators, it is contended, must not be "partial" to the appointing party, but they are authorized to be "sympathetic" to the interests or views of that side. This subtle distinction, however, is not tenable in practice.[17] Because of the difficulty of drawing this distinction, and given the danger of different parties having different expectations as to the kinds of "sympathy" that a party-designated arbitrator may display, there is much to be said for a system that frankly recognizes that impartiality can only be expected from the presiding arbitrator and accordingly permits the parties to circumscribe the impartiality norm to the latter. But if the law insists that the impartiality norm must apply to all the arbitrators, then the institution of the party-appointed arbitrator is quite dysfunctional. It is better for all the arbitrators to be designated by consensus.[18]

It is interesting to refer at this juncture to the practice of hiring sitting judges to arbitrate. As we saw in Chapter 1, in a number of countries including Sweden, Denmark, and Germany, judges may be chosen to arbitrate a dispute. This possibility is excluded, however, if the appointment is unilateral. Thus, in Sweden the law regulating public employment includes a provision barring employees from performing any activity that may adversely affect confidence in their impartiality or may harm the reputation of public authorities. A judge is thus generally considered to be prevented from accepting appointments from one party only.[19] The same understanding operates in Denmark.[20] In Germany, likewise, a judge can only be granted the required governmental authorization to serve as an arbitrator if he is appointed by both parties (or by a neutral institution).[21] So the underlying assumption in these countries seems to be, quite rightly, that unilateral designation is inimical to full and genuine impartiality.

In addition to enhancing impartiality, a system based on the joint appointment of arbitrators helps select the right combination of experts. Under such a system,

17 For a critique of this distinction, see Alan Scott Rau, "On Integrity in Private Judging," 14 *Arbitration International*, 115 (1998), pp. 230–231.

18 For a criticism of the practice of unilateral appointments, see Jan Paulsson, *The Idea of Arbitration* (Oxford: Oxford University Press, 2013), pp. 153–166, and pp. 276–283.

19 Madsen, *Commercial Arbitration in Sweden*, p. 136.

20 Steffen Pihlblad, Christian Lundblad, and Claus Søgaard-Christensen, *Arbitration in Denmark* (Copenhagen: DJØF Publishing, 2014), p. 46.

21 Kreindler, Wolff, and Rieder, *Commercial Arbitration in Germany*, p. 125.

arbitrators can be chosen in light of their complementary areas of expertise, instead of their sympathies toward the appointing parties.[22] Actually, it is advisable for the tribunal to include a generalist jurist who can interact with the more specialized experts. As was noted earlier, experts may suffer cognitive biases as a result of their narrow areas of knowledge and may be unduly inattentive to more general legal doctrines or principles.

In any event, where co-arbitrators are unilaterally nominated, the law should provide that the opinion of the president shall prevail if no majority can be formed.[23] A provision of this kind works as a safety valve. It ensures that, should co-arbitrators adopt a very partisan attitude, the president will not be forced to lean in favor of one of them to reach a majority. The president will instead be able to insist on the answer he or she deems correct and write the award accordingly.

All these considerations concerning impartiality and the various appointment methods are relevant when assessing the legitimacy of dissenting opinions. Under a system where the parties are allowed to unilaterally designate partial co-arbitrators, it is not much of a problem for such co-arbitrators to file dissenting opinions in favor of the party that appointed them. No one is to be surprised if a partial co-arbitrator issues a dissent in favor of the side that appointed him or her. Similarly, if the system is one under which all the members of the tribunal must be impartial, and all of them are jointly nominated by the disputants, dissenting opinions are not troublesome either. If an arbitrator issues a dissent in favor of one side, this is not interpreted as a sign of partiality, since such an arbitrator was hired by common agreement. If, in contrast, the arrangement is the third one we have considered, where all the members of the tribunal are required to be impartial, but the co-arbitrators are unilaterally designated by each of the parties, the publication of dissents may indeed undermine the integrity of the arbitral process. The legitimacy of arbitration is weakened if, as happens in actual practice, the dissents are almost always filed by one of the co-arbitrators to favor the party that selected him or her.[24]

22 Paulsson, *The Idea of Arbitration*, p. 280.

23 See, for instance, section 30 of the Swedish Arbitration Act, article 382(4) of the Swiss Code of Civil Procedure, and article 35(2) of the Spanish Arbitration Act. The ICC (International Chamber of Commerce) Rules also establish that if there is no majority, the award shall be made by the president of the arbitral tribunal alone. See Rule 32 (1).

24 For a criticism of the practice of writing dissenting opinions, based on this reason, see Alan Redfern, "The 2003 Freshfields-Lecture. Dissenting Opinions in International Commercial Arbitration: The Good, the Bad and the Ugly," 20 *Arbitration International*, 223 (2004), pp. 233–234. For a similar assessment in the field of investment arbitration, see Albert Jan van den Berg, "Dissenting Opinions by Party-Appointed Arbitrators in Investment Arbitration," in Mahnoush H. Arsanjani et al. (eds.), *Looking to the Future: Essays on International Law in Honor of W. Michael Reisman* (Leiden: Martinus Nijhoff Publishers, 2010), pp. 821–843.

3.4 DISCRIMINATORY ARBITRAL AGREEMENTS

One of the virtues of arbitration, as we discussed in Chapter 1, is related to the fact that the contending parties can appoint the individuals they deem most suitable to adjudicate the dispute, on account of their personal and professional traits. Are there limits, however, to the criteria that the parties may specify in their arbitration agreements, concerning the characteristics that arbitrators should or should not have? In particular, may the parties select or exclude arbitrators on grounds of race, gender, nationality, or religion?

The question can be posed in many jurisdictions, either because constitutional rights are taken to apply to arbitral agreements, or because ordinary legislation has been passed barring discrimination in a number of private spheres. If a rule against discrimination applies, what plausible justifications can the parties advance in defense of the selective or exclusionary criteria they have agreed upon? In the case of distinctions based on race and gender, it is hard to think of good grounds to support them. They are extremely rare in practice, in any event. Things are different, however, with respect to nationality and religion.

As to nationality, the issue arises primarily in the sphere of international commercial arbitration, which we will explore in Chapter 5. The point of requiring arbitrators to possess a particular nationality is to ensure that they will exhibit an adequate understanding of the law of the country or culture of one or all of the parties. Conversely, the reason why a particular nationality may be excluded by the disputants has to do with their wish to guarantee the neutrality of the arbitral forum. In order to preserve neutrality, they may prescribe that the sole arbitrator, or the president of the tribunal, or all the arbitrators, cannot have the nationality of any of the parties. These are legitimate concerns, and it seems unreasonable for law-makers or courts to render such contractual specifications invalid on equality grounds. A cardinal virtue of arbitration would be eliminated if they did so.

Religion is a more complex factor. As we will discuss in the next section, the parties sometimes indicate that they do not want arbitrators to resolve the dispute on a legal basis. Instead, they instruct arbitrators to decide according to their own sense of the equities of the case (arbitration *ex aequo et bono*). Most countries permit this kind of arbitration. If it is allowed, the door is then open for members of a particular religion to require arbitrators to adjudicate the controversy in light of the moral tenets of their religion. It seems reasonable, in this context, for the law to empower the parties to specify that the arbitrators should be members of the religious community the parties belong to. In this way, the parties make sure that there will be a good fit between the norms they want to get applied to the dispute and the characteristics of the persons who are selected to arbitrate it.

What if the parties opt for arbitration based on the law, however? Can they use criteria based on religion when picking arbitrators? A controversial case arose in the United Kingdom in this connection, concerning an arbitral clause attached to a joint venture agreement which provided that disputes would be resolved by three arbitrators, each of whom should be a respected member of the Ismaili community. Both contracting parties belonged to this community. At the same time, the joint venture agreement expressly stipulated that English law would apply to the contract. When a difference between the parties arose, one of them nominated an arbitrator who did not belong to the Ismaili community. That party argued that the arbitral clause was discriminatory and thus void. The Court of Appeal agreed: it held the clause invalid under the pertinent domestic legislation that bans employment discrimination. The Supreme Court overturned the judgment, however.[25] It maintained, first, that arbitrators are not employees of the parties. Second, more importantly for our purposes, it held that even if the employment anti-discrimination legislation applied, the parties had good grounds in this case to require arbitrators to belong to their community of faith. In particular, the Court said, "the parties could properly regard arbitration before three Ismailis as likely to involve a procedure in which the parties could have confidence and as likely to lead to conclusions of fact in which they could have particular confidence," even if English law governed the contract.[26] The decision was well received by the international arbitral community, which was rightly worried that the position of the Court of Appeal, if it had been upheld, would have drastically reduced the liberty of the parties to select the arbitrators they deemed most suitable, on grounds of religion, culture, or nationality.

All this is not to say that the law should allow an arbitral agreement to support the unfolding of a religious adjudicative process that deviates from mandatory norms that the state has good reason to lay down, concerning procedural fairness, absence of discrimination when assessing the evidence, and lack of coercion, for example.[27] It bears emphasizing, moreover, that in this discussion we are assuming that the dispute being referred to religious arbitration involves rights which the parties can contractually waive in advance. If, instead, mandatory rules govern the merits of the controversy, the state is entitled to further constrain arbitration, in order to ensure the correct application of such rules, as will be discussed later in the chapter.

3.5 SUBSTANTIVE NORMS AND REASONS IN ARBITRATION

Let us now turn to the body of substantive norms that arbitrators are instructed to apply to decide the merits of a given controversy. As just explained, in most legal

[25] See *Jivraj* v. *Hashwani*, Judgment of 27 July 2011, [2011] UKSC 40.

[26] Ibid., para. 70.

[27] For a discussion of some of the objections and problems that religious arbitration raises, see Ayelet Shachar, "Privatizing Diversity: A Cautionary Tale from Religious Arbitration in Family Law," 9 *Theoretical Inquiries in Law*, 573 (2008); Amanda M. Baker, "A Higher Authority: Judicial Review of Religious Arbitration," 37 *Vermont Law Review*, 157 (2012); and Michael J. Broyde, *Sharia Tribunals, Rabbinical Courts, and Christian Panels. Religious Arbitration in America and the West* (New York: Oxford University Press, 2017), pp. 205–235.

systems the parties can ask the arbitrators to decide the case in accordance with the law, but they can also direct them to decide the case *ex aequo et bono*. If the latter form of arbitration is selected, the arbitral decision is based on general intuitions of justice and fairness, which may differ from those embodied in the particular rules the state has adopted through its lawmaking processes.

It makes sense for legal systems to offer the contending parties this flexibility, when no mandatory law is at stake. Individuals have a basic right to organize their legal relationships as they see fit (provided that the interests of other individuals and general public interests or basic values are not compromised). Individuals must accordingly have the liberty to stipulate that, if a dispute arises in connection with a contract, the decision-maker shall not apply the law but shall instead rely on general principles of justice and fairness, taking into account the particular circumstances of the case. Actually, it would not be unreasonable for the law to take a further step and also allow the parties to ask *courts* (not just arbitrators) to adjudicate their case *ex aequo et bono* (when no mandatory norms are applicable). This is possible in Italy, for example.[28]

Arbitrators, of course, must respect the choice of the parties. If the latter have not opted for arbitration *ex aequo et bono*, the arbitrators are exceeding their powers if they issue an award that relies on their own sense of the equities of the case instead of applying the relevant corpus of legal rules. And the converse is also true. It is useful, in this connection, for the law to establish default rules, so that it is clear which kind of arbitration must unfold if the parties do not indicate anything in their agreement. The laws often provide that arbitration shall be based on the law, unless the parties expressly indicate otherwise. This is the case, for example, in those countries that follow the UNCITRAL Model Law.[29]

It is interesting to note in this regard that arbitration has become increasingly "legalized," especially in the field of international commercial transactions. In the past, "arbitrators were known more for their personal wisdom and gravitas than for their legal expertise."[30] Now they are chosen for their legal skills. As Yves Dezalay and Bryant G. Garth explain, "international commercial arbitration has clearly moved along a Weberian path to a more routine, judicialized form of dispute resolution, and the center of power of the field has shifted from the small group of Continental professors to the increasingly powerful transnational law firms dominated by the Anglo-Americans."[31] The charismatic notables, the "grand old men," have been replaced by legal technocrats.

28 Article 114 of the Code of Civil Procedure provides that the contending parties can require the courts to decide *secondo equità*, if the controversy involves waivable legal rights.

29 Article 28(3) of the UNCITRAL Model Law provides that "the arbitral tribunal shall decide *ex aequo et bono* or as *amiable compositeur* only if the parties have expressly authorized it to do so."

30 Joshua Karton, *The Culture of International Arbitration and the Evolution of Contract Law* (Oxford: Oxford University Press, 2013), p. 95.

31 Yves Dezalay and Bryant G. Garth, *Dealing in Virtue. International Commercial Arbitration and the Construction of a Transnational Legal Order* (Chicago: The University of Chicago Press, 1996), p. 63.

This is not to say that arbitrators are always expected to apply the law exactly in the same way as courts would apply it. Arbitrators are sometimes licensed to go further than courts. The case of inadequately specified contracts is illustrative. As Alan Rau explains, in some countries judges are reluctant to enforce such defective contractual agreements. They insist on their institutional inability to make contracts for the parties. Arbitrators, in contrast, can fulfill a broader task. It can be understood that they have been hired by the parties, not only to interpret the contract but also to complete it when important elements have been left unspecified. This is true in the United States, for example.[32] It is also the case in Sweden, whose legislation is very explicit in this regard: "In addition to interpreting agreements, the filling of gaps in contracts can also be referred to arbitrators."[33] Arbitrators are thus given greater authority than courts.[34] In other European jurisdictions, on the other hand, the powers of arbitrators are more closely mapped upon the sphere of action permitted to judges.

An important question we must now turn to is this: Ought arbitrators to state in a written opinion the reasons in support of their decision? The parties may want them to do so in order to understand why they have decided the way they have. The parties can thus check whether the arbitrators have taken their task seriously. If the award fails to address certain issues that were discussed during the proceedings, or if it reflects a lack of understanding of the case, or if the reasons given are contradictory, the disputants will conclude that the arbitrators have done a poor job. Of course, the party that prevails does not care very much about this. Before the award is made, however, the parties do not know whether they will find themselves on the winning side or on the losing side. So it is rational for them to force the arbitrators to explain themselves, to create the incentives for the latter to execute their assignment in earnest. Even if the parties have chosen *ex aequo et bono* arbitration, they may insist on reasoned awards. They are likely to be especially interested in being informed about the considerations of justice and fairness the arbitrators have taken into account in their decisions.

On the other hand, the parties may believe that it is not worthwhile to pay the extra money that writing a reasoned opinion entails. Or they may not wish to increase the time it takes to issue an award. If they have sufficient trust in the arbitrators, they may conclude that, all things considered, they are better off with a "naked" award, one that does not indicate the reasons that underpin the arbitral decision.

Or the disputants may doubt that requiring arbitrators to furnish grounds in a written opinion will really make a difference in practice. Alan Rau makes the interesting and controversial point that the American preference for naked awards in domestic

[32] Alan Scott Rau, *The Allocation of Power between Arbitral Tribunals and State Courts* (Leiden: Brill Nijhoff, 2018), pp. 200–208.

[33] See section 1, para. 2, of the Swedish Arbitration Act.

[34] Madsen, *Commercial Arbitration in Sweden*, p. 67.

arbitration is to be explained by the fact that American lawyers are rather skeptical about the capacity of reasons to constrain judges. They are more skeptical than their European counterparts, he argues. American legal education "has so carefully honed the skills of deconstructing judicial opinions, and so laboriously trained us [Americans] to debunk their explanatory power, that we can no longer believe in the presence of such opinions as an indispensable element of a just decision."[35]

Or the parties may think that the case is such a close one that reasons run out. When the reasons for and against the legal positions advanced by the parties seem to lead to a tie, arbitrators may render "Solomonic" judgments. Jon Elster has argued that it is actually part of reason's maturity to recognize its own limitations. We should be aware that we have an addiction to reason that needs to be held in check. When the costs of looking for further reasons clearly exceed the benefits, the most rational course of action is to "resist the sirens of reason."[36] Arbitration can be regarded by some parties as a space that is friendly to this type of rationality in very close cases.

So there are advantages and drawbacks to reasoned awards. As a matter of fact, there has been lots of variation in the law and actual practices in this regard, both across jurisdictions and over time. Historically, many arbitral awards were naked. The tendency in most jurisdictions, however, is for arbitral awards to be reasoned, particularly in international commercial arbitration. The laws in many countries and the rules of arbitral facilities typically establish reason-giving as a default rule. The UNCITRAL Model Law, for instance, provides that "the award shall state the reasons upon which it is based, unless the parties have agreed that no reasons are to be given."[37] The United States has joined this general trend in international commercial arbitration, though naked awards are still common in the domestic commercial sphere.[38]

In this connection we can appreciate, once more, how the differences between arbitration and litigation in court matter for constitutional purposes. Constitutions

35 Alan Scott Rau, "On Integrity in Private Judging," 14 *Arbitration International*, 115 (1998), p. 148.

36 Jon Elster, *Solomonic Judgements. Studies in the Limitations of Rationality* (Cambridge: Cambridge University Press, 1989), p. 117.

37 See article 31(2) of the UNCITRAL Model Law.

38 Thus, the Commercial Arbitration Rules and Mediation Procedures of the American Arbitration Association (AAA) (Rules amended and effective October 1, 2013) establish the naked award as a default rule: "The arbitrator need not render a reasoned award unless the parties request such an award in writing prior to appointment of the arbitrator or unless the arbitrator determines that a reasoned award is appropriate." See Rule 46(b). On the other hand, the international division of the AAA, the International Centre for Dispute Resolution, lays down the opposite default rule for international deals: "The tribunal shall state the reasons upon which an award is based, unless the parties have agreed that no reasons need be given." See article 30(1) of the International Arbitration Rules, which are included in International Dispute Resolution Procedures (Including Mediation and Arbitration Rules) (Rules amended and effective June 1, 2014). A similar default rule is contained in the AAA's rules regarding consumer contracts and employment contracts. See, respectively, Rule 43 (b) of the Consumer Arbitration Rules (Rules amended and effective September 1, 2014), and Rule 39 (c) of the Employment Arbitration Rules and Mediation Procedures (Rules amended and effective November 1, 2009).

often enjoin judges to provide reasons in justification for their decisions. This requirement serves two goals: first, the public can better monitor the performance of judges, since the latter have to explain themselves. This external check is important, given that judges can exercise their adjudicative powers over society as a whole. Second, reason-giving is necessary for judicial opinions to become the source of rules that supplement other sources of law through a system of precedents. Arbitration stands in stark contrast to litigation in these respects. First, arbitrators can exert no power over the members of the political community. If the disputants have trust in the arbitrator they have chosen and don't think it necessary to require him to give reasons, society need not interfere. Second, arbitrators are not expected to provide rules by way of precedents, so it is not problematic if they fail to spell out the grounds of their awards. In sum, for the same reasons that confidentiality in arbitration does not offend constitutional norms regarding publicity in adjudication, as we discussed in Chapter 1, the absence of explicit reasons in arbitral awards does not breach constitutional norms directing adjudicators to justify their decisions.

The Swiss Supreme Court, for example, has repeatedly held that the constitutional guarantee to a reasoned opinion, a guarantee that flows from article 29(2) of the federal Constitution providing that "each party has a right to be heard," does not apply in arbitration.[39]

From all this it does not follow, however, that the legislature is constitutionally barred from requiring arbitrators to state reasons. In Spain, Italy, and France, for example, the law establishes such a duty.[40] A plausible argument in its support is connected to the system of judicial review of arbitral awards that is in place. Depending on the particular grounds on the basis of which arbitral awards may be overturned by courts, it may be indispensable that arbitrators spell out reasons. In order to check whether due process rights have been respected, for instance, it is not really necessary for the award to be reasoned. The party that wishes to challenge the award can bring the necessary evidence to prove that there was a violation of due process, even if the award is a naked one. In contrast, if the law allows the parties to attack an award on the ground that the arbitrators have made a legal mistake when adjudicating the merits of the dispute, it seems necessary for the award to provide reasons. If the arbitrators do not explain the conclusions they have reached as to the facts, it is hard to see how judges can verify that the outcome fits with the applicable law. Judges cannot run a new trial and assess the evidence to ascertain the facts. As Hans Smit contends, "in the absence of reasons, the reviewing court cannot

[39] For references, see Gabrielle Kaufmann-Kohler and Antonio Rigozzi, *International Arbitration. Law and Practice in Switzerland* (Oxford: Oxford University Press, 2015), pp. 483–484.

[40] In Spain, the reason-giving requirement figures in article 37(4) of the Spanish Arbitration Act. In Italy, it is established in articles 823 and 829 of the Code of Civil Procedure. In France, the requirement applies to domestic arbitration, but it does not extend to international commercial arbitration. See articles 1482, 1483, 1492, and 1520 of French Code of Civil Procedure.

determine whether the arbitrators misapplied the law when it does not know what facts the arbitrators found."[41]

In general, there is a strong connection between reason-giving and the efficacy of external checks. It is small wonder that arbitrators were advised in the past not to reason their awards in order to make them harder to annul by courts. Conversely, the Arbitration Rules of the International Chamber of Commerce (ICC) require arbitrators to state reasons in their decisions.[42] The justification for this rule is that arbitral awards under the ICC can be scrutinized by an internal body (the International Court of Arbitration). In order for this kind of check to be feasible, the ICC requires awards to be reasoned.[43] In a similar spirit, the English Arbitration Act assumes there is a connection between arbitral reason-giving and judicial scrutiny. According to the Act, if it appears to the court that the award that a party has challenged does not contain reasons, or does not contain reasons in sufficient detail to enable the court properly to consider the challenge, "the court may order the tribunal to state the reasons for its award in sufficient detail for that purpose."[44] Consistently with this, the Act provides that if the parties agree to dispense with reasons for the arbitral award, the parties shall be understood to have agreed to waive their right to appeal to a court on a question of law.[45] The assumption, of course, is that judicial review of the legal merits of the award is only possible if the award states reasons.

So the discussion about the reason-giving requirement brings us to the issue of judicial nullification of arbitral awards.

3.6 JUDICIAL REVIEW OF ARBITRAL AWARDS

In many countries, the law provides that arbitral awards may be overturned by courts if one of the parties challenges their validity. Most often, the grounds for review are rather limited: they center on excesses of arbitral authority and breaches of due process. Judicial review of the merits of the case, in particular, is not possible, or is only allowed under rather strict conditions.

The availability of minimal judicial checks on arbitral decisions is generally consistent with the expectation of the parties. When the latter elect arbitration they do not wish courts to adjudicate their disputes, of course, but they do want courts to exercise some measure of control should arbitrators exceed their authority or commit significant procedural irregularities. This expectation prevails even in the domain of international commercial transactions, where the case for excluding

41 Hans Smit, "Mandatory Law in Arbitration," in George A. Bermann and Loukas A. Mistelis (eds.), *Mandatory Rules in International Arbitration* (Huntington: Juris, 2011), p. 225.

42 See article 32(2) of the ICC Arbitration Rules.

43 See Yves Derains and Eric A. Schwartz, *A Guide to the ICC Rules of Arbitration* (The Hague: Kluwer Law International, 2005), p. 309.

44 See section 70(4) of the Arbitration Act.

45 See section 69(1) of the Arbitration Act.

national courts is particularly strong for neutrality reasons, as we will discuss in Chapter 5. The failed Belgian experiment of 1985 serves as a good illustration of the need for the law to provide a certain degree of judicial supervision. The Belgian legislature decided to eliminate all right to have awards vacated in disputes between foreign parties, in the belief that many parties would appreciate the absence of judicial oversight and would consequently choose to seat their arbitration in Belgium. It turned out that total exclusion of judicial review was regarded as too risky by business managers. The new system discouraged arbitration in Belgium. The law was eventually changed in 1998 to reintroduce a safety net of judicial control (as a default rule).[46]

An interesting question to address in this regard is whether the parties should be entitled to shape the regime that applies to the annulment of arbitral awards. If the law enumerates certain grounds for impugning arbitral decisions, may the parties contract around the law in this connection? May they reduce such legal grounds? Alternatively, may they expand them? What reasons can the state invoke to bar these options?

Forbidding the parties to reduce the legal grounds for review is easy to justify when the grounds are connected to procedural norms that are mandatory, such as the norm that requires impartiality and fairness. If the parties are not entitled to waive in advance their right to an impartial arbitrator, they should not be authorized to give up in advance their derivative right to challenge the arbitral award on impartiality grounds. Similarly, since the authority of arbitrators stems from the agreement of the parties, an award must be open to judicial scrutiny if the arbitrators exceeded their powers.

It is doubtful, however, that the rule against reducing the grounds for judicial review is justified when the latter extends to the merits of the controversy. Suppose, for example, that the law permits an award to be challenged on the ground that the arbitrator has not applied the law correctly, or has not interpreted the contract correctly, or has made a mistake as to the facts. (The law may or may not require that the mistake be clear or grave). Why can't the parties contract around this legal ground? The English Arbitration Act, for example, offers parties some degree of flexibility in this regard. It permits a party to arbitral proceedings to appeal to the court on a question of law in some circumstances, but it also allows the parties to contract away from this ground for review in their arbitral agreement.[47]

46 On Belgium's failed experiment and the dangers of excluding all types of judicial review of arbitral awards, see William W. Park, *Arbitration of International Business Disputes. Studies in Law and Practice* (Oxford: Oxford University Press, 2006), pp. 17–18.

47 See section 69 of the Arbitration Act. The appeal can be brought with the agreement of all the parties to the proceedings, or with the leave of the court. Leave to appeal shall be given only if the court is satisfied, among other things, that the decision of the arbitral tribunal on the legal question "is obviously wrong," or the question is "one of general public importance and the decision of the tribunal is at least open to serious doubt."

Note that the non-waivable character of the impartiality requirement is crucial in this context. An impartial arbitrator that has conducted a fair proceeding is, of course, a fallible human being. He may make mistakes when adjudicating the merits of the dispute. Since he is impartial, however, it is not possible to know in advance in which direction he will err. The parties may therefore be willing to run the risk of a mistaken decision and opt for excluding judicial review. The parties distribute the risk equally. The law should accept this choice. What the law cannot do, in contrast, is to support an unfair process that is structurally biased to err against one of the parties, to the benefit of the other.

The European Court of Human Rights has had the opportunity to say something about the autonomy of the parties to waive in advance their right to contest the validity of arbitral awards. It did so, however, in a case involving international commercial arbitration, which is special in some important respects. In the *Tabbane* case, the Court held that Swiss law is not in breach of the European Convention on Human Rights when it permits parties who have no links to Switzerland to give up their right to request Swiss courts to annul an arbitral award made in Switzerland.[48] The European Court gave weight to the voluntary character of the waiver in the particular case. More importantly, the Court also noted that the waiver that Swiss law permits does not eliminate judicial control altogether, since Swiss courts (as well as the courts in other countries) retain their authority to review the validity of awards at the enforcement stage.[49] So the Court upheld the Swiss scheme of judicial checks on international arbitration, which is similar to that adopted by some other countries.[50]

What about the other possibility: Allowing the parties to expand the grounds for review? A good case can be made in favor of it. If the law enables the parties to supplement the grounds for review, they enjoy a richer set of options when selecting a mode of dispute resolution. Instead of a stark choice between litigation in court, on the one hand, and standard arbitration (with very limited judicial review), on the other, they have the possibility of picking an arrangement that is somewhere in between. In France, for example, arbitral awards can only be subject to annulment actions under limited grounds, but the parties are authorized to stipulate in their

[48] *Tabbane* v. *Switzerland*, no. 41069/12, Decision of 1 March 2016.

[49] As we will see in Chapter 5, the New York Convention of 1958 establishes in article V that international awards may be refused recognition and enforcement if certain grounds apply. Such grounds are very similar to those that empower the courts of the seat to nullify an award. They actually coincide with the grounds mentioned in the UNCITRAL Model Law for purposes of judicial review of awards. So the absence of judicial review by the courts of the seat does not mean total immunity from judicial control.

[50] In Sweden, for instance, certain grounds for judicial review of awards (but not all of them) can be excluded by the parties when none of them is domiciled or has its place of business in Sweden. Judicial checks will operate nevertheless at the enforcement stage. See section 51 of the Swedish Arbitration Act.

agreement that the award is susceptible to broader appeal.[51] In the United States, in contrast, federal law does not accommodate such preferences.[52]

It may be argued that arbitration is no longer a speedy mechanism to resolve disputes if parties are given the alternative of providing for greater review, including review for legal errors. But this objection assumes that the primary reason why parties are interested in arbitration has to do with the quick resolution of disputes. As explained in Chapter 1, the parties may lean toward arbitration for other reasons as well, having to do with expertise, competence, privacy, and confidentiality. Why shouldn't individuals be empowered to select a modality of arbitration that serves these other values, even if it does not guarantee the prompt settlement of the difference?

It may be contended that the parties should not be entitled to determine the institutional division of labor between arbitrators and courts, and should therefore not be allowed to expand the grounds for reversal of awards. As Alan Rau has convincingly argued, however, it is inconsistent for the law to prohibit such expansion, while permitting other choices that also determine the institutional division of labor between arbitrators and courts.[53] The parties, for example, may decide to ask arbitrators to settle the factual issues only, so that the parties can then go to court to have the legal issues adjudicated. This choice is typically respected by the law. Similarly, the parties may undertake to obtain a nonbinding opinion first, before the door is open for them to litigate the controversy. The law puts no obstacles to this preference either. This being the case, why shouldn't the law accept the parties' choice to enlarge the scope of judicial review of arbitral awards?

It is tempting to use a utilitarian argument here, according to which the parties should not augment the grounds for judicial oversight because that would generate additional burdens for courts. But this argument fails. First, those additional judicial burdens are less significant than the burdens courts would confront if the case were fully litigated, instead of arbitrated.[54] Second, even if the amount of judicial work actually grew, the increase would not be so significant as to justify restricting the right of the parties to shape the arbitral process in accordance to their needs. Third, if

51 See article 1489 of the Code of Civil Procedure. This article only applies to domestic arbitration. No agreement providing for broad appeal is possible with respect to an international arbitration. See article 1518.

52 The United States Supreme Court has held that the Federal Arbitration Act does not permit contractual expansion of the grounds for judicial review. See *Hall Street Associates L.L.C.* v. *Mattel, Inc.*, 552 U.S. 576 (2008). At the state level, however, some courts have read state legislation to allow for it. See, for instance, the decision of the Supreme Court of Texas, *Nafta Traders, Inc.* v. *Quinn*, 339 S.W.3d 84 (2011). Interestingly, the Court points out in its opinion that "as a fundamental matter, Texas law recognizes and protects a broad freedom of contract," and recalls that arbitration has been explicitly guaranteed by every Texas Constitution since 1845.

53 Alan Scott Rau, "Fear of Freedom," 17 *The American Review of International Arbitration*, 469 (2006), pp. 472–476.

54 Ibid., pp. 506–509.

we are to take into account the collective interests, we should include in the calculus the possibility that in some cases extensive judicial scrutiny of awards for legal error will afford courts the opportunity to refine and develop the relevant case law. This consideration points in favor of letting the parties select a broad type of review. Another potential utilitarian advantage of opening up this possibility is that the market for arbitrators might improve. As Tom Ginsburg argues, if the parties are permitted to designate the standard of review, good arbitrators can signal their status. "The good arbitrator who is confident in her abilities will not fear a high level of judicial scrutiny," while an arbitrator who is not skilled "might prefer a lower level of judicial scrutiny."[55]

It will not do to say that nothing prevents the parties from constructing a private system of review of awards that suits their preferences. It is certainly possible for parties to bring their dispute to an arbitral institution that grants parties the right to request an internal body to supervise the arbitral award on broader grounds than those specified in the law.[56] The fact that this possibility is available does not mean, however, that the parties should not be entitled to choose the other option – to ask courts, instead of an internal arbitral body, to do the checking (under such more extensive grounds). Review of the award by courts is qualitatively different from review by an arbitral institution.

All things considered, a strong case can be made that the right to arbitration does not merely protect the ability of the parties to elect arbitration in the abstract, but also the ability to shape the arbitral regime to a certain extent, concerning, in particular, the scope of judicial review of awards. It is interesting to note at this juncture that the French Constitution of 1795, the Spanish Constitution of 1812, and most nineteenth century Latin American constitutions that expressly enshrined the right to arbitration, accorded the parties significant leeway when it came to determining the supervisory role of courts. Those constitutions laid down the general rule that arbitral decisions would not be subject to appeal, but they explicitly allowed the parties to provide otherwise in their agreement.[57] So a degree of flexibility was built into the right to arbitration guaranteed in those constitutional charters.

55 Tom Ginsburg, "The Arbitrator as Agent: Why Deferential Review is Not Always Pro-Arbitration," 77 *University of Chicago Law Review*, 1013 (2010), p. 1024.

56 In recent years, for example, the American Arbitration Association has established Optional Appellate Arbitration Rules (Rules effective November 1, 2013), which provide for the possibility of challenging the award before an appellate arbitral panel that applies a standard of review greater than that allowed by existing federal and state statutes. The panel controls errors of law that are material and prejudicial, as well as determinations of fact that are clearly erroneous. This appeal mechanism is an option that can only be used if both parties consent.

57 See article 211 of the French Constitution of 1795, article 281 of the Spanish Constitution of 1812, article 158 of the Constitution of Costa Rica of 1844, article 58 of the Constitution of El Salvador of 1824, article 179 of the Constitution of Guatemala of 1825, article 67 of the Constitution of Honduras of 1825, and article 120 of the Constitution of Nicaragua of 1826.

3.7 WHEN MANDATORY LAW IS AT STAKE

We have so far explored the justifications for various constraints that arbitration laws may place on the arbitral process. Throughout the discussion, we have assumed that no mandatory law was applicable to decide the merits of the dispute. We must now discuss how these constraints fare when arbitration extends to matters that are governed by mandatory law. What happens, to go back to the examples mentioned earlier in the chapter, when arbitrators are called upon to adjudicate the claim that the contract contravenes anti-trust law, or that one of the parties has violated the statutory or constitutional right of the other party not to suffer discrimination on grounds of race, gender, or age?

When laws of this mandatory kind get arbitrated, the justification for the establishment of constraints is rather straightforward. There is no question that the state has a legitimate interest in ensuring the correct application of mandatory law by arbitrators. When mandatory norms apply, it is no longer the case that only rights the contending parties can sign away are implicated. Public interests and non-waivable rights of the parties themselves are involved, and they need to be properly preserved when arbitrators are called upon to adjust a difference. Recall that, in practice, arbitration is almost always based on a contractual clause adopted before the controversy breaks out. If the parties cannot derogate from mandatory rules in their contract, neither can they circumvent those rules indirectly, by way of an arbitral clause that will later trigger an adjudicative procedure that is not properly designed to guarantee the correct application of mandatory rules. Arbitration can penetrate areas governed by mandatory law only if it satisfies certain conditions that warrant its reliability as a mechanism to interpret the law and find the relevant facts. As Daniel Markovits has argued, if the role of arbitrators is simply to fill in the gaps of a contract, any procedure chosen by the parties will do. If, instead, arbitrators are asked to adjudicate non-waivable statutory rights, certain procedural guarantees must then be observed.[58]

The principle of the rule of law, which is commonly embodied in national constitutions, whether explicitly or implicitly, speaks in favor of the state taking measures to secure the ability of arbitration to properly enforce mandatory law. The constitutional principle of the rule of law should not be understood in a narrow sense, as if its only point were to ensure that governmental institutions act in accordance with the law. The principle has a broader reach: it also requires private persons to comply with the law. If arbitration were used by some actors to effectively exempt themselves from the operation of mandatory norms adopted by the state, the principle of the rule of law would be breached. The state cannot be indifferent to the issue whether arbitration is working properly as a mechanism to resolve disputes in accordance with mandatory law.

58 Daniel Markovits, "Arbitration's Arbitrage: Social Solidarity at the Nexus of Adjudication and Contract," 59 *DePaul Law Review*, 431 (2010), pp. 469–487.

Actually, in many jurisdictions, as the circle of arbitrable matters has become larger, the procedural constraints on arbitration have turned out to be stricter. Some scholars have criticized this move on the ground that it deprives arbitration of the flexibility and simplicity it traditionally displayed when compared to litigation in court.[59] We should applaud, however, arbitration's ability to adjust to new normative requirements. As Hiro Aragaki has argued, there is no "metaphysical essence" that arbitration risks losing when it transforms itself in new directions as the field of arbitrability expands.[60]

When mandatory law is implicated, the impartiality and fairness requirement is particularly easy to justify. Only a fair procedure that is conducted by an impartial arbitrator can be trusted with the enforcement of mandatory law. In addition to impartiality, other legal constraints can be justified when mandatory law governs the merits of the case. The law, for example, can establish that sole arbitrators must be lawyers. Someone who is not learned in the law is not well equipped to decide a dispute in light of mandatory law. If an arbitral tribunal is set up, the presiding arbitrator ought to be a lawyer, given their key role when it comes to ensuring the impartiality of the tribunal as a whole.

A difficult question, however, is whether judicial review of awards should encompass controlling the accuracy with which mandatory law has been applied. In many jurisdictions, the typical ground for annulment of an arbitral decision that violates mandatory law (or at least its core elements) is the "public policy" ground. The UNCITRAL Model Law, for example, sets this ground for review.[61] If such judicial scrutiny is legally available, a related question is how deferentially should judges control the awards that are challenged for contravening mandatory law.

Arguably, if the arbitral proceedings are conducted fairly, there is no structural reason to suspect that arbitrators will not apply and interpret mandatory rules adequately. One of the contending parties is normally interested in having the arbitrators apply a piece of mandatory law. It is not usually the case that both parties wish to escape from mandatory law through arbitration. If arbitral tribunals are chosen in the proper way, so that there is no bias in favor of one disputant over the other, and if the proceedings are fair, there is no general reason to believe that arbitrators will be prone to under-enforce mandatory law. They may make mistakes in individual cases, but no systematic bias against mandatory law is to be expected.[62]

In some exceptional cases, however, the parties may be using arbitration to conspire against the public interests. The law should establish mechanisms for the

59 See, for instance, Deborah R. Hensler and Damira Khatam, "Re-Inventing Arbitration: How Expanding the Scope of Arbitration Is Re-Shaping Its Form and Blurring the Line Between Private and Public Adjudication," 18 *Nevada Law Journal*, 381 (2018).

60 Hiro N. Aragaki, "The Metaphysics of Arbitration: A Reply to Hensler and Khatam," 18 *Nevada Law Journal*, 541 (2018).

61 See article 34 of the UNCITRAL Model Law.

62 See Alexander Greenawalt, "Does International Arbitration Need a Mandatory Rules Method?," in Bermann and Mistelis (eds.), *Mandatory Rules in International Arbitration*, pp. 152–155.

state authorities to react in that situation. At the enforcement stage, for example, judges may be empowered to deny the execution of the arbitral agreement or the award if they observe a violation of public policy, even if none of the conspiring parties makes the pertinent allegation.[63]

In defense of the general reliability of arbitration when it comes to the application of mandatory law, the argument has been made that the arbitral community as a whole has an interest in preserving arbitration as a flourishing legal institution. States have permitted arbitration to enter fields that are subject to mandatory norms on the assumption that arbitrators will properly take into account such norms. If states realized that arbitration was being used to sidestep mandatory norms, they would probably reverse the expansive trends in arbitration. They would reform the laws in order to confine arbitrability to those matters that are purely contractual and not governed by mandatory norms. The arbitral community is aware of this, so it has arguably significant institutional incentives not to under-enforce mandatory law.[64]

The fact that, in general, there is no structural reason to fear that arbitrators will be inclined to under-enforce mandatory law does not mean, however, that no judicial review of awards should operate. Even if arbitral procedures are generally reliable, a judicial second-look may be a reasonable constraint to place on arbitration. The law may provide for judicial oversight regarding any applicable mandatory rule, or may instead circumscribe review to those rules that are of cardinal importance to the legal order. The "public policy" ground for review that figures in the UNCITRAL Model Law, for example, as well as in many national laws, is often understood in this narrow sense.[65] The laws may also direct judges to review awards deferentially, so that only clear breaches of norms embodying public policies should cause the invalidation of an award.[66] In any event, as the boundaries of arbitration expand to

63 See, for instance, section 1060 of the German Code of Civil Procedure. Judicial enforcement of an award is denied if it leads to a result that is in conflict with public policy, even if the award has not been previously challenged by the parties. The enforcement court will consider the public policy ground on its own motion. See Kreindler, Wolff, and Rieder, *Commercial Arbitration in Germany*, pp. 358–359.

64 Luca G. Radicati di Brozolo, for example, points out that in international commercial arbitration "overriding mandatory norms cannot clearly be systematically ignored by arbitral tribunals." If such norms were ignored, "States and their courts would inevitably step in." Among other things, they might adopt "a much sterner approach to arbitrability, reversing the trend which, starting from *Mitsubishi*, has allowed disputes involving overriding mandatory rules to be freely brought to arbitration." Luca G. Radicati di Brozolo, "When, Why and How Must Arbitrators Apply Overriding Mandatory Provisions? The Problems and a Proposal," in Franco Ferrari (ed.), *The Impact of EU Law on International Commercial Arbitration* (Huntington: Juris, 2017), p. 379.

65 In Germany, for example, not every violation of mandatory rules results in a violation of public policy. The rules need to be of a special quality, involving the basis of public and economic life or fundamental ideas of justice. See, Kreindler, Wolff, and Rieder, *Commercial Arbitration in Germany*, pp. 348–349.

66 In Sweden, for instance, the Arbitration Act is explicit when it provides in section 33 that an award is invalid, among other reasons, if "the award or the manner in which the award arose, is clearly incompatible with the basic principles of the Swedish legal system." The same is true of the Danish Arbitration Act: the award must be "manifestly contrary to the public policy" of Denmark (see section

cover an increasing number of areas that are connected to mandatory rules, it is legitimate for the law to introduce additional checks, which may be more or less demanding.

Another constraint that is relatively easy to justify when mandatory law applies is the requirement that arbitrators reason their awards. Given the state's interest in securing the correct enforcement of mandatory norms, it seems warranted for the law to require awards to be reasoned, in order to make it feasible for judges to verify their conformity with the relevant public policies. If the award does not lay out the facts the arbitrators found after assessing the evidence brought to the proceedings, it is difficult to see how judges can be satisfied that the arbitrators applied mandatory law correctly. So there is a good instrumental justification for the state to force arbitrators to explain the reasons for their awards, even if this requirement increases the costs of arbitration for the parties.

In sum, we can reconstruct as follows the historical evolution that has unfolded in many legal systems. At first, arbitration flourished as an expression of freedom of contract. But this "thesis" produced an "antithesis," to put it in Hegelian terminology. The rise of the modern administrative state interrupted the growth of arbitration. Indeed, because the norms issued by the regulatory governmental branches were regarded not to be arbitrable, the space for arbitration was correspondingly reduced. As Yves Dezalay and Bryant G. Barth explain, "arbitration declined initially with the development of the New Deal in the United States and welfare states elsewhere. New regulatory regimes gained power at the expense of more private dispute resolution."[67] A "synthesis" was finally reached at a third stage: mandatory law was considered to be arbitrable, but the arbitral process was subject to more demanding prescriptions. Under the new arrangement, the parties do not enjoy the same degree of liberty they traditionally possessed when designing the arbitral process. If mandatory norms linked to public interests and values can apply to the merits of the dispute, a larger body of mandatory rules now governs the arbitral procedure.

3.8 CONSUMER AND EMPLOYMENT CONTRACTS

In the context of our discussion of mandatory law, we must briefly touch on consumer and employment contractual relationships. In both types of relationships, the contracting parties possess unequal bargaining power and the

37(2)(2)). In other countries, courts have introduced a very deferential standard through interpretation. In Switzerland, for example, the Supreme Court has said that awards in international arbitration can only be quashed, on the ground that they are incompatible with public policy, if they make "intolerable" errors that shock one's sense of justice. A number of commentators have criticized the Court for being too lenient, however. See Kaufmann-Kohler and Rigozzi, *International Arbitration*, pp. 488–508. French courts, in turn, have also set a minimal standard of review. The violation of an essential rule or fundamental principle must be "flagrant," "manifest"; it must *crève les yeux*. See Paris Court of Appeal, Judgment of 18 November 2004, *Thalès* v. *Euromissile*, No 2002/19606.

67 Dezalay and Barth, *Dealing in Virtue*, p. 312.

lawmakers have reason to be concerned about the consequences of such disparity. Typically, the laws provide that certain rights cannot be surrendered through contract, and they devise mechanisms to ensure their protection. Thus, governmental bodies are entrusted with policing compliance with the laws, or associations and private individuals are empowered to seek collective remedies in court. Whether and how consumer and employment disputes are amenable to arbitration is a complex question that needs to be answered in the context of each legal system. We cannot deal with the problem here in detail, given the large variety of arrangements that have been set up in different countries. But a few general ideas may be useful.

With regard to consumer arbitration, the first point to bear in mind is that the quality of consent to the contractual agreement is usually very poor. Consumer contracts are take-it-or-leave deals. Normally, consumers don't read the fine print, which they would hardly understand – or care about – if they did. This being so, the legislature has good reason to intervene and make sure that firms do not include unfair clauses.[68] The question, then, is whether the law should regard arbitral clauses to be unfair and should thus prohibit them.

A categorical ban on consumer arbitration is not easy to justify as a matter of principle. After all, arbitration is a form of resolving disputes that is agreed upon in many contractual settings, including those where the parties possess roughly equal bargaining power. It seems unreasonable to maintain that consumers would never have accepted any type of arbitration if they had had the opportunity to negotiate the arbitral clause on an individual basis.

What seems certainly warranted is for judges to scrutinize the specific terms according to which the consumer contract regulates the arbitral procedure, which may be unfair regarding the way in which arbitrators are appointed, the connections that arbitrators maintain with the business community, the limitations on the production of evidence, the place of arbitration, etc ... In addition, the law may establish specific requirements to protect consumers, such as the need for awards to be published. As Margaret Jane Radin argues, confidentiality in consumer arbitration is problematic, for "a firm that loses an arbitration because it has engaged in unfair or unethical business practices avoids having its reputation damaged by the publication of this fact."[69] Lawmakers may thus decide to introduce transparency in the sphere of consumer arbitration. A nuanced approach along these lines may be better than a categorical exclusion of consumer arbitration.

On the other hand, it may be countered that a case-by-case model is too difficult to implement. Too much uncertainty and inconsistency will be generated if courts are tasked with drawing the relevant distinctions. In light of this, a blanket prohibition of pre-dispute arbitration clauses in consumer contracts may ultimately be justified on

[68] For a general discussion, Margaret Jane Radin, *Boilerplate: The Fine Print, Vanishing Rights, and the Rule of Law* (Princeton: Princeton University Press, 2013).

[69] Ibid., p. 134.

institutional grounds. If it is assumed that the potential benefits of arbitration in this area are not worth its dangers, a prophylactic rule barring pre-dispute arbitration clauses may be the best answer to the problem.[70]

Still another possibility is for consumer arbitration to be heavily regulated and supervised by public authorities. The law may provide, for example, that arbitration procedures can only be initiated by consumers against traders, that such procedures must be free of charge or available at a nominal fee for consumers, and that consumers – but not traders – may still go to court if they disagree with the awards.[71] Alternatively, public authorities themselves may supply arbitral services, recruiting both public servants and private individuals to act as arbitrators. These public–private hybrid forms of consumer arbitration are a promising alternative to purely private ones.

Secondly, it is important to understand that the state needs to have effective instruments to deter businesses from engaging in conduct that violates the legal rights of consumers. In some countries, administrative agencies are basically in charge of this task. In other places, associations of consumers play a critical part in bringing suits against companies that insert abusive clauses in their contracts. Yet in other jurisdictions, class actions brought by individual consumers are the key tool to implement the public policy that the law embodies.[72] In the latter case, arbitration agreements are especially problematic. Indeed, if class actions are the primary devices the legal system has created to attack the problem of abuses, it is not acceptable for consumer contracts of adhesion to include arbitration clauses that allow the companies to escape the threat of class actions. The state would be justified

[70] On the plausibility of this approach, see Scott Rau, *The Allocation of Power between Arbitral Tribunals and State Courts*, pp. 103–104. Within the European Union, for example, a large variety of legislative approaches has emerged to comply with the Council Directive 93/13/EEC of 5 April 1993, on unfair terms in consumer contracts, which includes clauses "requiring consumers to take disputes exclusively to arbitration not covered by legal provisions" in an annex of terms "which may be regarded as unfair." Some countries have established a blanket ban on pre-dispute consumer arbitral clauses, while others have stipulated formal conditions or have called on judges to engage in a case-by-case inquiry. On these different approaches, see Gary Born, *International Commercial Arbitration* (Alphen aan den Rijn: Kluwer Law International, 2014), pp. 1018–1021.

[71] In Europe, for example, consumer arbitration of this kind is being promoted by the European Union. See Directive 2013/11/EU of the European Parliament and the Council of 21 May 2013 on alternative dispute resolution for consumer disputes and amending Regulation (EC) No 2006/2004 and Directive 2009/22/EC (Directive on consumer ADR). For a comparative study of the way this Directive is being implemented in different countries, see Pablo Cortés (ed.), *The New Regulatory Framework for Consumer Dispute Resolution* (Oxford: Oxford University Press, 2015).

[72] In the United States, for example, class actions are the main instrument to protect consumers. As Robert Kagan explains, Americans tend to distrust governmental institutions for purposes of securing social justice. The structure of the United States political system is very fragmented as a result of the horizontal and vertical separation of powers, so it is difficult for the government to execute a coherent normative program. In this context, courts need to be resorted to in order to constrain the actions of corporations. In contrast, in parliamentary democracies where power is more centralized, and where political parties are more cohesive, it is easier for the government to enact and carry out effective social policies. In such countries, class action litigation does not perform a central function in order to protect consumers, or simply does not exist. See Robert A. Kagan, *Adversarial Legalism. The American Way of Law* (Cambridge, Massachusetts: Harvard University Press, 2001), p. 120.

in banning such clauses, or conditioning their enforceability to the availability of class-wide arbitration.[73] As Margaret Jane Radin argues, it is a form of "democratic degradation" for firms to use private tools to do away with the public avenues of redress the state has designed to safeguard consumer rights.[74]

Similar considerations can be extended to employment contracts. The weaker bargaining position of employees when they enter agreements with their employers raises questions as to whether arbitral clauses contained in such contracts genuinely register the consent of the employees. It is also controversial whether their individual consent to arbitration can be expressed indirectly, through their labor representatives, when the latter engage in collective bargaining with employers and fix some of the terms of employment contracts. In a number of countries (France, Belgium, Italy, England, for example), these and other concerns have caused the legislature to deny the arbitrability of employment-related claims.[75]

It is particularly problematic for arbitration to be used by employers to shield themselves against various forms of collective action. If the legal system relies on collective judicial redress to preserve the non-waivable rights of employees, courts should not allow arbitral clauses contained in employment contracts to operate as barriers against this type of redress.[76] The principle of the rule of law requires the state to prevent arbitration from being used by employers as a means to insulate themselves from the strictures of mandatory law.

3.9 WHEN ARBITRATORS CONFRONT UNCONSTITUTIONAL LEGISLATION

We now shift to an interesting question that has arisen in connection to mandatory law: What should arbitrators do if they believe that the relevant piece of legislation that applies to the instant case is not in conformity with the constitution?

73 The position of the United States Supreme Court in this regard deserves criticism, for it has read the Federal Arbitration Act in such a way that it allows businesses to preclude class relief by means of arbitral clauses inserted in consumer contracts. See *AT&T Mobility LLC* v. *Concepcion*, 563 U.S. 333 (2011). For a criticism of the Court's case law in this area, see Alexandra Lahav, *In Praise of Litigation* (New York: Oxford University Press, 2017), pp. 25–27 and pp. 126–128. There is empirical evidence that suggests that arbitration is being used by companies to avoid class actions. See Theodore Eisenberg, Geoffrey P. Miller, and Emily Sherwin, "Arbitration's Summer Soldiers: An Empirical Study of Arbitration Clauses in Consumer and Nonconsumer Contracts," 41 *University of Michigan Journal of Law Reform*, 871 (2008). Not all companies do so, however. See Christopher R. Drahozal and Stephen J. Ware, "Why Do Businesses Use (or Not Use) Arbitration Clauses?," 25 *Ohio State Journal on Dispute Resolution*, 433 (2010), pp. 470–474.

74 Radin, *Boilerplate*, pp. 33–51 and 173.

75 For references, see Born, *International Commercial Arbitration*, pp. 1009–1010.

76 See, however, the decision of the Supreme Court of the United States in *Epic Systems Corp.* v. *Lewis*, 138 S.Ct. 1612 (2018). There is evidence that the enormous growth of employment arbitration in the United States in recent decades correlates with the availability of class-action waivers through arbitration. See Alexander J. S. Colvin, "The growing use of mandatory arbitration," Economic Policy Institute, Washington, DC, Report of April 6, 2018, available at www.epi.org/144131.

The answer is relatively unproblematic in those countries that have established a decentralized system of judicial review of legislation, as is typically the case in the American hemisphere, for example, under the influence of the United States. If all courts are authorized to set aside statutory provisions they deem unconstitutional, it seems natural to take the view that the same rule should apply to arbitrators. In Argentina, for example, where constitutional review is decentralized, arbitral practice has gone in this direction. Thus, legal provisions enacted by the government to confront the economic crisis of the early 2000s were set aside by arbitral tribunals in a number of cases on the rationale that they contravened the Constitution.[77]

When reviewing legislation for its constitutionality, arbitrators should arguably take into account what the relevant courts have said or are likely to say on the issue in light of existing precedents. It would generally frustrate the expectations of the parties for arbitrators to refuse to apply statutory provisions which the parties had envisaged as part of the law governing the contract. Unless the unconstitutionality of the relevant provision is rather clear against the background of judicial precedents, arbitrators should uphold its applicability.[78] Democratic considerations press in the same direction. It may be maintained that if judges are appointed through procedures that register the inputs of the democratic branches, they possess the requisite degree of democratic legitimacy to overturn a law enacted by a popularly elected parliament. Arbitrators do not have this legitimacy, however, since they are hired by the parties. Their ability to disregard statutes on constitutional grounds should therefore be more constrained.

The issue is more intricate in jurisdictions that have adopted a centralized system of constitutional review. Europe is strongly associated with this model, as was already mentioned in Chapter 2. In many European countries, a constitutional tribunal has been set up to check the validity of legislation. That tribunal is normally the only institution authorized to invalidate a statute (or a norm of equivalent rank) on account of constitutional infirmities. Consequently, if ordinary judges in charge of resolving a particular dispute consider that the applicable law is inconsistent with the constitution, they are required to raise a "constitutional question" to the constitutional court. The system of legislative review is thus centralized, to better serve legal certainty. There are also democratic reasons animating this institutional scheme: as a general rule, the members of the constitutional court are appointed through more democratic procedures than ordinary judges are, so it makes sense to bestow upon the former the exclusive power to invalidate a law approved by the parliament.[79]

77 See José Carlos Fernández Rozas, *Tratado del Arbitraje Comercial en América Latina* (Madrid: Iustel, 2008), pp. 311–315.

78 For an argument along these lines, in the context of international commercial arbitration, see Horacio A. Grigera Naón, "Should International Commercial Arbitrators Declare a Law Unconstitutional," in David D. Caron, Stephan W. Schill, Abby Cohen Smutny, and Epaminontas E. Triantafilou (eds.), *Practising Virtue: Inside International Arbitration* (Oxford: Oxford University Press, 2015), pp. 308–317.

79 On this democratic argument, see Victor Ferreres Comella, *Constitutional Courts and Democratic Values. A European Perspective* (New Haven: Yale University Press, 2009), pp. 98–103.

What should arbitrators do in such countries, if they confront a statute they take to be unconstitutional? Contrasting answers have been given in different jurisdictions. In Italy, for instance, arbitrators have been empowered to certify questions to the constitutional court.[80] The latter has reasoned that arbitrators and regular judges are to be treated the same way for these purposes. The advantage of this solution is that arbitrators can obtain an authoritative ruling by the constitutional tribunal at an early stage. If they comply with that ruling, the award is shielded against the risk that the losing party may later challenge it on constitutional grounds. This solution, moreover, has the virtue of consistency: if for reasons having to do with legal certainty and democracy only the constitutional court has been conferred the authority to cancel the effects of legislation, it makes sense for arbitrators to be enjoined to ask that court to intervene, whenever they believe the applicable statutory provision runs afoul of the Constitution.

In other jurisdictions, in contrast, such as Spain and France, arbitrators have not been allowed to certify questions to the constitutional court.[81] What are arbitrators supposed to do, then, if they reach the conclusion that the applicable statute is in breach of the constitution? Are they enabled to disregard the statute or must they apply it nevertheless? There has been debate on the matter.[82] Arguably, the most plausible thesis is that arbitrators may set aside legislation they deem unconstitutional, if their conviction on the issue is rooted in the constitutional court's jurisprudence. Forcing them to apply a statute they have good reasons to consider invalid would delay the final disposition of the case. Indeed, if arbitrators expressed and reasoned their belief that the statute they were bound to apply was unconstitutional in light of the court's precedents, they would be inviting a judicial challenge against the award. It seems better to allow arbitrators to refuse the application of the statute in such circumstances. This should be regarded as a second-best solution, however. In systems that follow the centralized model of constitutional review, the first-best solution is to enable arbitrators to raise questions to the constitutional court, for the reasons given above.

3.10 PRELIMINARY REFERENCES TO SUPRANATIONAL COURTS

A related problem refers to the applicability in arbitration of certain procedures that domestic judges can sometimes employ to request supranational tribunals to clarify the meaning of the law of the relevant international organization. In the case of the European Union, for instance, national judges may consult with the Court of Justice

80 See *sentenza* 376/2001, November 22, 2001.

81 See decision of the Spanish Constitutional Court, ATC 259/1993, July 20, 1993; and decision by French *Cour de cassation*, 11–40.030, June 28, 2011.

82 For a summary of the discussion, see Ignacio Torres Muro, *La legitimación en los procesos constitucionales* (Madrid: Reus, 2007), pp. 125–129. For an argument in favor of allowing arbitrators to disregard unconstitutional laws, see Paulsson, *The Idea of Arbitration*, pp. 231–255.

of the European Union any legal issues regarding the interpretation and validity of European Union law that applies to a given case. The treaties establish that this preliminary reference procedure can be triggered by "courts of Member States."[83]

May arbitrators use this procedure? The Court of Justice has answered in the negative. It has repeatedly held that arbitrators are not "courts" for these purposes.[84] To justify its position, the Court has reasoned that certain features must be present for an adjudicative body to qualify as a court. Arbitration exhibits some of these features, but not others. Thus, arbitrators are expected to be independent and apply the law after hearing the contending parties. They differ from courts, however, in two important respects: they are not permanent bodies established by law, and their jurisdiction is not compulsory.[85]

The Court's position on this issue, however, leads to an unsatisfactory state of affairs. If arbitrators cannot raise questions to the Court of Justice, the burden to secure the correct application of European Union law rests on the shoulders of the national judges that may later become involved with the arbitral process. Thus, when a party challenges the award, or when a party seeks its judicial enforcement, the court that is authorized to intervene can use the preliminary reference mechanism to have the Court of Justice address a controversial question under European Union law. This is not a very functional arrangement, for there is then a strong pressure coming from European Union law for domestic courts to have the authority to check arbitral awards (whether at the reviewing stage or at the enforcement stage) to control any errors in the application of European Union law.[86] This unduly delays the final resolution of the dispute, in a way that undermines one of the rationales of arbitration.

A possible alternative is for national laws to permit arbitrators to stay the proceedings and ask an ordinary court to certify a question to the Court of Justice of the European Union. This is the institutional scheme established in Denmark, for example, though it is not used in practice.[87]

83 See article 267 of the Treaty on the Functioning of the European Union.

84 See Judgment of 23 March 1982, C-102/81, *Nordsee* case. The Court has confirmed its holding in later cases. See, for instance, the Judgment of 27 January 2005, C-125/04, *Denuit and Cordenier* case.

85 Sometimes, however, the Court has applied its case law in a very relaxed manner, and has concluded that certain special types of arbitral bodies are established by law, are permanent, and enjoy compulsory jurisdiction. The Court of Justice has considered those bodies to be courts, and has accordingly allowed them to raise preliminary references. See, for example, Judgment of 13 February 2014, C-555/13, *Merck Canada* case, and Judgment of 12 June 2014, C-377/13, *Ascendi* case.

86 Thus, in its Opinion in the *Genentech* case, C-567/14, delivered on March 17, 2016, Advocate General Melchior Wathelet suggested that minimalist, deferential judicial review of awards is insufficient to protect European Law. The Court of Justice, however, avoided this issue in its judgment in this case. See Judgment of July 7, 2016.

87 Pihlblad, Lundblad, and Søgaard-Christensen, *Arbitration in Denmark*, p. 96. Article 27(2) of the Danish Arbitration Act provides: "If the arbitral tribunal considers that a decision on a question of European Union law is necessary to enable it to make an award, the arbitral tribunal may request courts to request the Court of Justice of the European Communities to give a ruling thereon."

A better solution would be to simplify things and enable arbitrators themselves to refer questions to the Court of Justice. A preliminary ruling would help arbitrators interpret European Union law in the right manner, thus enhancing the reliability of the arbitral process. Arbitrators should not be required to use this procedure, of course, in the same way that judges are generally not required to do so either. Arbitrators may prefer to adjudicate the European Union legal issues on their own.[88] But if a complicated issue arises, and the arbitrators think it proper to ask the Court, they ought to be able to avail themselves of this mechanism.[89]

We should bear in mind that European Union law has evolved dramatically over the years. In the past, it had a very small impact on private law, so it was very rarely the case that arbitrators handling a dispute between two private parties would have to take into account European Union law. Arbitration, moreover, was a relatively marginal mode of dispute resolution. The current situation is different. The domain of private law is increasingly regulated by norms issued by the European Union, so that it is becoming more and more common for arbitrators to have to consider them when adjudicating controversies. And the cases that are referred to arbitration are growing in number. European Union law and arbitration law, therefore, need to be better linked. The preliminary reference procedure is a central piece to ensure the necessary institutional fit.

In other supranational or international contexts, similar procedures have been designed. Within the framework of the Andean Community in Latin America, for example, domestic arbitrators have been conferred the authority to certify questions to the supranational Court.[90] Similarly, under the 1982 United Nations Convention on the Law of the Sea, certain controversies regarding the International Seabed Area can be referred to commercial arbitration. The arbitrators are bound to raise a question to the Seabed Disputes Chamber of the International Tribunal for the Law of the Sea, if they determine that their decision depends upon a ruling of the latter.[91]

In light of these comparative precedents, it would be a better arrangement in Europe for arbitrators to be authorized to certify questions to the Court of Justice of

88 There is a specific situation, however, where arbitrators would be required to certify questions to the Court of Justice. If they consider that a relevant law or decision of the European Union law is invalid, they should raise a question of validity to the Court. The latter has a monopoly when it comes to declaring the invalidity of European Union acts. See Judgment of 22 October 1987, C-314/85, *Foto-Frost* case.

89 For a defense of this proposal, see Carl Baudenbacher and Imelda Higgins, "Decentralization of EC Competition Law Enforcement and Arbitration," 8 *Columbia Journal of European Law*, 1 (2002), pp. 14–17; and Jürgen Basedow, "EU Law in International Arbitration: Referrals to the European Court of Justice," 32 *Journal of International Arbitration*, 367 (2015).

90 The Treaty that establishes the Court of Justice of the Andean Community has followed the European Union model in that it allows domestic courts to stay proceedings and ask questions to the Court of Justice of the Andean Community regarding Andean Community law. This preliminary reference procedure, the Court has held, can also be used by arbitrators. See, for example, its decision of May 13, 2014, 14-IP-2014.

91 See articles 187 and 188 of the United Nations Convention on the Law of the Sea.

the European Union. To the extent that the relevant norms issued by the European Union are mandatory in character, the available mechanisms to buttress the reliability of adjudicative processes should be fully employed.[92]

3.11 CONCLUSION

As this chapter has illustrated, arbitration is subject to limitations of various kinds. While the constraints that national legislation typically establishes are usually grounded in good reasons, others are not. The constitutionalization of the right to arbitration we explored in Chapter 2 makes it possible for statutory provisions to be tested against constitutional norms in a judicial forum. If the constitution enshrines the right to arbitration, the government is required to justify in court the constraints it establishes, whenever someone challenges their validity.

We have also taken note that the world of arbitration has been profoundly transformed as a result of the expansion of the space of arbitrability. Since mandatory law can now be arbitrated, including norms that are tied to critical public interests and values, the institutional and procedural requirements that apply to arbitration have become increasingly demanding, and rightly so.

[92] It is controversial whether the Court of Justice of the European Union could reconsider its case law on this matter. For a discussion, see Basedow, "EU Law in International Arbitration: Referrals to the European Court of Justice"; and Maciej Szpunar, "Referrals of Preliminary Questions by Arbitral Tribunals to the CJEU," in Ferrari (ed.), *The Impact of EU Law on International Commercial Arbitration*, pp. 85–123.

4

Arbitration and the Lawmaking Process

Our discussion so far has focused on the logic of arbitration as a method to settle disputes. Now we have to look at arbitration from another angle, to assess its relationship to the lawmaking process. Arbitration is remarkably different from adjudication by courts when it comes to the production of case law. While courts are expected to formulate rules through a system of precedents, in addition to resolving particular controversies, arbitration is only expected to do the latter. For a number of reasons we will examine in this chapter, arbitration is not well equipped to supply a consistent body of rules of general application. Some important normative consequences follow from this.

4.1 THE DUAL FUNCTION OF COURTS: DISPUTE RESOLUTION AND RULE FORMULATION

In a modern legal system, the judiciary performs two major tasks: it resolves disputes in accordance with the law, thus confirming the authority of the law in practice; and it develops the law through the formulation of rules. These two functions normally go together. Judges usually make their contribution to the lawmaking process in the context of particular controversies. Only rarely are judges requested to address legal issues in the abstract, with no reference to a given dispute (through the delivery of advisory opinions, for example).

In an advanced legal order, of course, legislative and administrative organs have an enormous lawmaking capacity. Much of the law in the modern world is issued by them. There is nevertheless a significant space for courts to originate norms on a case-by-case basis, by way of precedents. Whether the legal order belongs to the civil law or to the common law tradition may matter in terms of the way this judicial contribution is characterized.[1] But in both traditions it is plain that the jurisprudence worked out by courts shapes the law in a general fashion.

[1] For a comparative analysis of the relevance and weight of judicial precedents in various countries, see D. Neil MacCormick, Robert S. Summers and Arthur L. Goodhart (eds.), *Interpreting Precedents. A Comparative Study* (New York: Routledge, 1997).

Within the judiciary, distinctions may have to be drawn when assessing the relative importance of these two functions. Because courts are structured in a hierarchical manner, it is possible to portray the basic assignment of lower courts differently from that of the highest courts (the courts of appeal and the supreme court). The dominant responsibility of lower courts typically consists in the resolution of disputes in light of the law, whereas the production of rules through case law is a key function of the highest courts. This contrast, of course, is a matter of degree. Lower courts also contribute to the life of the law, although their impact may be less significant. In any event, the critical point is that the judiciary as a whole discharges a dual task.

There seems to be broad consensus among commentators on this matter, although the emphasis they place on each of these functions varies. For some scholars, dispute resolution is the main job of the judiciary. Martin Shapiro, for instance, notes that courts of appeal create law through precedents, but takes this activity to be distant from the inner logic of adjudication. He writes that "most high courts of appeal are barely courts at all," the reason being that "while in form they may be engaged in finally resolving one particular dispute between two particular litigants, their principal role may be to provide uniform rules of law."[2]

For other scholars, in contrast, it is precisely the production of rules to clarify and operationalize the law that needs to be highlighted in order to capture the nature of adjudication. Owen Fiss, for example, is of the view that "dispute resolution may be one consequence of the judicial decision," but the role of courts is "to give the proper meaning to our public values." The judiciary does this "by enforcing and thus safeguarding the integrity of the existing public norms or by supplying new norms."[3]

Whatever relative weight must be accorded to these two functions, there is no doubt that the judiciary carries out both of them. A tension is felt at some point, however. In so far as a court is to adjudicate a particular dispute, it is proper that the contending parties are the ones entitled to participate in the proceedings with their factual and legal arguments. To the extent, however, that a court renders a decision that creates a precedent with binding effects on future parties, there is a potential problem in the way the judicial process is designed: the individuals that will be affected in the future take no part in the proceedings generating the relevant judicial precedent.

It is interesting to recall, in this connection, Lon Fuller's theory of adjudication, which is based on the axiom of individual participation: the party whose interests are affected must be given the opportunity to present proofs and reasoned arguments in court for a decision in his favor. According to Owen Fiss, one of the implications of Fuller's individualist conception, if taken to its logical extremes, is that it would be

[2] Martin Shapiro, *Courts. A Comparative And Political Analysis* (Chicago: The University of Chicago Press, 1981), p. 56.

[3] Owen Fiss, "The Forms of Justice," in Owen Fiss, *The Law As It Could Be* (New York: New York University Press, 2003), p. 25.

unacceptable for courts to originate norms through precedent. A legal precedent, after all, will bind parties that have not been heard by the court that lays it down. For it to be legitimate, adjudication would have to be reduced to a form of arbitration. Fiss comments: "It is no mere happenstance that Fuller spent a great deal of his professional life as an arbitrator."[4]

Actually, Fiss contends that dispute resolution is such a marginal aspect of adjudication that it is an "extravagant use of public resources" for judges to hear cases that do not "threaten or otherwise implicate a public value," as when disputes are confined to the interpretation of the words of a contract, for example. It is in this context that arbitration enters the picture. Fiss maintains that "it seems quite appropriate for those disputes to be handled not by courts but by arbitrators."[5]

Arbitration, indeed, is primarily concerned with the resolution of controversies. Its basic mission is not the generation of rules to properly construe, implement, and enrich the existing body of law. Let us see why this is so.

4.2 ARBITRATION'S INABILITY TO PRODUCE RULES THROUGH A SYSTEM OF PRECEDENTS

For a well-functioning system of precedents to emerge from a collection of decisions, several conditions need to be satisfied. The arbitral regime meets some of them to a certain extent, but fails to satisfy all of them to a sufficient degree.

First, the decisions that are to be the source of rules must come in the form of reasoned opinions that explain the facts and invoke the relevant law. In the absence of reasons of this sort, there is no way rules can be extracted from a multiplicity of discrete decisions. As was explained in Chapter 3, arbitration varies a lot in this regard, both across jurisdictions and over time. In many places, arbitral awards are naked – they provide no reasons at all. In others, reasons are required or expected. There is a trend, we also noted, toward reason-giving, especially in international commercial arbitration.

Second, the opinions need to get published for rules to materialize through a system of precedents. Arbitration generally comes short of this requirement, since confidentiality is very common in arbitral proceedings. As we saw in Chapter 1, however, the laws in many jurisdictions are evolving toward transparency in some specific fields, such as consumer law. In the realm of international transactions there is also a tendency toward publication of awards. The fact that the

[4] Fiss, "The Forms of Justice," p. 36. Fuller, however, accepted that the production and development of norms is part of the judicial task. It would be wrong to read him to endorse the thesis that the only responsibility of courts is to settle disputes. For a convincing reconstruction of Fuller's conception, see Robert G. Bone, "Lon Fuller's Theory of Adjudication and the False Dichotomy between Dispute Resolution and Public Law Models of Litigation," 75 *Boston University Law Review*, 1273 (1995).

[5] Fiss, "The Forms of Justice," p. 26.

decisions are usually reported in redacted form, so that the identities of the parties are concealed, is not a problem for purposes of the production of norms.[6]

Third, adjudicators need to have the right incentives to look beyond the specific case they are handling and think in terms of general rules that can be projected onto the future. According to William Landes and Richard Posner, arbitrators do not have such incentives.[7] Arbitrators are paid by the parties to decide a particular dispute, not to think deeply about the shape of the rule that should govern future controversies. Arbitrators, moreover, may fear that a clear holding of a general kind will make them less likely to be hired as arbitrators in later disputes, if such a holding disfavors a class of people that may be potential clients. So we cannot expect arbitrators to give us much in terms of precedents, which are technically "public goods": a precedent creates positive externalities for people who have contributed nothing to the process through which the precedent has been generated.

We should not overlook, however, an incentive that goes in the opposite direction: arbitrators are sometimes jurists who wish to build and augment their reputation through doctrinally sophisticated awards that are taken into account in professional legal circles. This is particularly true in the field of international commercial arbitration.[8]

There is a fourth condition, finally, that is of critical importance for the development of a system of precedents: there must be a central body with the power to harmonize the discordant interpretations of the various decision-makers. Arbitration does not satisfy this requirement at all. In some spheres of economic activity, arbitrators are part of an informal network of decision-makers, but they are not organized in a hierarchical structure. Arbitral institutions, in turn, administer and supervise arbitral proceedings, but no internal arbitral tribunal has been set up to settle interpretive controversies among arbitrators, as a supreme court does with respect to the judgments of lower courts. Nor is there a higher authority that connects the different arbitral facilities to bring about interpretive harmony. No overarching institution has been erected to scrutinize all the awards for conformity with substantive law. Arbitral tribunals, moreover, are not permanent. Arbitrators are selected to decide a particular case. Once they have done so, their authority comes to an end. It is hard to secure consistency when the bodies making decisions are so ephemeral.

6 Mark Weidemaier, "Toward a Theory of Precedent in Arbitration," 51 *William & Mary Law Review*, 1895 (2010), p. 1921, notes that the publication of awards is sometimes not necessary: their accessibility to the community of arbitrators may be sufficient. In systems where a few arbitrators capture a large share of the arbitration business, he explains, past awards can be taken into account even in the absence of publication. This is a rather extraordinary situation, however.

7 William M. Landes and Richard A. Posner, "Adjudication as a Private Good," 8 *Journal of Legal Studies*, 235 (1979).

8 On this point, see Gilles Cuniberti, "Beyond Contract – The Case for Default Arbitration in International Commercial Disputes," 32 *Fordham International Law Journal*, 417 (2008), pp. 456–457.

So, all things considered, it is safe to conclude that the arbitral regime is not well-suited to formulate rules through the generation of a system of precedents.

Should we be concerned about this "precedential deficit"? Generally speaking, the answer is no. Regular courts are intensely occupied with many disputes that raise all sorts of legal issues. Courts are thus in a position to furnish the array of rules that arbitration cannot engender. If judges hear a sufficient number and variety of cases to produce such rules, the weakness of arbitration in jurisprudential terms is not problematic.[9]

We cannot exclude the danger, however, that arbitration will be so widely used in some specific sectors that courts will no longer have the opportunity to develop case law properly. In such circumstances, it is justified for the legislature to declare the relevant claims to be non-arbitrable, especially if they are connected to mandatory law. Alternatively, the legislature may establish that judicial review of awards will be broader when arbitration operates in those specific sectors. Some scholars worry, for example, that the explosion of consumer arbitration in the United States may be impeding the operation of the common-law system of precedent as regards consumers.[10] As a response, federal legislation could be enacted barring consumer arbitration or providing for fuller judicial review of the legal merits of arbitral awards. Similarly, there were once concerns in England about the generation of judicial precedent in admiralty, commodities, and insurance cases. The legislature restricted the ability of parties in arbitration to waive their right to appeal arbitral awards on points of English law in such areas. It was felt that courts needed to speak about such matters to keep English common law alive and attuned to changing circumstances. In 1996, however, the legislature eliminated such restriction.[11] In the same vein, some critics of the Delaware state-sponsored arbitration program that was mentioned in Chapter 1 argued that it was a bad idea to encourage contending parties to refer cases to Chancery judges in arbitration. Because of the confidential nature of the arbitral proceedings conducted by judges in that program, Delaware was running the risk of degrading the continued maintenance and development of its corporate common law.[12] So although the shortcomings of arbitration in terms of the production of precedents are generally not problematic, it may sometimes happen that the wells feeding the judicial formulation of rules become so dry that restrictions on arbitration need to be established.

9 A study conducted in the United States by Chistopher Drahozal, for example, concluded that "only in relatively limited areas does it appear that arbitration might completely remove cases from the courts." See Christopher R. Drahozal, "Is Arbitration Lawless?," 40 *Loyola of Los Angeles Law Review*, 187 (2006), p. 210.

10 See Margaret Jane Radin, *Boilerplate: The Fine Print, Vanishing Rights, and the Rule of Law* (Princeton: Princeton University Press, 2013), p. 135.

11 See William W. Park, *Arbitration of International Business Disputes. Studies in Law and Practice* (Oxford: Oxford University Press, 2006), pp. 153–154.

12 See, for instance, Brian J. M. Quinn, "Arbitration and the Future of Delaware's Corporate Law Franchise," 14 *Cardozo Journal of Conflict Resolution*, 829 (2013), pp. 856–874.

There is an additional consideration to keep in mind when thinking about the normative consequences of arbitration's inability to achieve consistency in the application of the law. When it comes to courts, consistency is commonly valued, not only because it brings with it legal certainty, but also because persons should be treated equally. It is indeed a breach of equality for a decision-maker to apply the same law differently to two individuals, when the cases they are involved in are identical in all relevant legal aspects. The judiciary, of course, does not consist of a single court. It comprises many different courts, which often produce disparate outcomes. The underlying aspiration, however, is that a sufficient degree of convergence will ultimately be secured through the appellate system. Even if there are many courts, all of them are part of the same organization, and they should speak with one voice. Ronald Dworkin captured this aspiration when he developed his idea of law as integrity.[13]

In the arbitral domain, however, the different arbitrators are not interconnected, as already noted. They are not part of an institutional unit. So if various arbitrators, within the area of discretion that the relevant law accords them, decide cases differently, the sense of unfairness is less acute: the parties realize that they are being treated differently by separate decision-makers who do not speak in the name of a larger institution. Even if the decisions being compared have been made by arbitrators chosen with the help of the administrative structures of the same arbitral center, this link is insufficient to create the necessary institutional wholeness that can trigger the unfairness objection.

4.3 THE INDEPENDENCE OF ARBITRATORS: TOO LITTLE, TOO MUCH?

Against the background of the topics we have studied so far, what can be said about the degree of independence arbitrators enjoy? For purposes of our discussion, we should distinguish two kinds of independence: "party detachment" and "political insularity," to use Owen Fiss's terminology.[14] With respect to the judiciary, the first kind refers to the extent to which judges are independent from the parties to the controversy. The second concerns independence from political institutions and the public in general.

According to Fiss, independence as party detachment is uncompromising in its demands. "The more detachment from the parties the better," he writes.[15] Political insularity, in contrast, is necessary, but too much of it may be a bad thing. Fiss explains:

[13] See, generally, Ronald Dworkin, *Law's Empire* (Cambridge, Massachusetts: Harvard University Press, 1986).

[14] Owen Fiss, "The Right Degree of Independence," in Owen Fiss, *The Dictates of Justice. Essays on Law and Human Rights* (Dordrecht, Republic of Letters, 2011), pp. 13–29.

[15] Ibid., p. 13.

> We want to insulate the judiciary from the more popularly controlled institutions, but at the same time recognize that some elements of political control should remain. We must accommodate two values –not just judicial legitimacy, but popular sovereignty as well- and this requires us to optimize, rather than to maximize, this form of independence. In contrast to party detachment, it is simply not true that in a democracy the more political insularity the better. What we need is the right degree of insularity.[16]

Fiss enumerates some of the ways in which judges are subject to political control: the political branches have a say in the appointment process; they exercise power over judicial finances; they can reverse judicial rulings through legislative or constitutional amendments; and they can create obstacles to the enforcement of judicial decisions.

If we compare arbitration to adjudication by courts, we can see that the first form of independence is structurally weaker in arbitration: arbitrators are appointed by the disputants, whereas judges sitting in permanent courts are not. In the previous chapter we already discussed the procedures for selecting arbitrators in light of the impartiality norm. Let us focus here on the other side of the coin, independence understood as political insularity.

As far as political insularity is concerned, arbitrators are actually *more independent* than judges, since some of the instruments that the political institutions can use to check courts are not applicable against arbitrators. The political branches, in particular, have no say in the appointment process, and they have no control over arbitral finances. There is still the possibility, however, for the legislature to intervene to counteract arbitral rulings. Is the high level of political independence that arbitrators are granted normatively acceptable?

In answering this question, we must be sensitive to the reason why courts need to be linked to the democratic institutions. The reason, basically, is that courts engender rules through case law. If the only function judges discharged was the settlement of controversies, they could be accorded maximum political insularity. But the generation of norms requires a certain measure of democratic legitimacy. Since the dispute resolution function and the lawmaking function are placed in the same hands, a balance needs to be struck between normative considerations pulling in opposite directions. We are inclined to move in the direction of strong political independence to the extent that judges adjudicate specific disputes, but we are eager to move in the opposite direction in so far as judges participate in the lawmaking process.[17] The point of equilibrium need not be the same for all courts. In some countries, for example, supreme court (or constitutional court) judges are selected

[16] Ibid., p. 20.

[17] As Martin Shapiro observes, two conflicting goals are involved in the debate about judicial independence from politics: we want the disputes between two parties to be resolved by an independent third party, but we also want lawmakers (including courts) to be responsible to the people. Martin Shapiro, *Courts. A Comparative and Political Analysis*, p. 34.

through procedures that are more open to the inputs of the political branches than the procedures employed to recruit the rest of judges.

So what about arbitrators? As we saw in earlier chapters, arbitrators are generally directed by the parties to follow the law enacted by the political organs as interpreted and developed by public courts. Insofar as arbitrators decide in this way, no democratic checks are necessary. The checks on courts are the important ones, since courts are the source of the rules arbitrators will be using to interpret and apply the law. We should therefore not be worried that the political branches don't get to appoint arbitrators.

Sometimes, however, arbitrators experiment with novel solutions to legal problems, especially when the parties instruct them to decide *ex aequo et bono*. Arbitration can serve as a laboratory for trying new ideas without affecting the entire judicial system, much in the same way that federalism has traditionally been said to permit individual member states to experiment with new policies without putting the rest of the country at risk.[18] In that scenario, it seems reasonable for the political branches to wait and see in what directions courts elaborate their doctrines in reaction to specific arbitral developments. If courts finally embraced the legal constructions advanced by arbitrators, the political bodies could then intervene through the usual legislative mechanisms. In the same vein, if arbitrators generally interpreted the law in a given sector differently than courts, and the parties that resorted to arbitration structured their behavior accordingly, the legislature would have reason to enter the scene and speak its will, if it disagreed with the legal interpretations arbitrators were converging upon.

4.4 CONCLUSION

Within the sphere of private law, arbitrators cannot be expected to supply a consistent body of rules by way of precedents. Because arbitral tribunals are not hierarchically organized permanent bodies, they are not well suited to the rule formulation enterprise. This jurisprudential deficit is not problematic, however, to the extent that courts are being asked to adjudicate a sufficient number and variety of cases allowing them to furnish case law pertaining to all the relevant fields. The fact that arbitrators do not contribute to the production of legal rules, moreover, makes it easier to justify their being placed in an institutional space that is very distant from the political process. From this perspective, their high level of political insularity is not objectionable.

18 The classic defense of the role of states in federal systems as laboratories of democracy appears in a dissenting opinion by Justice Louis Brandeis in *New State Ice Co.* v. *Liebmann*, 285 U.S. 262 (1932).

5

The Special Case of International Commercial Arbitration

For a variety of reasons we have explored in Chapter 1, arbitration plays a notable role in the domestic sphere. As we will discuss in this chapter, arbitration becomes even more important when it involves private transactions of an international character. Although we have already mentioned international commercial arbitration at different junctures, it is time to discuss it more thoroughly.[1]

Arbitration, indeed, is quite popular among businesses operating in international settings. When the contracting parties come from different countries, or when the contract exhibits some other foreign element, arbitration is often selected to adjust differences. In addition, where states act in their commercial capacity, as opposed to their sovereign capacity, arbitration clauses are often inserted in the international agreements they enter into. Practitioners sometimes say that arbitration "is the only game in town" on the international commercial stage. This is probably an exaggeration. We do not have comprehensive data to gauge the degree to which arbitration is actually favored over litigation.[2] But there is no doubt that arbitration is a key element of international trade.

Most commonly, the contracting parties stipulate in their agreement the specific city where their arbitration will be seated if a dispute arises. The seat of the arbitration is not necessarily the place where the hearings will be held. By choosing the seat the parties basically select the country whose laws will apply to the arbitral process and whose courts will have jurisdiction to review the validity of the award if one of the parties challenges it. The most popular arbitral venues include Paris,

[1] For a comprehensive treatment of international commercial arbitration, see Gary Born, *International Commercial Arbitration* (Alphen aan den Rijn: Kluwer Law International, 2014). For a useful introduction, see Nigel Blackaby and Constantine Partasides QC with Alan Redfern and Martin Hunter, *Redfern and Hunter on International Arbitration* (Oxford: Oxford University Press, 2015). For a collection of essays, see William W. Park, *Arbitration of International Business Disputes* (Oxford: Oxford University Press, 2006). A study of international commercial arbitration in a context of comparison with international litigation can be found in George A. Bermann, *International Commercial Arbitration and Private International Law* (Leiden: Brill Nijhoff, 2017).

[2] For a discussion of the limitations of the available empirical studies on the matter, see Thomas Hale, *Between Interests and the Law. The Politics of Transnational Commercial Disputes* (Cambridge: Cambridge University Press, 2015), pp. 40–44.

London, Geneva, New York, Stockholm, Hong Kong, and Singapore. A number of arbitral centers have become prominent in this field, such as the International Court of Arbitration of the ICC (the International Chamber of Commerce), the London Court of International Arbitration, the Arbitration Institute of the Stockholm Chamber of Commerce, the International Center for Dispute Resolution (which is the international division of the American Arbitration Association), the Singapore International Arbitration Centre, and the Hong Kong International Arbitration Centre, among others. To facilitate the arbitration of international contractual claims, the UNCITRAL (United Nations Commission on International Trade Law) adopted in 1976 a set of arbitral rules (revised in 2010) which the parties can incorporate in their agreements by reference, regardless of whether they resort to an arbitral center or choose *ad hoc* arbitration instead.

Why is arbitration particularly attractive in the international commercial context? Among the reasons often mentioned, two of them stand out. First, arbitration benefits from the existence of the New York Convention of 1958 on the Recognition and Enforcement of Foreign Arbitral Awards, which gives arbitration certain advantages over adjudication in court. Second, arbitration can be resorted to in order to create a neutral forum where disputes involving international private deals can be adjudicated in an objective manner. Surveys conducted among international commercial arbitration stakeholders reveal that these two factors play a critical part in their choices to arbitrate disputes.[3] We will next discuss them in some detail.

5.1 THE NEW YORK CONVENTION OF 1958: AN EFFECTIVE LEGAL INSTRUMENT FOR THE ENFORCEMENT OF ARBITRAL AGREEMENTS AND AWARDS

Arbitration enjoys great protection under international law as a result of the adoption of the New York Convention of 1958 on the Recognition and Enforcement of Foreign Arbitral Awards. The states that have subscribed to this Convention pledge to enforce arbitral agreements and awards. Arbitral awards, in particular, can only be refused recognition and execution on very limited grounds, which are enumerated in the Convention (in article V). Interestingly, these grounds are congruent with the grounds for judicial nullification of awards listed in the UNCITRAL Model Law.

The New York Convention was adopted by the United Nations on the basis of a draft submitted by the International Chamber of Commerce. Treaties on the

[3] The "2018 International Arbitration Survey: The Evolution of International Arbitration," released by the Queen Mary University of London School of International Arbitration, available at www.arbitration.qmul.ac.uk/research/2018/, asked respondents about the three most valuable characteristics of international arbitration. "Enforceability of awards" was chosen by 64 percent of respondents, while "avoiding specific legal systems/national courts" was chosen by 60 percent. "Neutrality" was mentioned by 25 percent, and "confidentiality and privacy" by 36 percent.

matter had already been negotiated under the League of Nations: the 1923 Geneva Protocol on Arbitration Clauses and the 1927 Geneva Convention Relating to the Execution of Foreign Arbitral Awards. The New York Convention went further, however, in the extent to which it facilitated arbitration of transborder disputes. We can see, once more, how private actors often need the backing of public institutions for market transactions to develop in an effective manner. Without the Convention, many commercial deals would not be entered at all, or would only be entered at higher costs.

The Convention has been extraordinarily successful in terms of its membership: most countries in the world (161, as of April 1, 2020) have ratified it. Even during the Cold War, this international instrument facilitated East-West trade. Commercial entities of the communist countries often used arbitration institutions (especially the Stockholm Chamber of Commerce) to adjudicate differences with their Western counterparties.[4]

Indeed, in the field of international transactions, arbitration has a clear advantage over litigation in court. While the New York Convention is widely accepted across the world, no equivalent treaty to protect choice-of-judicial forum agreements has received broad support. The Hague Convention of 2005 on Choice of Court Agreements, in particular, which entered into force on October 1, 2015, has been ratified by very few countries.[5] It is thus risky for the contracting parties to adopt clauses specifying that the courts of a given country will have jurisdiction to decide disputes. The courts of that country may ultimately refuse to hear a case for lack of sufficient links.[6] In the absence of international treaties covering the controversy, the contracting parties cannot be sure the designated judiciary will accept to adjudicate it, or that other courts will refrain from deciding the case in deference to the chosen court.

To be sure, some countries are eager to open their judiciaries to international disputes. The specialized commercial courts in London and New York have traditionally been ready to adjudicate them. There is actually a recent trend in different parts of the world to attract international litigation. Singapore is a remarkable example of this. In 2015, this country opened the Singapore International Commercial Court, a division of the Singapore High Court seeking to become a dispute resolution hub catering to international disputes with an Asian connection. Interestingly, this new body is comprised of both national judges and foreign judges, so-called "international judges." Singapore is not alone in these efforts to attract litigation business: Qatar, Dubai, Amsterdam, Paris, Frankfurt, among other places, have also been introducing new courts and procedural arrangements of diverse kinds

4 Hale, *Between Interests and Law*, p. 32.

5 As of April 1, 2020, only Mexico, Singapore, Montenegro, the members of the European Union, and the European Union itself, have done so.

6 On this risk, see Park, *Arbitration of International Business Disputes*, p. 374.

to facilitate international litigation.[7] So things may change in the coming years in terms of how often the parties prefer arbitration to litigation. So far, however, arbitration has enjoyed an advantageous position, since the parties know for sure that the arbitral seat they specify in their agreement will be respected by the adjudicators.

A similar asymmetry emerges when arbitral awards and court judgments need to be enforced in a foreign country. While the New York Convention facilitates the execution of arbitral awards, the prospects are not so good with regard to court judgments. The Hague Convention of 1971 on the Recognition and Enforcement of Foreign Judgments in Civil and Commercial Matters, which entered into force on August 20, 1979, has obtained few ratifications.[8] A new international agreement on this matter has recently been adopted, the Hague Convention of 2019 on the Recognition and Enforcement of Foreign Judgments in Civil or Commercial Matters, but it has not yet entered into force. It is generally hoped that it will attract a larger number of states than the previous Convention. There are certainly bilateral treaties facilitating the execution of judicial decisions, but these instruments are not as effective as a widely supported global treaty would be.

So the international legal infrastructure that has been built so far has not put arbitration and litigation on an equal footing. It would be a clear improvement, of course, to introduce changes to level the playing field between these two dispute-resolution mechanisms. Within the European Union, for example, an effective legal regime has been set up for the enforcement of forum selection clauses and judgments.[9] As a result, arbitration and adjudication by courts are treated more equally within the region. This is a welcome move. Arbitration has its own natural virtues – there is no need to protect it artificially. States should be willing to ratify global treaties aimed at facilitating the recognition and enforcement of choice-of-forum agreements and court judgements.[10] There may be dignitarian reasons that explain states' reluctance to do so. As Jens Dammann and Henry Hansmann have suggested, empowering arbitration may be easier for states than empowering foreign courts: "It is one thing for a government to recognize that its citizens might prefer to have their commercial disputes handled by private arbitrators in a foreign country than by the local public courts; it is another thing to recognize that its citizens might prefer the foreign country's public courts to the local public courts." The latter

7 For an overview of this new landscape, see Pamela K. Bookman, "The Adjudication Business," 45 *The Yale Journal of International Law*, 227 (2020).

8 As of April 1, 2020, the countries that have ratified the Convention are Albania, Cyprus, Kuwait, The Netherlands, and Portugal.

9 See Regulation (EU), No 1215/2012 of the European Parliament and of the Council of 12 December 2012 on jurisdiction and the recognition and enforcement of judgments in civil and commercial matters (recast).

10 For an interesting proposal to go further and facilitate resort to foreign courts even when the underlying dispute is domestic, see Jens Dammann and Henry Hansmann, "Globalizing Commercial Litigation," 94 *Cornell Law Review*, 1 (2008).

seems to affect national pride: it "looks more like conceding that foreign government might be superior to local government."[11] Whatever the explanation for this governmental stance, the normative case remains that states should not artificially privilege arbitration on the international stage by failing to properly buttress global litigation.

5.2 THE NEW YORK CONVENTION AS A CONSTITUTIONAL CHARTER

In addition to the procedural benefits that arbitration derives from the New York Convention, the latter can be interpreted to impose substantive restrictions and requirements on national arbitration laws. To the extent that this is so, the Convention performs a "constitutional" function: although national legislatures enjoy regulatory leeway, they need to observe certain limits.

It is certainly an open question which are, specifically, the constraints and requirements that the Convention lays down. Commentators disagree on the issue. And there is no central tribunal located in the international sphere with the task of fixing the Convention's meaning. The Convention does not contain a dispute settlement clause entrusting an international organ with the resolution of disputes among treaty partners regarding its interpretation and application. Within the United Nations, UNCITRAL (the United Nations Commission on International Trade Law) can make recommendations concerning the Convention, but it has no authority to issue binding interpretations. The job of construing and applying the treaty is thus assigned to the multiplicity of national judiciaries that get involved with the arbitral process.[12]

The New York Convention, for example, delegates to the national laws the task of regulating the conditions arbitral agreements must meet in order for them to be valid and enforceable. It may be argued that states are not totally free when they establish rules on this matter. If a domestic statute, for instance, prohibited the contending parties from agreeing to appoint foreigners to serve as arbitrators, it would arguably contravene the Convention.[13] More generally, Gary Born contends that arbitral agreements should only be declared invalid "under generally-applicable, internationally-neutral contract law defenses that do not impose discriminating burdens or requirements on the formation or validity of agreements to arbitrate."[14]

Similarly, the New York Convention can be read to constrain states with respect to the legal grounds for nullification of arbitral awards. The general assumption is that

11 Ibid., p. 25.

12 Scholars working in the field of international commercial arbitration have been debating for a long time which of the national legal systems that are potentially applicable in a given case is more strongly connected to the arbitral process. For a discussion of the issue, see Emmanuel Gaillard, *Legal Theory of International Arbitration* (Leiden: Martinus Nijhoff Publishers, 2010).

13 Born, *International Commercial Arbitration*, pp. 1740–1743.

14 Ibid., p. 840. For a skeptical view of Gary Born's thesis, see Alan Scott Rau, *The Allocation of Power between Arbitral Tribunals and State Courts* (Leiden: Brill Nijhoff, 2018), pp. 541–543.

the awards can only be reversed by the courts of the country where the arbitration is seated.[15] The laws of that country will specify the circumstances under which awards may be overturned by domestic courts. Arguably, there are limits to such legislative choices. As Gary Born points out, the Convention must be taken to exclude certain grounds for the annulment of awards as inconsistent with the spirit of the Convention, which seeks to buttress international arbitration. By way of illustration, he claims that it would be against the Convention for national law to provide for *de novo* judicial review, or to require the application by arbitrators of a domestic procedural code, or to empower judges to disregard the parties' choice of seat or language of the arbitration.[16]

It can be maintained, furthermore, that the Convention establishes limits on states in the other direction: the laws of the arbitral seat must make judicial review of awards possible. Some measure of judicial control must be established. Otherwise, the complex system that the Convention has set up to facilitate the recognition and enforcement of awards is undermined. Indeed, the judges who are asked to recognize and enforce foreign awards (the "secondary jurisdiction") will be less eager to do so if no judicial check is available in the country where the arbitration was seated (the "primary jurisdiction"). As Michael Reisman has argued, "in the absence of even the possibility of an exercise of a primary jurisdiction, the degree of review in the secondary jurisdiction will probably (and, indeed, should) be greater."[17] This runs counter to the underlying logic of the Convention, which aims to reduce the obstacles to the execution of foreign awards.

If we accept, in the light of these arguments, that the New York Convention places both negative limits and positive obligations on national legislatures, the Convention's effect is somewhat similar to that of a constitution that guarantees a right to arbitration of the sort we discussed in Chapter 2. Of course, the New York Convention does not explicitly recognize a right to arbitration. But it does presuppose that arbitration is an institution linked to private autonomy, an institution whose integrity can only be preserved if states refrain from imposing unreasonable constraints on the arbitral process and if they honor certain positive obligations.

The Convention will produce different legal effects in various countries depending on the kind of authority that international treaties are generally awarded within the respective domestic legal order. Quite often, national legislation must be interpreted in such a way that conflicts with international treaty obligations are avoided. If a conflict appears, however, different countries follow contrasting rules. In some jurisdictions, national legislation overrides an earlier treaty, while in others

15 See article V(1)(e) of the New York Convention.

16 Born, *International Commercial Arbitration*, pp. 3168–3173.

17 Michael Reisman, *Systems of Control in International Adjudication and Arbitration. Breakdown and Repair* (Durham: Duke University Press, 1992), p. 130.

it is the treaty that prevails.[18] In countries that belong to the latter group, the national judiciary can thus be empowered to disregard a provision of the domestic arbitration law that is deemed to breach the New York Convention. If so, the practical effect of judges using the Convention to test national laws is similar to that of judicial review of legislation in light of a constitutional right to arbitration.

We can also appreciate the constitutional nature of the New York Convention from a different angle. As we saw in Chapter 1, there are good reasons supporting the claim that private parties have a basic right to arbitration. This right, as we discussed, requires for its satisfaction the establishment of a legal and institutional framework without which arbitration cannot normally get off the ground. When we extend these ideas to the international commercial domain, we should take note of the great complexity of the legal and institutional arrangements that arbitration requires. In particular, a dense web of treaty relationships needs to be created, and courts in different jurisdictions have to lend their support to the arbitral process. The New York Convention is the cornerstone of the current system, without which the right to arbitration in connection to international private transactions would not be honored in practice. It is "constitutionally necessary," therefore, for a treaty like the New York Convention to exist. If the legal and institutional network that the governments have jointly created at the international level were dismantled, the right to arbitration would be infringed upon.

Actually, because the New York Convention is doing an acceptably good job in this connection, it is plausible to argue that states have a duty to become parties to it, in order to contribute to the maintenance and improvement of the arbitral system. When discussing the duties of states under international law, Ronald Dworkin postulated the "principle of salience," under which states have sometimes the duty to endorse the efforts that other states have successfully made to set up international legal structures. As he argued,

> if a significant number of states, encompassing a significant population, has developed an agreed code practice, either by treaty or by other form of coordination, then other states have at least a prima facie duty to subscribe to that practice as well, with the important proviso that this duty only holds if a more general practice to that effect, expanded in that way, would improve the legitimacy of the subscribing state and the international order as a whole.[19]

There is, of course, no court in the world one can have recourse to, in order to force governments to establish and maintain in good shape a system like the one that has been formed under the New York Convention. But the fact that no judicial remedy is available does not mean that states are not legally required to construct

18 For a general comparative view of the relationships between international treaties and national law in domestic jurisdictions, see James Crawford, *Brownlie's Principles of Public International Law* (Oxford: Oxford University Press, 2012), pp. 62–111.

19 Ronald Dworkin, "A New Philosophy for International Law," 41 *Philosophy & Public Affairs*, 2 (2013), p. 19.

and administer a framework that makes arbitration possible when people interact across borders. In general, individual rights are the source of different waves of obligations that governments must comply with, some of which are more specific and amenable to judicial protection, while others are more structural in nature and less open to judicial enforcement.[20]

It would be unreasonable to contend that the right to arbitration is at work when private transactions take place within the domestic sphere, while it vanishes when the underlying transactions have links to more than one country. What governments do on the global stage can matter a lot when it comes to individual rights. If arbitration is to be protected as an expression of private autonomy, certain legal consequences must follow regarding the international conduct of states.

This argument applies to the right to judicial protection as well. Because private parties often enter the international domain, governments must create a legal architecture that facilitates access to foreign courts, judicial assistance, and enforcement of foreign judgments. The fact that the current system is defective, especially in comparison to the arbitral regime, is ultimately a "constitutional" problem: the fundamental right to judicial protection is not fully satisfied as a result of the limitations of the existing legal order.

Note that the constitutional argument in support of international arbitration and the central importance of the New York Convention is not a utilitarian one. The point is not that arbitration (as well as courts) are necessary to promote international trade. States may or may not want to open their economies to foreign business. There is no fundamental right to enjoy open economies. But to the extent states carve out a space for international transactions to develop, they must ensure that private parties that engage in such transactions will be able to exercise their right to an impartial adjudication of disputes. Both courts and arbitral tribunals have a role to play in fulfillment of this right. Of course, if private parties know that the existing adjudicative mechanisms are in good shape, they will be more eager to engage in transborder commercial deals. There is evidence, for example, that the adoption of pro-arbitration policies boosts international trade. Ratifying the New York Convention, in particular, appears to notably increase a country's foreign trade.[21] From a constitutional perspective, however, what matters is whether states are effectively securing the fundamental right of private individuals to an impartial adjudication of their contractual rights. It is in this sense that the New York Convention partakes of a constitutional quality.

[20] See Jeremy Waldron, "Rights in Conflict," in Jeremy Waldron, *Liberal Rights: Collected Papers (1981–1991)* (Cambridge: Cambridge University Press, 1993), pp. 203–224.

[21] For a discussion on this empirical issue, see Thomas Hale, "What is the Effect of Commercial Arbitration on Trade?," in Walter Mattli and Thomas Dietz (eds.), *International Arbitration and Global Governance: Contending Theories and Evidence* (Oxford: Oxford University Press, 2014), pp. 196–213.

5.3 ARBITRATION AND THE NEUTRALITY OF THE LAW

Let us now discuss the second advantage that arbitration exhibits in the international commercial arena: its neutrality from a national point of view. The parties to an international contract usually want their potential disputes to be settled according to a procedure that is detached from local judicial authorities. Arbitration can be used to create such a "neutral forum." It is important to realize that the kind of neutrality that matters in this context does not refer to the lawmakers, but to the adjudicators. Arbitration promises neutrality, not because a special kind of law is chosen to govern the underlying contract, but because a special forum is constructed to settle the controversy. We will first examine the connection between neutrality and substantive law, and will then proceed to discuss the neutrality of the forum in the next section.

The basic point to bear in mind, indeed, is that the neutrality that arbitration serves does not depend on the substantive law that arbitrators apply. Suppose that the seller in an international sales contract comes from country A, while the buyer comes from country B. The law of country A is not necessarily biased in favor of the class of sellers. It may actually give them less protection than the law of country B. The seller might prefer to choose the law of country B for this reason.

In general, private law tends to be neutral regarding nationality. Each legal order realizes a particular conception of justice and privileges some interests over others. It is certainly not neutral from a moral point of view. But because both nationals and foreigners can easily occupy any of the diverse legal positions regulated by private law (sellers and buyers, to continue with the same example), it is unlikely that the stronger protection that a particular legal position enjoys is connected to nationality. In many private law contexts (but not in all of them), the lawmaker works under a certain veil of ignorance: it does not know whether it is mostly foreigners or citizens that will be "favored" by its laws on contracts.

A party may certainly wish to subject the contract to the law he is most familiar with. This will typically be the law of his country, or a law similar to it.[22] This has nothing to do with neutrality, however. A party may feel more comfortable with a law he knows about, to reduce the risk of legal surprises. But this does not mean that a different law would have been tilted against him from a substantive point of view.

The nationality of the law may also matter in other situations. If the parties do not indicate which law applies to their transaction, for example, the arbitrators may be reluctant to choose the law of the country of one of the parties. They may rather select the law of a third country, or rely on international contract law instruments, or even on unwritten principles of *lex mercatoria*.[23] Other times, even if a particular law has been determined by the parties to govern the contract, the arbitrators may be inclined to explain in their award that the result they have reached would not have

[22] Joshua Karton, *The Culture of International Arbitration and the Evolution of Contract Law* (Oxford: Oxford University Press, 2013), p. 119.

[23] Ibid., p. 120.

been different if the law of the country of the losing party had been applied. Such clarification may help enhance the legitimacy of the decision in the eyes of the party that suffers a legal defeat.[24] In a similar spirit, arbitrators may try to interpret the applicable law in a conceptually fresh manner: they may seek to translate the local categories of domestic law into more universal concepts that lawyers and litigants from different nations can grasp.[25] These are all reasonable strategies to fortify the authority of the award in a global setting. But they are not really necessary to generate substantive neutrality.

5.4 ARBITRATION AND THE NEUTRALITY OF THE FORUM

What is really critical in the world of international commerce is the neutrality of the adjudicative forum. When private parties of different nationalities enter a contract, they have good reason to attach an arbitration clause to it, to keep away from domestic courts. When a party litigates before the courts of the country of the other party, he or she may feel foreign there. Those courts will follow procedures the foreign party is likely to be unfamiliar with. The language to be employed in the course of the litigation is usually the local one. And local lawyers will have to be hired. Arbitration, in contrast, opens a space for adjudicative neutrality. A neutral country can be chosen as the seat of the arbitration. The proceedings are agreed upon by the parties. No local language needs to be used. And there is no requirement to employ local lawyers.

Of course, arbitration cannot be completely neutral from a cultural perspective when the parties come with diverse backgrounds. If a Western company enters into an agreement with a Chinese company, for instance, seating the arbitration in Switzerland will attract Western legal conceptions that are different from those that would guide an arbitration seated in Beijing. Some degree of neutrality can nevertheless be achieved through arbitration. Singapore and Hong Kong, for example, are often chosen as a "compromise" between Western and Chinese companies. Both places are culturally similar to the Chinese mainland, yet both are governed by legal systems strongly influenced by the legacy of British colonialism.[26] Similarly, although in many cases arbitral procedures are the upshot of a synthesis of common law and civil law conceptions regarding adjudication, the parties and their lawyers may feel more or less comfortable with the way arbitrators run those proceedings, depending on how far they deviate from the way of doing

[24] Ibid., p. 140.

[25] In general, a comparative law approach to legal problems can be liberating. As Konrad Zweigert and Hein Kötz explain, comparative law can "facilitate the mutual comprehension of jurists of different nationalities and allay the misunderstandings which come from the prejudices, constraints, and diverse vocabularies of the different systems." See Konrad Zweigert and Hein Kötz, *An Introduction to Comparative Law* (Oxford: Oxford University Press, 1998), p. 46.

[26] Hale, *Between Interests and Law*, p. 340.

things in a specific legal culture.[27] Some lawyers, for example, are of the view that the rules developed by arbitral practices so far have been too heavily influenced by common law precepts. Those lawyers have proposed the introduction of new rules, to encourage tribunals to take a more active role in managing the cases, as traditionally done in many civil law countries.[28]

There is a connected consideration that figures prominently in the justifications that are commonly marshaled to support international arbitration. It is often reasonable, it is argued, for the parties to fear that local courts will be skewed in favor of local litigants. Gary Born, for example, writes in his influential treatise: "One of the central objectives of international arbitration agreements is to provide a neutral forum for dispute resolution." Domestic courts are distrusted: "If nothing else, an instinctive mistrust of the potential for home-court bias usually prompts parties to refuse to agree to litigate in their counter-party's local courts."[29] In the same vein, Alan Redfern and Martin Hunter argue that it is better for the parties to establish a neutral arbitral tribunal "than it is to entrust the resolution of the dispute to the courts of one of the parties, which may lack experience of commercial matters or which may, quite simply, be biased in favour of the local party."[30] William Park, in turn, writes that "arbitration clauses in cross-border contracts are usually prompted by apprehension about the real or imagined bias of foreign judicial proceedings."[31] Similarly, Jan Paulsson explains that "it is unusual for parties of different nationalities to agree to the jurisdiction of a national court." "Either party is disinclined to accept the courts of the other."[32] As a result, arbitrability (that is, the range of matters that the law allows private parties to submit to arbitration) is often deemed especially broad in connection with international business transactions, "where it is important to avoid nationalistic turf wars."[33] According to Paulsson, we can debate about the advantages of arbitration in the domestic setting. Is it really quicker, less expensive, less disruptive because of confidentiality, etc..? "In international arbitration," however, "all these elements of evaluation fade into relative insignificance when

27 On the merger of common law and civil law procedural traditions in arbitration, see Gabrielle Kaufmann-Kohler, "Globalization of Arbitral Procedure," 36 *Vanderbilt Journal of Transnational Law*, 1313 (2003).

28 See, in particular, the "Rules on the Efficient Conduct of Proceedings in International Arbitration (Prague Rules)," drafted by a working group formed by representatives from thirty, mainly civil law, countries, available at www.praguerules.com.

29 Born, *International Commercial Arbitration*, pp. 73–74.

30 Blackaby and Partasides QC with Redfern and Hunter, *Redfern and Hunter on International Arbitration*, p. 39.

31 Park, *Arbitration of International Business Disputes*, p. 232. Park refers to an interesting article by Kevin M. Clermont and Theodore Eisenberg, "Xenophilia in American Courts," 109 *Harvard Law Review*, 1120 (1996), which found that in federal civil actions in the United States foreigners fare better than domestic parties, part of the reason being that their fear of the American civil justice system causes them to continue to final judgment only when they have particularly strong cases. William Park, ibid., p. 232, footnote 66.

32 Jan Paulsson, *The Idea of Arbitration* (New York: Oxford University Press, 2013), p. 174.

33 Ibid., pp. 102–103.

contrasted with a criterion that is dominant here although it is, by definition, irrelevant in the national context. . . . That unique criterion is neutrality."[34]

So it appears that arbitration is chosen, to a significant extent, in order to transcend local biases. Consistent with this, it has become standard practice for the presiding arbitrator to be selected from a nation, region, and culture different from those of the parties. The disputants often appoint co-arbitrators of their own nationality, in order to make sure that their respective cultural or legal perspectives are represented. But the general presumption is that the presiding arbitrator will not share the nationality of one of the parties.[35] The UNCITRAL Model Law, for example, provides that the court or authority that is asked to appoint arbitrators shall take into account "the advisability of appointing an arbitrator of a nationality other than those of the parties," in the case of a sole or presiding arbitrator.[36] Actually, Jan Paulsson goes further and suggests that arbitration agreements should include the prescription that no arbitrator may possess the nationality of any party.[37]

Arbitration, of course, cannot dispense with local courts entirely. The danger of favoritism is therefore still present. When a foreign award needs to be enforced by domestic courts, for example, the New York Convention permits the latter to deny enforcement on "public policy" grounds.[38] The risk exists that judges will apply this vague standard in an arbitrary manner in order to favor the local party. Public policy exceptions may thus serve as a cover for "xenophobic bias."[39] This danger could only be avoided if an international court were created with the exclusive jurisdiction to determine the enforceability of international awards under the New York Convention.[40]

5.5 OVERCOMING LOCAL BIASES: EXTERNAL AND INTERNAL STRATEGIES

Let us assume that the neutrality argument in favor of international commercial arbitration is basically correct. In particular, let us accept that there is indeed a significant risk of local favoritism on the part of domestic judiciaries. This assumption should drive us to critique the existing legal structures. Indeed, if national courts have a propensity to favor the locals, we should acknowledge that

34 Jan Paulsson, "International Arbitration is not Arbitration," *Stockholm International Arbitration Review* 1(2008:2), p. 2.

35 Catherine A. Rogers, *Ethics in International Arbitration* (Oxford: Oxford University Press, 2014), pp. 94–95.

36 See article 11(5) of the UNCITRAL Model Law.

37 Paulsson, *The Idea of Arbitration*, p. 281.

38 See article V(2) of the New York Convention.

39 Paulsson, *The Idea of Arbitration*, p. 206.

40 For a proposal to set up an International Court of Arbitral Awards, endowed with such jurisdiction, see Stephen M. Schwebel, *Justice in International Law. Further Selected Writings* (Cambridge: Cambridge University Press, 2011), pp. 246–254.

the level of civilization we have reached is not very high. What should be done? We can distinguish two basic kinds of strategies to confront this problem.

5.5.1 *External Strategies*

The first type of strategy, which we may call "external," seeks to create decision-making institutions that are removed from the local players. Arbitration in the international business sphere is an example of such a strategy. Arbitration, of course, is only a fragmentary solution to the neutrality problem, since it mainly covers, in practice, contractual disputes. Arbitration does not apply to many other controversies involving citizens of diverse nationalities. If a local pedestrian suffers injuries caused by a foreign driver, for example, the action for damages will most likely be heard by domestic courts. Indeed, it is rare for arbitration to be agreed upon after the controversy breaks out. With respect to criminal law, local courts will be in charge, since criminal law cannot be arbitrated. The same is true of many other branches of the law. To be sure, public international law puts some limits on the arbitrary treatment of foreigners by local courts. It does so by means of the "denial of justice" doctrine.[41] This doctrine addresses rather extreme cases of abuse, however, and is insufficient to neutralize all forms of local favoritism.

We might therefore consider the possibility of creating "international courts" to adjudicate disputes involving litigants of different nationalities. Much in the same way that federal courts in the United States have jurisdiction to decide controversies between citizens of different states, we might think it a good idea to establish a web of international courts to settle disputes confronting individuals of different nationalities.[42] Or the courts of a neutral country may be chosen as the adjudicative forum, an option that is underused in practice owing to the limitations of the international legal infrastructure we discussed earlier.

Alternatively, we may want to leave matters in the hands of local courts, but put the latter under the supervision of a supranational tribunal that is made up of judges of different nationalities. Within the framework of the European Union, for example, the potential prejudices against outsiders are in part counteracted by European Union law, which protects the principle of no discrimination on grounds of nationality. European Union law is regularly applied by domestic courts, but there is a more "neutral" tribunal in Luxembourg, the Court of Justice of the European Union, made up of judges of the different member states. This Court ensures the uniform interpretation of European Union law, and has some ability to guide domestic courts into objective legal outcomes. Another option is to set up an

41 See, generally, Jan Paulsson, *Denial of Justice in International Law* (Cambridge: Cambridge University Press, 2005), and Berk Demirkol, *Judicial Acts and Investment Treaty Arbitration* (Cambridge: Cambridge University Press, 2018).

42 See article III, section 2, of the Constitution of the United States, establishing that the judicial power of the United States shall extend to controversies between citizens of different States.

international human rights court with jurisdiction to scrutinize whether state judges have respected the right not to be discriminated against on grounds of nationality. The European Court of Human Rights, for instance, can play a role in this respect, although it is a very limited one.

It is important to observe that in the field of public international law, which we will study in later chapters, we can also discern an impulse toward externality. Within the framework of the WTO (World Trade Organization), for example, citizens whose governments are parties to a dispute (or whose governments are third parties entitled to intervene in the proceedings because they have a substantial interest in a matter) cannot serve on an adjudicative panel that is concerned with that dispute, unless the contending parties agree otherwise.[43]

Similarly, when a difference between two states is referred to the International Court of Justice (ICJ), the latter is quite external in terms of nationality. All (or almost all) its members are nationals of states other than the contending parties. This seeks to ensure objectivity. Externality is marginally qualified, however, since judges of the nationality of each of the parties to a controversy retain their right to sit in the case before the Court. Moreover, if the Court includes on the bench a judge of the nationality of one of the contending parties, the other party may choose a person to sit as an *ad hoc* judge in the case. If neither party has a judge of its nationality, each may choose a person to sit as a judge.[44] Experience has shown that *ad hoc* judges rarely vote against their country.[45] This feature of the Court has historically elicited criticism. Hans Kelsen, for example, was critical of the institution of *ad hoc* judges.[46] So was Hersch Lauterpacht, who wrote that international judges should have a "clear individual consciousness of citizenship of the *civitas maxima*."[47] As citizens of the world, they should regard the international community to be an entity as real as any sovereign state, with an equal claim to allegiance. Legal institutions that perpetuate the idea that judges represent national interests should therefore be eliminated, according to Lauterpacht.

We can observe a similar tendency toward externality in the context of investor-state arbitration, which we will study in Part II of this book. Under the ICSID Convention, for example, the majority of arbitrators must be nationals of states other than the respondent state and the home state (from which the investor comes). This is the rule, unless each member of the tribunal has been appointed by the agreement

43 See article 8(3) of Annex 2 of the WTO Agreement: Understanding on Rules and Procedures Governing the Settlement of Disputes.

44 See article 31 of the Statute of the ICJ. The *ad hoc* judge, however, need not be a national of the state which appoints him or her.

45 Henry G. Schermers and Niels M. Blokker, *International Institutional Law* (Leiden: Martinus Nijhoff Publishers, 2011), pp. 486–487.

46 Hans Kelsen, *Peace Through Law* (Chapel Hill: The University of North Carolina Press, 1944), p. 63.

47 Hersch Lauterpacht, *The Function of Law in the International Community* (Hamden, Connecticut: Archon Books, 1966; originally published by Oxford University Press, 1933), p. 233.

of the two contending parties.[48] If the award is later challenged before an ICSID annulment committee, none of the members of the committee can be a national of the respondent state or the home state.[49]

At the domestic level we can also find examples of institutional arrangements that are designed to transcend nationality-based partisanship, at least to a certain extent. The Constitutional Court of Bosnia and Herzegovina, for instance, consists of nine judges. Six of them are citizens of that state, while the rest are foreigners. In practice, two judges are Bosniaks, two are Croats, and two are Serbs, so that the three largest ethnic groups in the country are equally represented. The remaining three members of the Court are appointed by the President of the European Court of Human Rights, after consultation with the presidency of Bosnia and Herzegovina. These members cannot be citizens of Bosnia and Herzegovina or of its neighboring states. Such external voices are expected to introduce a measure of objectivity and to help overcome deadlocks in adjudication in a country that has experienced great violence among various ethnic groups. The Court is thus not purely external in its composition, but it comprises elements of externality.[50]

So several examples can be given to illustrate strategies of the external kind that have been implemented in different adjudicative settings in order to transcend local biases.

5.5.2 *Internal Strategies*

A completely different approach to attack the problem of national bias is "internal." It seeks to transform the attitudes and beliefs that lead to local prejudices. Instead of looking for external institutions to realize impartiality, the plan is to introduce the necessary internal changes in order to push national institutions in the direction of impartiality. The idea is that citizens should be educated into the belief that all human beings have an equal moral standing and should therefore be treated equally under the law. Judges and juries should be trained and urged to be impartial when they interpret and administer the law in specific disputes. The fact that one of the parties to the controversy comes from a foreign country is to be made completely irrelevant when the law needs to be applied.

It is interesting to recall, in this regard, the transformation of British judicial processes at the end of the nineteenth century, evolving from a model exhibiting a certain degree of externality to a model of pure internality. Traditionally, "mixed juries" made up of natives and aliens were used in Great Britain to try cases involving

48 See article 39 of the ICSID Convention.

49 See article 52(3) of the ICSID Convention.

50 For a discussion of the composition of this court, in light of the consociational nature of the political structures set up in the country, see Christopher McCrudden and Brendan O'Leary, *Courts and Consociations: Human Rights versus Power-Sharing* (Oxford: Oxford University Press, 2013), pp. 39–42.

a national and a foreigner.[51] This institution was finally abolished in 1870, in part because it proved difficult to find foreign jurors, and in part because no reason was thought to exist to question the capacity of British people to act in a fair and open-minded manner. Thus, during the legislative debates at the House of Lords, the Earl of Derby argued that "it is stigmatizing ourselves as a nation very unjustly to assume that the prejudice against foreigners is such that an alien on his trial will not have a fair trial before British subjects."[52]

Actually, there are grounds to believe that, in spite of all the glaring imperfections of our world, we have made moral progress in this regard. The circle of people whose interests we take into account when making decisions has expanded. We do not care only about members of our family, or of our tribe. We are also sensitive to the interests of much wider groups.[53] Various forces have contributed to this enlargement, including the universal character of scientific inquiry, the interconnectedness that comes from international trade, and the emergence of political movements that have organized their activities in the international arena, concerning human rights, the environment, conditions of labor, and a host of other issues. These forces have gradually brought to the public mind the idea of the unity of humankind.[54] There are, of course, limits to our capacity to take care of others. In the adjudicative context we are talking about, however, what we need is not the expansion of love or emotional empathy. The aim is more modest: human beings should develop a basic sense of fairness, out of which they should be willing to respect the legal rights of foreigners, when controversies involving the latter are to be settled under the law.

This basic sense of fairness is sometimes missing in adjudicative processes, even in mature liberal democracies. A famous case often mentioned in the arbitral literature is *Loewen Group* v. *the United States*.[55] This case concerned a claim by a Canadian company against the United States under NAFTA (the 1992 North American Free Trade Agreement). The company had been sued in Mississippi by a local business competitor. The whole trial was pervaded by references to the nationality of the defendant. The lawyer for the plaintiff compared the struggle of his client to heroic efforts against the Japanese during the war. The jury verdict awarded 500 million dollars to the local business, an extremely exaggerated amount given the nature of the dispute. Arbitrators in an investor-state proceeding later concluded that the conduct of the trial judge was so flawed that it constituted miscarriage of justice.

51 See Marianne Constable, *The Law of the Other: The Mixed Jury and Changing Conceptions of Citizenship, Law and Knowledge* (Chicago: The University of Chicago Press, 1994).

52 Cited in Constable, *The Law of the Other*, p. 145.

53 For a good discussion of this process, see Steven Pinker, *The Better Angels of Our Nature: Why Violence Has Declined* (New York: Penguin Books, 2011).

54 For an account of the different sources of moral universalism in modern history, see Mark Mazower, *Governing the World. The History of an Idea* (New York: The Penguin Press, 2012), pp. 31–115.

55 *Loewen Group Inc. and Raymond L. Loewen* v. *United States of America*, ICSID Case No. ARB (AF)/98/3, Award, 26 June 2003.

(They did not grant a remedy, however, since they were of the view that the investor had not exhausted the available local procedures.)

This case, however, is not representative of the kind of trial that a foreigner can normally get in the United States, or in other liberal democracies. The objectivity that national courts can display, which is the result of a long process of internal moralization of political communities, should not be underestimated.

An interesting question is whether it is possible to follow the external strategies and the internal strategies at the same time. They may actually be in tension. The more we insist on external tribunals, made up of judges or arbitrators with a different nationality than that of the disputants, the more we reinforce the expectation that national bias is inevitable at the domestic level. By the same token, in the intergovernmental international sphere, the more we insist on the need to counteract the risk that judges sitting in international tribunals will be biased in favor of the country of their nationality, the more we may be contributing to maintaining a culture in which partiality because of nationality is likely to be expected.[56] There is no easy way out of this dilemma.

5.6 INTERNATIONAL ARBITRATION AND THE LAWMAKING PROCESS

Let us now shift to the role of international commercial arbitration when it comes to the development of the law. The division of labor between arbitrators and judges we discussed in Chapter 4 is roughly the same when the disputes refer to international deals. International commercial arbitration is "international" only in the sense that the transaction or the dispute is connected to two or more countries. But the parties usually select the substantive law of a particular country to govern the contract. Therefore, the ideas advanced previously can be extended here: even if arbitrators do not produce a consistent body of rules, there is no ground for concern, in so far as regular courts at the national level are furnishing the necessary case law.

The clear tendency, indeed, is for private actors to subject their international contracts to national law. One of the hallmarks of arbitration in the international context is the ample liberty the parties enjoy to determine the domestic law that will govern the contract. Arbitrators will normally respect that choice, provided the relevant norms of a mandatory character are observed, whereas if the dispute were referred to a court, the law of the forum might require that the chosen law bear some relationship to the forum. Arbitration thus secures a great variety of alternatives when selecting the country whose laws will apply to the contract. There is such a wide range of possibilities that the parties do not need to look beyond domestic law to find what they want. As a matter of fact, commercial players very rarely pick

[56] For an argument along these lines, see Tom Dannenbaum, "Nationality and the International Judge: The Nationalist Presumption Governing the International Judiciary and Why It Must Be Reversed," 45 *Cornell International Law Journal*, 77 (2012).

"transnational law" in the form of international *lex mercatoria*. Thus, only in 2 percent of all disputes referred to ICC arbitration in 2018 had the parties chosen non-state law to govern the contract.[57] This is consistent with data reported in earlier years. As Christopher R. Drahozal notes, "the available empirical evidence reveals only very limited use of transnational commercial law in international commercial arbitration." In effect, "few parties contract out of national law."[58] This is not surprising, since it is too risky for the parties to subject their contracts to vague principles of international *lex mercatoria*, or even to the UNIDROIT Principles of International Commercial Contracts, which is a more precise and articulated text produced by the International Institute for the Unification of Private Law, an intergovernmental organization based in Rome. The legislation and case law that states have developed over many decades of experience affords better protection to private parties.[59]

Consistently with this, the contracting parties generally expect arbitrators to apply the law they have chosen in light of the jurisprudence worked out by the competent national courts. As George Bermann observes, "freedom of arbitrators to apply the law in ways that differ from the way in which courts would apply it does not figure prominently among the reasons why parties choose arbitration over national court litigation."[60] In actual practice, arbitrators consult and cite national court decisions to support their interpretations of national law. They are less likely to refer to the occasionally available arbitral awards that may be relevant for construing that law. They pay significant attention to previous awards only when they have to address issues that are specific to arbitration law.[61]

Of course, the quality of national law differs from country to country. Companies in the shipping and insurance industries, for example, often elect English law, even if neither party is English, since that law is very developed in the commercial sectors involved.[62] In such cases arbitrators are not likely to introduce qualifications to the existing body of case law produced by English courts. On the other hand, if the law picked by the parties is rather outdated when it comes to commerce in general or a particular sector of commercial activity, some interpretive adjustments will be necessary. A cosmopolitan arbitrator, sensitive to the needs of international commerce, may be more willing than national courts to update the law through flexible interpretation.[63] The UNCITRAL Model Law provides, in this regard, that "in all

57 See "ICC Dispute Resolution 2018 Statistics," p. 13, available at www.iccwbo.org/dr-stat2018.

58 Christopher R. Drahozal, "Contracting out of National Law: An Empirical Look at the New Law Merchant," 80 *Notre Dame Law Review*, 523 (2005), p. 551.

59 See Born, *International Commercial Arbitration*, pp. 2759–2767. See, also, Michael Reisman, "Soft Law and Law Jobs," 2 *Journal of International Dispute Settlement*, 25 (2011).

60 Bermann, *International Arbitration and Private International Law*, p. 482.

61 Ibid., pp. 484–486.

62 See Karton, *The Culture of International Arbitration and the Evolution of Contract Law*, p. 70.

63 Ibid., pp. 110–111.

cases, the arbitral tribunal shall decide in accordance with the terms of the contract and shall take into account the usages of the trade applicable to the transaction."[64]

The bottom line is that contracting parties and arbitrators generally rely on the body of law supplied by national authorities. It is worthy of note that amiable composition clauses, which instruct arbitrators to decide *ex aequo et bono*, have never been common in international commercial contracts. They are nowadays even less popular than in the past.[65] Only in one case, for example, out of a total of 842 cases filed with the ICC in 2018, did the contract require arbitrators to decide *ex aequo et bono*.[66]

As a result of all this, it is hard to accept the proposition that international arbitrators are originating a body of law that is greatly autonomous from national law, covering all relevant aspects relating to the validity and enforcement of contracts. Scholars who have examined the principles announced by arbitral jurisprudence have come up with the following list, which will read very familiar to anyone who has studied national contract law:[67] (a) *pacta sunt servanda*; (b) performance must be carried out in good faith; (c) *force majeure* is a defense of contractual nonperformance; (d) conduct may be deemed tacit acceptance of modifications of contract; (e) interpretations of contractual clauses which have the effect of cancelling contractual terms, or of making them redundant, are to be avoided; (f) the party that alleges facts to support a claim has the burden of proof; (g) the legal nomenclature misused by the parties to classify their contract should be disregarded; (h) use of goods implies acceptance; (i) parties have a duty to mitigate damages; (j) damages for contractual breach are limited to foreseeable consequences; (k) parties have a right to raise a defense of compensation or set-off; (l) no party may rely on its own inconsistency to the detriment of another; (m) contracts are unenforceable if their purpose is contrary to international morality, such as demanding or accepting bribes. Now, the specific scope and effect of all these principles may vary from country to country, but it is obvious that arbitrators have drawn from national legal sources when crafting them.

There is no weighty reason, one is authorized to conclude, to raise democratic concerns in the international commercial context on account of the role of arbitrators in the lawmaking process. Arbitrators are not creating a new body of private law that is unhooked from democratically enacted law and judicial case law. In some instances, arbitrators may refine at the margins the law that the parties have selected, if such law needs interpretive updating. But the general principles arbitrators invoke are extracted from national laws. So the basic engines of the lawmaking machine are still national legislatures and national courts.

64 See article 28(4) of the UNCITRAL Model Law.

65 See Karton, *The Culture of International Arbitration*, p. 152; and Blackaby and Partasides QC with Redfern and Hunter, *Redfern and Hunter on International Arbitration*, p. 4, footnote 9.

66 See "ICC Dispute Resolution 2018 Statistics," p. 13.

67 See Park, *Arbitration of International Business Disputes*, pp. 542–555.

5.7 CONCLUSION

We have seen in this chapter that arbitration is particularly popular when parties engage in international commercial dealings. The existence of the New York Convention and the need to construct a neutral adjudicative forum explain the appeal of arbitration. It may be argued, however, that the international legal order is defective because of the more favorable treatment it grants arbitration over litigation at the global stage. The neutral forum argument in favor of arbitration, in turn, raises intricate questions about the best strategies to achieve objectivity in a world where the nationality of adjudicators seems to make a difference. There is less cause for concern, on the other hand, regarding the risk that arbitrators may be producing a corpus of transnational law that is out of sync with democratically enacted domestic law.

With this, we have concluded our discussion of arbitration in the sphere of private law. We now proceed to explore investment treaty arbitration in Part II of the book.

PART II

Investment Treaty Arbitration

6

The Rise of Investment Treaty Arbitration

The use of arbitral procedures to settle differences between foreign investors and host governments has sparked great controversy in recent years. The discussion has not been confined to academic and professional circles. It has entered the wider public sphere, as various political parties and social movements have attacked investor-state arbitration on the ground that it serves the interests of powerful global investors to the detriment of the regulatory capacity of democratic nations.

This part of the book is devoted to this deeply contested modality of arbitration. We will focus on three issues. The first concerns the compatibility of the investment regime with constitutions governing liberal democracies, which typically proclaim the right to equality. Since investment treaties only cover foreign investors, the question arises whether such treaties breach the constitutional norm barring discrimination on grounds of nationality. How can investment treaties be squared with the constitution in this regard?

The second issue relates to the production of arbitral jurisprudence and the democratic checks it should be subject to. As we will see, arbitrators enjoy a considerable amount of discretion when adjudicating disputes in this field. The principles they have to interpret commonly speak at a high level of abstraction. Are arbitrators capable of supplying a consistent body of case law to secure a sufficient degree of uniformity in the application of the law? And what mechanisms are available for the political branches to check arbitral jurisprudence, if they disagree with the direction it takes?

The third question refers to the interaction between the investment legal regime and other branches of international law. Does it make sense for investor-state arbitration to be resorted to when the states involved belong to a supranational organization that is grounded in the principle of mutual trust, as is true of the European Union? And how should arbitrators deal with cases implicating human rights norms, including norms safeguarding public health, the environment, worker rights, etc . . .? These questions must be addressed against the general background of international law, which exhibits tendencies toward regionalization and fragmentation.

We will address the first issue in the next chapter, and we will then proceed to explore the other questions in Chapters 8 and 9. Before we do that, we need to identify the core features of investment treaties and investor-state arbitration, in order to understand what makes this type of arbitration so special. We do so in this chapter.

6.1 THE FOUNDATIONS OF THE INTERNATIONAL INVESTMENT REGIME

When private individuals or entities invest in a foreign country, the risk exists that the domestic authorities in that country will exercise their governmental powers in ways that unduly harm the investments. The authorities may engage in discriminatory or arbitrary practices, or they may expropriate assets without justification or against no compensation. Local courts, in turn, may fail to fully protect the rights of investors when complaints are lodged against the host government. A solution to this problem has been worked out at the level of public international law.[1]

The international community has developed some customs that protect foreign investors. States, for example, are under the duty to guarantee investors full protection and security, must accord them a minimum standard of treatment, and cannot take their property without paying adequate compensation. The specific content of these customary norms is uncertain, however. The conceptions endorsed by the United States and Western Europe in the nineteenth century were contested by Latin American nations. They were also called into question by African and Asian countries in the twentieth century, when the process of decolonization took place.[2] In 1974, the challenge by developing nations against Western conceptions of private property was expressed in a United Nations General Assembly resolution entitled "The Charter of Economic Rights and Duties of States," which included a controversial article providing that compensation for expropriated property should be determined "under the domestic law of the nationalizing State and by its

[1] For a comprehensive exposition of this area of the law, see Rudolf Dolzer and Christoph Schreuer, *Principles of International Investment Law* (Oxford: Oxford University Press, 2012); Zachary Douglas, *The International Law of Investment Claims* (Cambridge: Cambridge University Press, 2009); Jeswald W. Salacuse, *The Law of Investment Treaties* (Oxford: Oxford University Press, 2015); and M. Sornarajah, *The International Law on Foreign Investment* (Cambridge: Cambridge University Press, 2017). For an illuminating study that integrates the law in this field with economic theory and political analysis, see Jonathan Bonnitcha, Lauge N. Skovgaard Poulsen, and Michael Waibel, *The Political Economy of the Investment Treaty Regime* (Oxford: Oxford University Press, 2017). See, also, Jonathan Bonnitcha, *Substantive Protection under Investment Treaties. A Legal and Economic Analysis* (Cambridge: Cambridge University Press, 2014).

[2] M. Sornarajah, *Resistance and Change in the International Law on Foreign Investment* (Cambridge: Cambridge University Press, 2015), pp. 89–94.

tribunals."[3] This was part of the "New International Economic Order" that developing countries were struggling to bring about.

Because of the uncertain scope of international customary law in this area, states have entered into international treaties of various types in order to specify the protections foreign investors are entitled to. Many states, for example, have subscribed to bilateral investment treaties (BITs) affording substantive protections to individuals and companies that are nationals of those states. Some countries, moreover, have signed broader treaties on free trade which contain chapters on investments. The international instruments that cover investors may also be multilateral, such as NAFTA (the 1992 North America Free Trade Agreement), which will be replaced by USMCA (the 2018 United States-Mexico-Canada Agreement), the 1991 treaty establishing MERCOSUR, and the 1994 Energy Charter Treaty, for example.

The first bilateral instrument of this kind was signed by Germany and Pakistan in 1959. Most investment treaties were originally concluded among developed and developing nations. In their competition for external capital, developing countries were bound to make credible commitments to treat foreign investors fairly.[4] The 1990s witnessed an explosion of investment agreements. A liberalized global economy was the order of the day. Some nations adopted international treaties to "lock in" the liberalizing reforms they had already implemented domestically.[5] In the 1990s, moreover, a large number of agreements were also concluded among developing countries, as well as among developed ones. So the investment regime that has finally emerged is not only a North-South phenomenon, as it has expanded to cover both South-South and North-North relationships. As a result, more than 3000 investment agreements are currently in force.

This is in keeping with the reduction of ideological divisions in the world we have observed in recent decades. As Barry Buzan and George Lawson point out, in the wake of the market reforms in China in the late 1970s and the collapse of communism in Eastern and Central Europe in 1989, capitalism has become the dominant model to shape economic life. "Almost every state organizes its economy through market logics and takes part in global regimes around trade, production and finance."[6] Contrasting forms of capitalism have appeared, but they converge upon certain basic rules buttressing the global economy. The investment treaty regime is an instance of this convergence.

[3] See article 2(2)(c) of the Charter, General Assembly Resolution 3281 (XXIX), adopted on 12 December 1974.

[4] On this competition for capital, see Zachary Elkins, Andrew T. Guzman, and Beth A. Simmons, "Competing for Capital: The Diffusion of Bilateral Investment Treaties, 1960–2000," *University of Illinois Law Review*, 265 (2008).

[5] On this strategy, see Bonnitcha, Skovgaard Poulsen, and Waibel, *The Political Economy of the Investment Treaty Regime*, pp. 218–220.

[6] Barry Buzan and George Lawson, *The Global Transformation. History, Modernity and the Making of International Relations* (Cambridge: Cambridge University Press, 2015), p. 281.

From a historical point of view, the foundations of the network of international agreements protecting investments can be traced back to the many friendship, commerce, and navigation treaties concluded by the United States after the Second World War, as part of the international liberal strategy envisaged by Presidents Franklin D. Roosevelt and Harry Truman.[7]

One of the striking characteristics of the investment regime that has been erected on the international plane is the absence of a universal treaty to support it. While international trade is governed by a set of global agreements instituting the WTO (World Trade Organization), the protection of foreign investments is instead grounded in a multiplicity of treaties signed on a bilateral, regional, or sectoral basis. Efforts to come up with a global investment treaty have historically failed. In 1995, for example, the Organization for Economic Cooperation and Development (OECD) launched negotiations to draw up the MAI (Multilateral Agreement on Investment), an investment treaty of global reach. Anti-globalization NGOs in Europe and the United States organized street protests against the initiative, and the French government led by Prime Minister Lionel Jospin decided not to take part in the ongoing negotiations. The proposal finally came to nothing.[8]

So instead of a global treaty, there exists a vast web of international instruments covering investors. A common pattern can be discerned, however. The investment treaties tend to incorporate similar principles, even if distinct qualifications and exceptions are set out. This commonality of language generates "network effects." As Santiago Montt explains, states benefit from the economies of scale that derive from a global regime based on agreements that use the same terms. The first treaty is an esoteric document that nobody knows how it will work. As more treaties are signed, the practice under one treaty has repercussions on the general practice.[9]

A number of factors have pushed things in a homogenizing direction, which Stephan Schill has studied in detail.[10] In 1967, for example, the OECD issued a draft Convention on the Protection of Foreign Property. This draft influenced the Model BITs many countries adopted later, thus introducing a degree of homogeneity into the system.[11] In addition, Schill explains, most-favored-nation clauses are often included in BITs. Such clauses extend to the investors of the contracting states any better protections granted to the investors of third countries. A level playing field

7 On the historical impact of the international agreements signed by the United States on the later generation of bilateral investment treaties, see Kenneth J. Vandevelde, "The Liberal Vision of the International Law on Foreign Investment," in C. L. Lim (ed.), *Alternative Visions of the International Law on Foreign Investment. Essays in Honour of Muthucumaraswamy Sornarajah* (New York: Cambridge University Press, 2016), pp. 43–68.

8 On the failure of the MAI, see Antonio R. Parra, *The History of ICSID* (Oxford: Oxford University Press, 2017), pp. 183–185.

9 Santiago Montt, *State Liability in Investment Treaty Arbitration. Global Constitutional and Administrative Law in the BIT Generation* (Oxford: Hart Publishing, 2009), pp. 83–123.

10 Stephan W. Schill, *The Multilateralization of International Investment Law* (Cambridge: Cambridge University Press, 2009).

11 Ibid., pp. 39–40.

is accordingly created for all foreign investors, thus generating multilateral effects in the treaty network.[12]

To understand the legal force of investment agreements, it is critical to observe that states cannot unilaterally alter them. Amendment requires the consent of the other treaty partner (or partners). A country may legally withdraw from a treaty after a period of notice has elapsed, but the existing investments will still be covered for many years. This means that the state is subject to an important set of substantive constraints. Investment treaties record strong political precommitments regarding the protection of foreign investors. Their "constitutional" force is thus quite apparent.[13]

Actually, from an international legal perspective, investment treaties prevail over national constitutions in the event of a conflict. A state cannot, of course, validly conclude a treaty that breaches its own constitution. National courts can intervene to stop that. But if a treaty is properly adopted, the state cannot later rely on national constitutional norms to justify a breach.[14] In particular, if a country amended its constitution in a direction that wronged foreign investors, the investment agreement would work as a shield. The treaty in that case would operate somewhat similarly to "intangibility clauses," which are sometimes included in national constitutions to entrench certain basic principles against repeal or erosion by constitutional amendment.[15] To be sure, the treaty can ultimately be terminated, whereas intangibility clauses arguably cannot. Still, for the typically long duration of an investment treaty, the effects are comparable: the political branches exercising the constitutional amendment power are being constrained by external norms. The fact that the domestic legal order may insist that a constitutional amendment ranks higher than a treaty does not undermine the latter's authority under international law. A state cannot be released from its international obligations through unilateral actions, such as the modification of its own constitution. Domestic courts may have to abide by the constitution resulting from the internal reform, but international adjudicators will ascertain the state's liability for breach of the treaty, the national constitution notwithstanding.

So far we have examined the sources and force of the substantive rules that protect investments. What about the procedures to secure compliance with such rules?

[12] Ibid., pp. 121–196.

[13] For a constitutional reading of the international investment regime, see David Schneiderman, *Constitutionalizing Economic Globalization. Investment Rules and Democracy's Promise* (Cambridge: Cambridge University Press, 2008). Schneiderman is critical of the "disabling effect" of international treaties. He argues that these treaties operate as constitutional instruments that severely limit the capacity of democratic institutions to regulate the market.

[14] See article 27 of the 1969 Vienna Convention on the Law of Treaties: "A party may not invoke the provisions of its internal law as justification for its failure to perform a treaty."

[15] For an overview of such clauses, see Yaniv Roznai, *Unconstitutional Constitutional Amendments. The Limits of Amendment Powers* (Oxford: Oxford University Press, 2017). For objections against their adoption, see Richard Albert, *Constitutional Amendments. Making, Breaking, and Changing Constitutions* (New York: Oxford University Press, 2019), pp. 194–202.

Investor-state arbitration enters the picture here. As we will see next, this is a very special kind of arbitration.

6.2 WHAT IS SPECIAL ABOUT INVESTOR-STATE ARBITRATION?

Many investment treaties contain clauses enabling investors to take the host state before an international arbitral tribunal. Different arbitration forums have been set up for this purpose. Chief among these is ICSID (the International Centre for Settlement of Investment Disputes), which was created by the Washington Convention of 1965 under the auspices of the World Bank.[16] Although the Bank had not been given the explicit authority to draw up the ICSID Convention, member states shared the view that the Bank had an implicit power to do so, to further its foundational objectives of promoting investment and development.[17] In addition to ICSID, other facilities administer investment disputes, such as the International Court of Arbitration of the ICC (the International Chamber of Commerce), the London Court of International Arbitration, the Arbitration Institute of the Stockholm Chamber of Commerce, and the Permanent Court of Arbitration, among others. When parties turn to these arbitral institutions, they often choose to follow the UNCITRAL Arbitration Rules. These Rules are also available when the contending parties do not select an arbitration center.

It is important to note that in the past, when investor-state arbitration did not exist, a foreign investor would have to refer its dispute with the host government to the local courts. If the decisions made by the judicial authorities failed to secure compliance with the applicable international norms, the investor would then request its home state to assert diplomatic protection against the host state. The home government would thus "espouse" the investor's claim, and would start proceedings or negotiations with the other state. There was no guarantee, however, that the home state would actually espouse the investor's claim. For political reasons, for example, the government might think it better not to enter into an international conflict with the other nation. The less powerful the investor, the less likely the government would want to run into problems. Even if the home state endorsed the claim, the resolution of the dispute between the two states need not consist in the payment of a sum of money by way of compensation. And even if monetary redress was achieved, the sum was to be paid to the home state, not the investor, who might end up receiving nothing.

Things changed dramatically with the introduction of investor-state arbitration. Under the new arrangements, the investor is entitled to directly take the host state

16 On the origins of ICSID, see Parra, *The History of ICSID*, pp. 1–107. For a detailed analysis of the ICSID Convention, see Christoph H. Schreuer, Loretta Malintoppi, August Reinisch, and Anthony Sinclair, *The ICSID Convention. A Commentary* (Cambridge: Cambridge University Press, 2009).

17 Parra, *The History of ICSID*, pp. 26–27.

before an international tribunal. The investor does not depend on diplomatic protection to file grievances. The ICSID Convention actually provides that the home state cannot give diplomatic protection to an investor that has consented to submit or has submitted a dispute to arbitration. Only if the arbitral award later rendered in that case is not complied with by the host state may the home state assert that kind of protection.[18] In addition, the general rule is that the investor is not bound to exhaust local remedies before he can bring a claim to international arbitration. Under the ICSID Convention, for example, the default rule is that exhaustion of local administrative or judicial remedies is not required, unless the relevant states indicate otherwise in the pertinent legal instruments.[19]

As already mentioned, ICSID is the major arbitral institution in the investment field. This forum is open to states that have ratified the ICSID Convention. The vast majority of countries in the world (154, as of 1 April 2020) have done so. Since the 1990s, there has been a dramatic increase in the number of arbitration cases brought to ICSID. For many years since the first case was registered in 1972, very few cases were referred to the Centre. The 1990s witnessed a rapid growth of arbitration. As of December 31, 2019, 745 cases had been registered.[20]

For ICSID arbitral proceedings to be instituted against a state, it is necessary, of course, for the disputants to consent. As repeatedly noted in previous chapters, arbitration is an adjudicative mechanism grounded in the joint will of the parties. The investor undoubtedly expresses its consent by filing a request for arbitration. The state's consent, in turn, is normally given before the dispute arises. Sometimes, the contract between the government and the investor includes the pertinent arbitration clause. Other times, national law provides that the state agrees to arbitrate particular classes of disputes with foreign investors. Most frequently, however, the state's consent is to be found in an international treaty (a BIT, for example) that the state has signed with the other state the investor comes from. It is the latter modality of arbitration that has caused an enormous expansion of ICSID cases.[21]

18 See article 27 of the ICSID Convention

19 See article 26 of the ICSID Convention.

20 See "The ICSID Caseload – Statistics (Issue 2020–1)," available at www.icsid.worldbank.org.

21 During the first decades, ICSID arbitration was rooted in arbitral clauses inserted in contracts between foreign investors and host governments. A very limited number of controversies were referred to ICSID at that time. In the 1990s the situation changed dramatically: investment treaties started to be invoked as a source of arbitral authority. The first case where a complaint by an investor was accepted on this basis was *Asian Agricultural Products Ltd (AAPL)* v. *Republic of Sri Lanka*, ICSID Case No. ARB/87/3, Final Award, 27 June 1990. This was the starting point for an enormous expansion of ICSID arbitration. On this evolution, see Sornarajah, *Resistance and Change in the International Law on Foreign Investment*, pp. 136–146. For an early discussion of the radical transformation that was afoot, see Jan Paulsson, "Arbitration Without Privity," 10 *ICSID Review. Foreign Investment Law Journal*, 232 (1995). The idea that investment treaties could be the source of ICSID jurisdiction had already been suggested in 1967 by Aron Broches, the architect of the ICSID Convention and the first Secretary-General of ICSID. See Parra, *The History of ICSID*, p. 104.

As is true of arbitration in general, in investment treaty arbitration the contending parties pick the adjudicators. The default rule under the ICSID Convention is that the tribunal shall consist of three arbitrators, one arbitrator appointed by each party and the third, who shall be the president of the tribunal, appointed by agreement of the parties.[22] If no consensus is reached, the Chairman of the Administrative Council can be asked to make the appointment.[23] The President of the World Bank is *ex officio* Chairman.[24] In practice, the Chairman has always relied on the recommendation of the Secretary-General of ICSID in deciding on the appointments.[25] The Secretary-General, in turn, is elected by a majority of two-thirds of the representatives of the states that are parties to the ICSID Convention, upon the nomination of the Chairman.[26]

One of the remarkable things about ICSID arbitration is that the award issued by the arbitrators can only be reviewed by an "annulment committee" within ICSID. No national court is authorized to check the validity of the award. National courts, moreover, cannot refuse to enforce it. The New York Convention of 1958, which enumerates some grounds for denying enforcement of arbitral awards under national law, does not apply here. The ICSID Convention applies instead. Every country that has subscribed to the ICSID Convention must recognize an award rendered pursuant to it as binding, "and enforce the pecuniary obligations imposed by that award within its territories as if it were a final judgment of a court in that State."[27] The reason behind this rule is that the ICSID arbitral process is not seated in any domestic legal system, but is instead anchored in the sphere of public international law.[28] The decision it generates is thus immune from national checks.[29]

22 See article 37(2) of the ICSID Convention.

23 See article 38 of the ICSID Convention.

24 See article 5 of the ICSID Convention.

25 Parra, *The History of ICSID*, p. 295.

26 See article 10 of the ICSID Convention.

27 See article 54(1) of the ICSID Convention.

28 On the international law nature of ICSID arbitration, see Eric De Brabandere, *Investment Treaty Arbitration as Public International Law. Procedural Aspects and Implications* (Cambridge: Cambridge University Press, 2014).

29 If only the host state or the home state, but not both, is a party to the ICSID Convention, there is the possibility of using the so-called ICSID Additional Facility Rules, which are of a different nature. The arbitration process is then connected to a particular domestic legal system. The courts of the seat that has been chosen get the authority to review the award, in light of national arbitration laws. The enforcement of the award, moreover, can be denied by local courts, on the basis of the legal grounds mentioned in the New York Convention. The ICSID Additional Facility was introduced in 1978 to expand the Center's activities in the investment field. On its origins, see Parra, *The History of ICSID*, pp. 128–137. Similarly, when investor-state controversies are arbitrated outside the ICSID framework (when the UNCITRAL Arbitration Rules are employed in an *ad hoc* arbitration, for example, or when an arbitral institution different from ICSID is resorted to), the arbitration needs to be seated in a national legal system. The courts of that nation will have the authority to review the award, and the New York Convention will apply when enforcement of the award is sought.

Investor-state arbitration is an important instance of the gradual empowerment of private persons under public international law.[30] It fits well with general trends toward the "humanization" of international law.[31] In the domain of human rights, in particular, we have witnessed the emergence of legal regimes that entitle private individuals to sue states before an international tribunal. The European Court of Human Rights is the most prominent example in this regard. The African Court of Justice and Human Rights is a more recent instance. The other side of the coin is that individuals have also duties under international law, violation of which may lead to the imposition of criminal penalties. Thus, the International Criminal Court has jurisdiction to try persons charged with the gravest crimes of concern to the international community: genocide, war crimes, crimes against humanity, and the crime of aggression.

These are all outstanding developments. The fact that private persons can derive rights from international rules, which they can invoke before international courts or arbitral tribunals, is a key feature of the modern legal world. The individual has been brought back to the realm of public international law, after being expelled from it during the nineteenth century, when legal positivism reached its climax.[32] We can no longer view the "law of nations" as being exclusively concerned with the relations between states.

Of course the picture we get from all this reveals the moral imperfections of the existing political and legal structures. While investors enjoy robust protection under a dense web of treaties enabling them to bring claims before international tribunals, other people who are more in need of help – refugees being a compelling example – have not been empowered to directly seek justice in international tribunals. No human rights court of a universal reach, moreover, has been founded. So we cannot ignore that the "humanization" of international law we can discern is limited and fragmentary, and does not express an attractive choice of moral priorities. This being said, the general trend toward opening international arrangements to private persons, including investors, is worthy of support.

A significant difference remains, however, between international law and domestic constitutional law in this regard. In the international sphere, private persons do not (yet) have a "fundamental right" of access to international tribunals. If they have

30 For a detailed and careful account of the increasing relevance of private persons in international law, see Kate Parlett, *The Individual in the International Legal System* (Cambridge: Cambridge University Press, 2011). Parlett explains that at the beginning of the twentieth century, only two international tribunals were designed in such a way that private persons had access to them: the proposed International Prize Court, based on the 1907 Hague Convention that was never ratified, and the Central American Court of Justice. An important step was taken later on, during the interwar period, when international claims commissions were set up, and private parties were allowed to bring cases to them, involving private disputes resulting from interstate war.

31 Theodor Meron, *The Humanization of International Law* (Leiden: Martinus Nijhoff Publishers, 2006), pp. 324–327.

32 On this evolution, see Jan Klabbers, Anne Peters, and Geir Ulfstein, *The Constitutionalization of International Law* (Oxford: Oxford University Press, 2009), pp. 157–179.

standing to sue a government before an international tribunal, this is because the states concerned have decided to grant them such ability through the pertinent treaty.[33] The grant can be withdrawn at any time, if the treaty is modified or terminated. Moreover, there is a glaring gap in international law: private persons have not been accorded the right to bring cases against international organizations (unless such organizations have a supranational character, as is the case with the European Union, for example, or unless the dispute concerns the administrative staff of an international organization).[34] In contrast, in a polity governed by a liberal constitution, private individuals are recognized a fundamental right to judicial protection. The ordinary legislature is not free to deny individuals, whose legal rights or interests are affected, standing to sue the government in order to obtain judicial redress. Restrictions may be imposed, but they need to be justified, since a fundamental right of access to justice is at stake.

Another notable characteristic of investor-state arbitration is the usually vertical nature of the underlying legal relationship that is adjudicated. The controversy to be settled generally involves a private actor, on the one hand, and a government, on the other. The government typically acts in its public law capacity – it exercises "power" over the investor. There is thus a vertical relationship between the contending parties, which stands in stark contrast to the horizontal character of the underlying transactions in other arbitral contexts. In the field of private law, the parties are situated on the same plane, formally speaking at least. Similarly, in the area of public international law, as we will see in Part III of this book, the contending states interact horizontally. Investor-state arbitration is thus completely different, in so far as it refers to a vertical relationship. Actually, at the domestic level, the law in many countries does not permit governmental authorities to submit to arbitration controversies involving decisions those authorities have made in their public law capacity. In other nations, significant limits and conditions have been stipulated.[35] It is remarkable, indeed, that so many nations in the world have nevertheless agreed to sign investment treaties containing investor-state arbitral clauses.

With all these notes by way of introduction, let us now turn to the question whether the investment regime and the arbitral arrangements that have been adopted are in harmony with the principle of equality commonly embodied in domestic constitutions of the liberal-democratic type.

[33] See Parlett, *The Individual in the International Legal System*, p. 122.

[34] For a criticism of this limitation, see Klabbers, Peters, and Ulfstein, *The Constitutionalization of International Law*, p. 132.

[35] For a comparative study of the arbitrability of disputes involving public authorities, see Stephan W. Schill (ed.), *The Comparative Constitutional Law of Private-Public Arbitration* (Oxford: Oxford University Press, forthcoming, 2021).

7

Privileging Foreign Investors?

The Equality Challenge

The international instruments described in the previous chapter benefit foreign investors exclusively. They do not apply to local investors. How can this different treatment be justified from a constitutional perspective? Constitutions in liberal democracies typically announce the principle of equality and bar discrimination on grounds of nationality. Are investment treaties in breach of equality?

The challenge cannot be easily disposed of with the argument that centers on the idea of reciprocity. Suppose Argentina and the United States conclude an investment treaty that is based on reciprocity. This means that the protections conferred on the investors coming from the United States are the same ones that are extended to investors coming from Argentina. This reciprocity, however, does not eliminate the discrimination that locals (in both countries) suffer, when compared to foreign investors (from both countries). The fact that there is equality at one level (when comparing United States and Argentine nationals investing abroad) does not exclude lack of equality at another level (when comparing national investors to foreign investors).

So what can be said in defense of the special rules that apply to foreign investors? What is the legitimate purpose that may justify the existence of such rules? In the discussion that follows, we will address the issue from the standpoint of a national court called upon to review the conformity of an investment treaty with the constitutional principle of equality.

7.1 ATTRACTING FOREIGN INVESTMENTS OR ENSURING EQUALITY?

It is commonly said that the point of investment treaties is to stimulate the flow of foreign investment, which is conducive to economic prosperity. The treaties themselves often mention goals of an economic nature. The preamble of the ICSID Convention, for example, refers to "the need for international cooperation for economic development, and the role of private international investment therein." The BITs are often more specific about their purposes. The preamble to the United

States-Argentina BIT of 1991, for example, recites that the parties recognize that agreement upon the treatment to be accorded to investments "will stimulate the flow of private capital and the economic development of the Parties." In turn, "the development of economic and business ties," the preamble goes on, "can contribute to the well-being of workers in both Parties."

Now, is it possible to justify the special treatment that foreign investors are afforded on the instrumental ground that it helps attract foreign capital? This justification is problematic from a constitutional perspective. The goal of increasing the inflow of external capital is legitimate, but using a device that entails a differential treatment based on nationality is a questionable strategy. Discrimination on grounds of nationality is a serious matter. The government must have powerful reasons to justify normative distinctions based on this factor. Are the reasons linked to the goal of attracting investment strong enough?

The answer hinges, first of all, on an empirical question. How good are investment treaties when it comes to inducing foreign investors to bring their assets? The available empirical literature fails to substantiate the proposition that investment treaties are key tools to attract foreign capital. Investors take into account many variables before they decide where to place their assets. The fact that the recipient state has subscribed a treaty protecting investments, though not an irrelevant factor, is not a critical one. Jonathan Bonnitcha, Lauge N. Skovgaard Poulsen and Michael Waibel have carefully studied the body of empirical research on this matter. Their conclusion is that "taken together, the literature suggests that investment treaties do have an impact on *some* investment decisions in *some* circumstances, but that they are unlikely to have a large effect on the majority of foreign investment decisions."[1]

We must also assess the broader consequences of the instrumental strategy under consideration. If foreign investors are overprotected when compared to national investors, no level playing field is secured for them to compete fairly in a free market. The market cannot operate efficiently if some actors can count on the application of rules guaranteeing an economic compensation if certain governmental measures are taken, while other actors are excluded from the application of such rules. In some extreme scenarios, moreover, feelings of hostility against foreigners may develop in the recipient country if the existence of disparate rules is common knowledge. This may be a source of unrest. The larger the percentage of private assets that end up being in the hands of foreign companies, the greater is the risk of political instability.[2] So we need a more persuasive theory to support the investment legal regime against the equality challenge.

An alternative theory to answer the equality objection is this: investment treaties seek to guarantee effective equality between foreign and local investors. Equality is

1 Jonathan Bonnitcha, Lauge N. Skovgaard Poulsen and Michael Waibel, *The Political Economy of the Investment Treaty Regime* (Oxford: Oxford University Press, 2017), p. 166 (emphases in the original).

2 See Thomas Piketty, *Capital in the Twenty-First Century* (Cambridge, Massachusetts: Harvard University Press, 2014), pp. 70–71.

the critical governmental interest that justifies the formally unequal treatment between the two classes of investors. On this account, the special rules that apply to foreign investors are designed to realize effective parity. The assumption is that outsiders are in a more vulnerable position than locals when it comes to the protection of their interests against domestic authorities. It is in order to equalize things that governments grant foreign investors some special safeguards through the adoption of international treaties. The latter may or may not ultimately contribute to stimulating capital flows. If they do, this is a desirable side effect. Indeed, as mentioned in Chapter 6, many countries entered into investment treaties expecting they would thereby help attract foreign capital. But success in enticing foreign investment is neither a necessary nor a sufficient condition, from a constitutional point of view, to warrant the establishment of special rules for foreign investors. The justification is instead tied to the need to bestow upon foreign investors the same degree of protection that national investors enjoy.

This is a plausible theory, but we need to unpack the grounds and conditions upon which it can be accepted. In what respects are foreign investors vulnerable? It is sometimes said that they are vulnerable for political reasons, since they are not allowed to participate in the political process with their vote. The European Court of Human Rights, for example, has sometimes insisted on the need to be careful when private property of foreigners is affected, given their weakness as a result of their not being entitled to vote.[3] Several arbitral tribunals have made the same point.[4] This connects with John Hart Ely's influential theory of constitutional review, which calls for heightened judicial scrutiny of those laws that harm aliens, in view of the fact that the latter cannot participate in the political process with their votes.[5] In the investment context, however, the right to vote is largely irrelevant. Most investors are corporations, and corporations, whether local or foreign, do not have a right to vote. Actually, the right to vote is not so important in order to protect one's interests. Political influence can be exerted in other ways. Corporations, in particular, often have plenty of money to lobby the government or use the media to affect public opinion.[6]

Still, we cannot rule out the possibility that foreigners will suffer discrimination. In some political contexts, the government may be inclined to issue regulations that indirectly protect local businesses against competition from outsiders. Or the government may be tempted to distribute the costs of public policies in an unfair manner, making foreign investors bear a disproportionate burden in comparison

3 See *James and Others* v. *the United Kingdom*, no. 8793/79, Judgment of 21 February 1986.

4 For references, see Gus Van Harten, *Sovereign Choices and Sovereign Constraints* (Oxford: Oxford University Press, 2013), p. 77, note 168.

5 John Hart Ely, *Democracy and Distrust. A Theory of Judicial Review* (Cambridge, Massachusetts: Harvard University Press, 1980), pp. 161–162.

6 For a persuasive argument that the right to vote is irrelevant in the investment context, see David Schneiderman, "Investing in Democracy? Political Process and International Investment Law," 60 *University of Toronto Law Journal*, 909 (2010).

to local ones. When measures of this sort are enacted, domestic courts may not be reliable enough to check their validity. The risk cannot be excluded that the government will exercise influence on courts to rule in its favor, or that courts will be too deferential toward the government, or that the interests of foreign investors will be underestimated, perhaps unconsciously. If the private and public interests at stake are very large, the risk of bias entails serious consequences.

Whether this risk should be a matter of grave concern depends on the context, of course. It varies according to the country, the historical moment, the political circumstances, the particular kind of investment, etc ... In many places, at many times, there is no significant danger that foreign investors will be mistreated on account of their nationality. After all, states have an incentive to treat current foreign investors properly not to discourage further investments. States suffer reputational costs if they exhibit hostility.[7] But the prospect of discrimination cannot be excluded altogether. Incentives based on reputation cannot do all the work to eliminate significant risks. As Charles N. Brower and Sadie Blanchard point out, "in practice, reputational effects and community pressure have proven inadequate against hostile actions of host states against foreign investors."[8] It is true that several studies suggest that host states do not tend to treat foreign investors less favorably than locals. As Jonathan Bonnitcha, Lauge N. Skovgaard Poulsen and Michael Waibel explain, however, an important flaw in those studies is that "they do not distinguish between the treatment of foreign investments covered by investment treaties and the treatment of those that are not," and therefore "it is not possible to determine whether the existence of investment treaties is one of the reasons why these aggregate studies suggest that foreign investors do not suffer from post-establishment discrimination."[9] So we cannot dismiss the risk of discrimination altogether in the absence of investment treaties.

In light of all this, and given that the stakes are often very high in investment disputes, it is constitutionally reasonable for countries to conclude international agreements promising foreign investors that a neutral body will adjudicate the disputes that may arise with the host government, under treaty norms that cannot be unilaterally altered. The ultimate goal being pursued is effective parity of treatment.

It is important to observe that the equality-based justification of investment agreements is not inconsistent with the fact that such agreements do not limit themselves to guaranteeing foreign investors "national treatment" (which means that foreign investors will be treated like national ones). The investment treaties

7 As Bonnitcha, Skovgaard Poulsen and Waibel explain in *The Political Economy of the Investment Treaty Regime*, p. 133, "a rational state considering whether to expropriate a particular investment will take into account the impact of its decision on other investors contemplating new investments."

8 The Honorable Charles N. Brower and Sadie Blanchard, "What's in a Meme? The Truth about Investor-State Arbitration: Why It Need Not, and Must Not, Be Repossessed by States," 52 *Columbia Journal of Transnational Law*, 689 (2014), p. 703.

9 Bonnitcha, Skovgaard Poulsen, and Waibel, *The Political Economy of the Investment Treaty Regime*, pp. 150–151.

typically go further: they grant protections whose force does not depend on any comparison between foreigners and locals. The provision prescribing that property cannot be expropriated without compensation, for example, safeguards a substantive right, regardless of whether the governmental measure under review is discriminatory or not. The same is true of the provision guaranteeing fair and equitable treatment, which protects, among other things, basic components of the rule of law. This protection kicks in even if there is no discrimination between foreigners and locals. Actually, these protections overlap with rights commonly embodied in national constitutions, such as the rights to property and due process, which are conceptually independent from the right to equality. But all this is not in tension with the equalization theory. What this theory holds is that special substantive and procedural rules need to apply to foreigners in order to ensure they will enjoy the same level of protection as national investors. The protections themselves are not only about equality, but the reason why special rules have been adopted to cover foreign investors is related to equality.

So if we understand the purpose and effect of the international treaties on investment to be structural parity between foreign and local investors, the equality objection can be answered. The constitutional principle of equality is not being contravened. Investment treaties actually derive from the constitution an important measure of legitimacy, insofar as they contribute to realizing equality.

A theory along these lines has been partially relied upon by some constitutional courts when ruling on the validity of investment agreements. The French Constitutional Council, for example, has upheld the constitutionality of the CETA (the 2016 Comprehensive Economic and Trade Agreement between Canada and the European Union) on equality grounds. The Constitutional Council has reasoned that the purpose of the treaty is to grant foreigners the same rights national investors enjoy. In its opinion, the Council makes reference to Point 6 (a) of the "Joint Interpretative Instrument" on the CETA, which states in relevant part that the "CETA will not result in foreign investors being treated more favourably than domestic investors."[10]

In a similar vein, the Constitutional Court of Colombia has upheld the 2014 BIT between Colombia and France against objections based on the right to equality.[11] In its judgment, the Court notes that the general purpose of the BIT is to promote the rule of law, the internationalization of economic relations, and economic and social development. But these goals are not sufficient to justify a disparate treatment between investors. The Court insists that foreign investors cannot be granted a higher degree of protection than national investors are accorded under the domestic constitution. The Court cites the French Constitutional Council's opinion on the CETA as persuasive authority in this regard.[12] In order to avoid

10 See *Décision* no 2017–749 DC, July 31, 2017, paras. 35–40.

11 Sentencia C-252/19, June 6, 2019.

12 Ibid., para. 117.

constitutional frictions, the Colombian Court explicitly conditions the validity of the BIT to the insertion of a common interpretive statement by the treaty partners clarifying that the BIT should not be read to give foreign investors greater rights than those that flow from the domestic constitution.[13] To this end, the Court summarizes its own doctrine about indirect expropriation and legitimate expectations, and declares that for the BIT to be in conformity with the constitution it cannot be taken to deviate from such doctrine, since otherwise the principle of equality would be breached.[14]

By way of contrast, the Court of Justice of the European Union avoided the deep questions concerning equal treatment when it had to review the conformity of the CETA against European Union legal standards, a review that the Belgian government had requested.[15] The Court accepted that article 20 of the Charter of Fundamental Rights of the European Union (which provides that "everyone is equal before the law") is relevant to test the CETA's validity. But the Court confined its inquiry to the narrow question of whether the fact that Canadian investors (foreigners) will be able to resort to the CETA tribunals to challenge European Union measures, while investors from European Union member states (locals) will not be entitled to do so, offends equality. According to the Court, the answer is no, the reason being that the situation of the two groups of investors is not comparable: while the CETA grants substantive protection to Canadian investors against European Union acts, it does not extend that protection to European Union investors.[16]

By reasoning in this manner, however, the Court circumvented the basic equality issue in play. Of course, if we assume that it is acceptable for the CETA to grant Canadian investors, but not European investors, a substantive legal remedy against European governmental measures, it follows quite naturally that a specific procedure must be made available to Canadian investors who wish to pursue that remedy. The critical question, however, is whether such disparity in substantive protection is warranted. What is the justification for limiting the CETA substantive protections to foreign investors? The Court, unfortunately, remained silent on this issue.

It bears mentioning that Advocate General Yves Bot addressed the issue more thoroughly in his Opinion on the CETA delivered on January 29, 2019.[17] He argued there that foreign investors need special protection because they assume the risks and costs of an investment in a foreign economic area, in a legal environment they are unfamiliar with.[18] Relations between Canada and the European Union, moreover, are not based on mutual trust.[19] Furthermore, he claimed, the different treatment is objectively justified by the purpose of encouraging foreign

13 Ibid., paras. 92–123.
14 Ibid., paras. 174–215, and 257–284.
15 Opinion 1/17, of 30 April 2019.
16 Ibid., para. 181.
17 See Opinion of Advocate General Bot, delivered on 29 January 2019.
18 Ibid., para. 207.
19 Ibid., para. 208.

investment.[20] The latter line of argument is controversial, for the reasons mentioned before. In any event, it is regrettable that the Court shied away from the important issues concerning equality that the Advocate General discussed in his Opinion, which go to the very foundations of the investment treaty regime.

7.2 AN IMPLICIT ASSUMPTION

The equality-based theory presented above needs to be refined in an important respect. So far we have implicitly assumed that local investors are treated fairly by the domestic legal system, so that it is just right to confer the same level of protection on foreign investors. Sometimes, however, this assumption does not hold. The domestic legal system may exhibit flaws in terms of the degree of protection it affords local investors.

A decision rendered by the Colombian Constitutional Court in 1996 is instructive in this context.[21] The Court had to review the constitutionality of an investment agreement between Colombia and the United Kingdom. One of the legal issues that arose concerned the right of investors to receive compensation in the event of an expropriation. The agreement clearly established this right, while the Colombian Constitution explicitly licensed the legislature, on equity grounds, to determine the cases in which no compensation ought to be paid. An absolute majority of both chambers of Congress was required to issue such a law providing for no compensation. The Constitution, moreover, stipulated that the grounds invoked by the legislature were not justiciable.[22] Although there was no consensus among legal commentators as to the meaning and scope of this constitutional provision, the Court concluded that the investment treaty was incompatible with it. The Court held that the legislature had the constitutional authority to issue a non-compensation law, and this authority could not be waived through the signature of an international treaty. In order to reinforce its conclusion, the Court invoked the constitutional right not to be discriminated against on grounds of nationality.[23] Indeed, the Court reasoned, the effect of the treaty was that investors who were nationals of the United Kingdom were offered better terms, in Colombia, than investors who were Colombian citizens: the former, but not the latter, were guaranteed the right to obtain compensation whenever an expropriation of their assets took place.

Three judges filed a dissenting opinion. They basically argued that the Constitution did not bar Colombia from signing international agreements whose effect was to restrain the discretion of the national legislature. Such restrictive effect is a natural consequence of international instruments, they pointed out. The dissenters, moreover, reasoned that foreigners are in a weaker position than nationals

20 Ibid., para. 209.
21 Sentencia C-358/96, August 14, 1996.
22 See article 58, paras. 5 and 6, of the Colombian Constitution (before it was amended in 1999).
23 This right is guaranteed in article 13 of the Colombian Constitution.

because they do not have the right to vote, so it makes constitutional sense to make up for this weakness through international instruments. There is, after all, a whole branch of international law that has traditionally covered the status of foreigners, on the understanding that private persons need protection when they are abroad. The dissenting judges also insisted on the need to attract investments in order to improve the national economy in a globalized world, and recalled that the Constitution instructs the government to "promote the internationalization of political, economic, social and ecologic relationships."[24]

Interestingly, the upshot of the Court's decision (as well as later decisions concerning BITs with Cuba, Peru, and Spain) was the amendment of the Colombian Constitution in 1999, in order to eliminate the possibility for the legislature to issue laws that exclude compensation in certain expropriation cases. So the treaties with Great Britain and other countries ultimately triggered a constitutional reform that raised the level of protection for both foreign and national investors. If we believe that the domestic Constitution was defective when it established the terms under which private property could be taken, we should welcome the constitutional changes that were later introduced.[25]

In any event, the Colombian case illustrates this general point: the equality-based theory in support of the investment treaty arrangements only makes sense if the domestic legal system is sufficiently protective of the rights of local investors. To a large extent, this theory is an updated version of the "Calvo doctrine," which is associated with Carlos Calvo, a prominent nineteenth-century Argentinean jurist. Under this doctrine, foreign investors are not to be given rights greater than those available to nationals. The underlying assumption is that the set of national laws and institutions that safeguard the economic rights of local investors are in good shape and certainly comply with international standards.[26]

[24] See article 226.

[25] On these constitutional developments in Colombia, see David Schneiderman, *Constitutionalizing Economic Globalization. Investment Rules and Democracy's Promise* (Cambridge: Cambridge University Press, 2008), pp. 164–181. Schneiderman is critical of the constitutional reform of 1999. He argues that the earlier constitutional provision that empowered Congress to exclude compensation in some cases was defensible, in light of a conception of private property that insists on the social function of this right (pp. 59–60). It may be countered, however, that the social function conception of property, which is accepted in a number of countries, should be interpreted to allow the government to establish general regulations imposing significant burdens on property-owners in the name of public interests. If an expropriation does occur in a given case, however, it seems to amount to a violation of private property and the rule of law for the legislature to pass a statute exempting the government from paying compensation and preventing courts to rule on the constitutionality of such exemption. On this interpretation of the social function theory of property, there is no reason to regret the 1999 amendment to the Colombian Constitution. Of course, there are alternative theories of property, as Schneiderman rightly points out. The interpretation I am assuming here would need to be justified against its rivals. But this question is beyond the scope of this book.

[26] For a careful description of the traditional Calvo doctrine and its modern incarnation, see Santiago Montt, *State Liability in Investment Treaty Arbitration. Global Constitutional and Administrative Law in the BIT Generation* (Oxford: Hart Publishing, 2009), pp. 31–82.

This assumption was also part and parcel of the conception animating the friendship, commerce, and navigation treaties the United States promoted after the Second World War. As Kenneth Vandevelde explains, the policy of the American government was to project United States constitutional principles abroad. The idea was to safeguard the rights of foreign investors, but not to grant them greater protection than local investors are accorded under United States law. It was clearly assumed that American law adequately preserved private property, freedom of contract, due process, equality, and other values. This understanding of the point of investment treaties was reaffirmed in 2002, when Congress enacted legislation (the "Bipartisan Trade Promotion Authority Act") establishing that the investment chapters in free trade agreements signed by the United States were not to provide greater substantive rights for foreign investors in the United States than United States investors possessed under American law.[27] With this goal in mind, the 2004 United States Model BIT included an annex (Annex B) clarifying that non-discriminatory regulatory measures would only amount to indirect expropriation "in rare circumstances." The annex incorporated American constitutional takings jurisprudence, when it instructed arbitrators to take into account the degree of interference with property rights, the character of the governmental measure (its purpose and context), and whether the measure interfered with reasonable and investment-backed expectations. The more recent Model BIT of 2012 is to the same effect. When it comes to indirect expropriation, therefore, foreign investors are not to be awarded a level of protection higher than that provided under American constitutional doctrine. In the preambles to a number of treaties the United States has concluded in recent years, it is explicitly declared that foreign investors are not being accorded greater substantive rights than domestic investors are granted under American law.[28]

A similar assumption underlies the position currently endorsed by the European Union. The official understanding is that "Union agreements should afford foreign investors the same high level of protection as Union law and the general principles common to the laws of the Member States grant to investors from within the Union, but not a higher level of protection."[29] The presupposition, again, is that European constitutional law secures an acceptable level of protection for investments.

In sum, for the equality-based theory to work its normative effects we must enrich it with the assumption that the domestic legal system adequately safeguards investor rights in general.

27 Kenneth J. Vandevelde, "The Liberal Vision of the International Law on Foreign Investment," in C. L. Lim (ed.), *Alternative Visions of the International Law on Foreign Investment. Essays in Honour of Muthucumaraswamy Sornarajah* (New York: Cambridge University Press, 2016), p. 63.

28 See, for example, the Preamble to the 2019 United States-Korea Free Trade Agreement.

29 See Recital 4 of Regulation (EU) No 912/2014 of the European Parliament and of the Council of 23 July 2014 establishing a framework for managing financial responsibility linked to investor-to-state dispute settlement tribunals established by international agreements to which the European Union is party.

Now, what would happen if this assumption did not hold in a given country? Would investment treaties be constitutionally acceptable nevertheless, in spite of the fact that foreign investors would end up being treated better than locals? Notice that if foreign investors are treated "adequately" while locals are treated "inadequately," the former are getting better treatment than the latter. This is not an easy question. On the one hand, it may be pointed out that investment treaties preserve basic rights of the kind typically recorded in national constitutions (such as the right not to be expropriated without compensation, and the right to due process, for example). This being so, the treaties should be allowed to stand even if their protections do not extend to locals. The situation where the basic rights of one group are secured while those of another group are not is normatively better, we might say, than the situation where the basic rights of neither group are. It may be claimed, moreover, that the local investors are in a better position than outsiders to work out political solutions to improve the domestic legal system and thus achieve parity of treatment. Furthermore, the fact that foreign investors are adequately protected while locals are not may prompt the latter to undertake actions to revamp the legal order. On the other hand, it may be countered that the breach of equality is too serious to be justified on these various grounds.

To make things more complicated, it is hard to imagine that a national court that is called upon to rule on the constitutional validity of an investment treaty will explicitly recognize the fundamentally defective nature of the internal legal system, in terms of the degree of protection it affords investors. A court that is part of a gravely flawed system is unlikely to transcend and criticize it in a judicial opinion. It is one thing for a national court to acknowledge the risk that foreign investors might be treated unfairly, in an opinion justifying the governmental signature of an investment treaty to deal with that problem. It is quite another for a national court to recognize the systematic failure of the constitutional order to secure the basic rights of investors in general.

A connected question is this: What happens when the courts of country A can correctly assume that the basic rights of local investors are adequately protected under national law, but no similar assumption can be extended to the legal system of country B, with which country A has concluded an investment treaty? Arguably, the case for the constitutionality of the treaty in country A gets reinforced in this "asymmetric" scenario. The reason is this: for the rights of investors from country A to be adequately hedged when they invest in the legally defective system of country B, country A needs to conclude a treaty with country B. Country A must then accept, out of reciprocity, that investors from country B investing in country A will also be covered by the treaty. So, in this situation, courts in country A can rely on an additional ground, different from the equality theory explored so far, to support the constitutional validity of the investment treaty.

It is important not to confuse this additional, specific argument with the more simplistic argument based on reciprocity that we rejected at the beginning of the chapter. That argument, you will recall, said that there is no equality problem at all in the investment field, since foreign investors are treated exactly the same way, no matter their nationality, by the relevant international agreement. The argument was not convincing, since the uniformity of treatment among foreign investors does not negate the existence of disparate rules on another level: while foreign investors are covered by the treaties, locals are not. In the asymmetric scenario we are now considering, in contrast, the argument takes a different shape. The equality problem is fully acknowledged. The fact that there is reciprocity does not eliminate it. Reciprocity, however, figures in a broader argument that supports the constitutionality of the treaty as a means to buttress the basic rights of nationals when they invest in a foreign country whose legal order is seriously faulty.

Note that, in the asymmetric context we are contemplating, the courts in country B will be facing the situation we referred to earlier: they cannot hold the assumption that the legal system is sufficiently protective of the rights of investors in general. As I suggested, however, it is unlikely that a court that is part of that system will recognize such a fundamental failure.

In any event, we will continue our conversation here on the understanding that the presupposition can indeed be entertained that local investors in the country whose courts are being asked to rule on the constitutionality of an investment agreement are sufficiently protected by national law. Let's see what consequences follow from an equality-based theory that incorporates such an assumption.

7.3 DOCTRINAL CONSEQUENCES

The equality-based theory in support of investment treaties generates some important consequences for the adjudication of investor-state differences. Arbitrators in charge of resolving such differences must work out a jurisprudence that is aligned with the equalization theory. The basic principle that should guide their doctrinal constructions is equality.

To this end, arbitrators should pay attention to the constitutional doctrines developed by judges in well-functioning liberal democracies. If foreign investors are not to be overprotected, arbitrators should develop interpretations that are in harmony with the basic rules and principles national courts have shaped when adjudicating similar types of disputes. Comparative law has a critical role to play in this regard. It gives arbitrators useful information about the approaches commonly taken by domestic courts when dealing with analogous issues.[30]

In this connection, Jan Kleinheisterkamp has proposed organizing an international commission of experts and government officials from different countries

[30] See, generally, Stephan Schill (ed.), *International Investment Law and Comparative Public Law* (Oxford: Oxford University Press, 2010). See, also, Montt, *State Liability in Investment Treaty Arbitration*, pp. 371–372.

tasked with studying a representative number of well-functioning domestic legal systems. The commission would distill from national legal orders a body of principles that could be extended with the pertinent qualifications to the international investment field.[31] The commission would publish the results of its comparative research in the form of an articulated set of "Principles of Investment Protection." Such Principles would have the weight of soft law, helping arbitrators to properly construe investment treaties. If these guidelines were followed, foreign investors would not be afforded greater protection than they could legitimately expect in a properly regulated market.

A key component of the domestic constitutional doctrines arbitrators should take a look at is the analytical framework judges employ when reviewing governmental measures. In many jurisdictions, courts use the principle of proportionality.[32] This principle requires the reviewing institution to verify that the measure called into question is (i) suitable to attain a legitimate goal; (ii) necessary (meaning that there is no less restrictive alternative), and (iii) balanced (in the sense that the benefits obtained are greater than the harms imposed). There is much to be said in favor of transferring this technique to the arbitral forum.[33] If the principle of proportionality is correctly applied, all the relevant interests that pass the test of legitimacy can be taken into account. The interests of the investors affected by a particular measure are balanced against the general interests the measure seeks to preserve. Jonathan Bonnitcha objects, however, that "under the proportionality approach, the focus is on the extent of the interference with the investment, rather than the costs and benefits for the full range of affected actors." As a result, "the determination of liability under the proportionality approach gives a greater weight to the interests of the investor than would an overall assessment of the costs and benefits of the conduct in question."[34] It is not clear, however, why the principle of proportionality should cause arbitrators to neglect the full range of interests involved. The government can bring to the arbitral table all the interests it strives to satisfy. The inquiry under proportionality is certainly triggered by the claim of the investor, but the focus of the analysis can be as broad as the government wants it to be, by way of the justifications it advances to support the rules or decisions being challenged.

31 Jan Kleinheisterkamp, "Investment Treaty Law and the Fear for Sovereignty: Transnational Challenges and Solutions," 78 *The Modern Law Review*, 793 (2015).

32 For a detailed description of the birth and evolution of the principle of proportionality in different regions of the world, see Aharon Barak, *Proportionality. Constitutional Rights and their Limitations* (Cambridge: Cambridge University Press, 2012), pp. 175–210. See, also, Alec Stone Sweet and Jud Mathews, *Proportionality Balancing and Constitutional Governance. A Comparative and Global Approach* (Oxford: Oxford University Press, 2019).

33 See Caroline Henckels, *Proportionality and Deference in Investor-State Arbitration. Balancing Investment Protection and Regulatory Autonomy* (Cambridge: Cambridge University Press, 2015); and Gebhard Bücheler, *Proportionality in Investor-State Arbitration* (Oxford: Oxford University Press, 2015).

34 Jonathan Bonnitcha, *Substantive Protection under Investment Treaties. A Legal and Economic Analysis* (Cambridge: Cambridge University Press, 2014), p. 306.

A related question concerns the standard of review. When state measures are called into question, external scrutiny can be more or less strict. How deferentially should arbitrators exercise review?[35] The equality-based theory suggests arbitrators should display the same degree of deference toward the political branches that constitutional judiciaries generally practice. Arbitrators should not apply a more intense type of scrutiny. That would end up overprotecting foreign investors. Arbitrators should not be more passive either. If they resort to the principle of proportionality, in particular, they should apply it fully, taking all the analytical steps this principle incorporates. Caroline Henckels, however, is of the view that arbitrators ought to focus on the issue whether the measure is suitable and necessary, and should abstain from judging whether the measure is a balanced one.[36] Her main argument is that international arbitrators are not embedded in a political system, and should thus apply a more relaxed type of scrutiny. But if we accept that the ultimate justification of the investment legal regime is to secure foreigners the same level of protection that local investors enjoy, arbitrators should not be more deferential than national judiciaries are. Arbitrators are certainly detached from the national political process, but that is precisely the reason we rely on them to ensure objectivity when the party affected by the governmental measure is a foreigner.

So arbitrators have good reason to draw from the intellectual resources that common constitutional traditions supply. This is not to say that arbitrators are to borrow domestic constitutional doctrines in an unqualified manner. In the first place, the textual formulation of the principles embodied in the investment treaties may be different from national constitutional clauses. Although the principles overlap to a large extent, the relevant texts often exhibit variations. The normative standards arbitrators are directed to apply, moreover, differ from constitutional norms in an important respect: they are basically liability rules, which require the host state to pay compensation if it has impaired the rights of the investor.[37] Domestic courts, on the other hand, can resort to a richer set of remedies to redress violations of constitutional rights. Importantly, courts can quash the governmental measures deemed to breach constitutional precepts. This contrast in the nature of the rules to be applied may account for

35 On the need for arbitrators to be sensitive to questions concerning deference and standards of review, see Stephan W. Schill, "Deference in Investment Treaty Arbitration: Re-conceptualizing the Standard of Review," 3 *Journal of International Dispute Settlement*, 577 (2012); and Julian Arato, "The Margin of Appreciation in International Investment Law," 54 *Virginia Journal of International Law*, 545 (2014). As Julian Arato explains, some arbitrators have recently imported the "margin of appreciation doctrine" developed by the European Court of Human Rights. As he explains, however, this doctrine expresses no unified approach to the standard of review issue. Arbitrators ought to be more specific when they refer to the tests to be used for assessing the validity of governmental measures.

36 Henckels, *Proportionality and Deference in Investor-State Arbitration*, p. 171.

37 On investment treaty protections as liability rules, see Bonnitcha, *Substantive Protection under Investment Treaties*, pp. 58–62.

differences in the contours of the legal doctrines developed by arbitrators and national judges respectively.

In spite of these qualifications, however, a basic equivalence in the level of protection of foreign and national investors must be achieved. The impulse must be for arbitrators to generate a jurisprudence that affords the two groups of investors roughly the same treatment. To this end, a more fluent dialogue between arbitrators and national judges must unfold. Thus, if a national court has to review the constitutionality of a governmental measure that has already moved foreign investors to institute arbitral proceedings against the host state (or is likely to move them to do so in the future), the court should take into account the applicable investment treaty when reasoning its way toward the conclusion that the measure is or is not in conformity with the constitution. Even if the treaty is not part of the constitution being adjudicated, it should be given some weight. The court should assume that arbitrators will pay attention to what the court says about the treaty. The Spanish Constitutional Court, for example, missed a great opportunity in a case it decided in 2015 involving the constitutionality of a 2013 emergency decree that introduced important changes to the existing renewable-energies regulation.[38] The Court's holding that the decree did not violate legitimate expectations was not sufficiently reasoned, as the dissenting judges rightly noted, and it paid no attention to the relevant investment treaties. The Court seemed not to be aware that Spain was being sued by foreign investors in international arbitration forums, and that it was important for the Court to offer a convincing reasoning in its opinion in support of the validity of the challenged decree, an opinion which arbitrators would afterwards read.

Arbitrators, in turn, should not disregard what national judges have said concerning the constitutionality of a measure which foreign investors claim to run afoul of an international investment treaty. If the arbitrators reach a different outcome than the national judiciary, they ought to explain why. The German Constitutional Court, for example, has ruled on the validity of certain legislative changes adopted in 2011 to accelerate the end of nuclear power plants. The Court has recognized investors the right to compensation for the costs generated by the legislative reforms under certain conditions.[39] Arbitrators are now hearing an Energy Charter Treaty case brought by Vattenfall, a Swedish state-owned company, against Germany, for the damages caused by those reforms.[40] If the arbitrators come up with a different conclusion than that of the German Constitutional Court, they should explain in some detail why they do so. Even if no perfect uniformity can be achieved in all cases, stronger efforts should be made to reduce discrepancies in practice.

38 See STC 270/2015, December 17, 2015.

39 See BVerfG, Judgment of 6 December 2016, 1BvR 2821/11.

40 See *Vattenfall AB and others* v. *Federal Republic of Germany*, ICSID Case No. ARB/12/12.

7.4 IS THE ARBITRAL SYSTEM SKEWED IN FAVOR OF FOREIGN INVESTORS?

Assuming an equality-based constitutional justification of the investment treaty regime, we must now take up an issue that figures prominently in current debates about investor-state arbitration. Critics contend that arbitrators are interpreting and applying the relevant treaties in ways that are too friendly to foreign investors.[41] As a result, the ability of democratic governments to regulate matters in the public interest (to protect the environment, public health, labor standards, national security, for example) is curtailed in an unjustified manner, and local investors are discriminated against.

Critics claim that the explanation for this investor-friendliness lies in structural features of the arbitral system. Arbitrators are interested in making arbitral institutions attractive to investors. The more cases that are brought to them, the more money they will make. It is only investors, however, that file complaints. Arbitrators must accordingly see to it that investors be satisfied with the jurisprudence being produced. The system is thus skewed. Judges, on the other hand, are more likely to be balanced in their interpretation of the law, since their future salaries do not depend on who tends to win cases.[42]

This is an interesting thesis, but there are reasons to cast some doubts on it. First, it is true that arbitrators have an incentive to make arbitration attractive to investors, since the latter are the ones who decide whether or not to refer cases. But a different incentive works in the opposite direction: arbitrators should not make states upset about the system, since they can ultimately pull out of it, as some have started to do in a more or less gradual manner. Ecuador, Venezuela, and Bolivia, for example, have withdrawn from ICSID. Australia, in turn, refrained from inserting investor-state arbitration clauses in some international agreements, such as the 2004 Free Trade Agreement with the United States, and the 2014 Economic Partnership Agreement with Japan, though it later incorporated such clauses in the 2014 Free Trade Agreement with Korea and the 2015 Free Trade Agreement with China.[43] And

41 See Schneiderman, *Constitutionalizing Economic Globalization. Investment Rules and Democracy's Promise*; and M. Sornarajah, *Resistance and Change in the International Law on Foreign Investment* (Cambridge: Cambridge University Press, 2015), pp. 191–299.

42 For an objection along these lines, see Gus Van Harten, *Investment Treaty Arbitration and Public Law* (Oxford: Oxford University Press, 2007), pp. 172–175. Van Harten, however, seems to suggest that there is a problem of "perceived bias" (p. 173), but not necessarily of actual bias. He asserts that most arbitral awards are fair and balanced. He writes: "Indeed, it is a testament to the sense of fairness of arbitrators that the reasoning in most awards is not strongly skewed in favour of claimants and that it often reflects an appreciation of the complex policy issues that arise in regulatory adjudication." Awards that defer to host governments "demonstrate clearly that many arbitrators will put their integrity and that of the system ahead of the interests of their industry" (p. 174). For a more recent study on this matter, see Gus Van Harten, "Arbitrator Behaviour in Asymmetrical Adjudication (Part Two): An Examination of Hypotheses of Bias in Investment Treaty Arbitration," 53 *Osgoode Hall Law Journal*, 540 (2016).

43 For an overview of current movements to withdraw from the investment regime, see Sornarajah, *Resistance and Change in the International Law on Foreign Investment*, p. 5.

in the context of the renegotiation of NAFTA, Canada has decided to opt out of investor-state arbitration under the new treaty, USMCA (the 2018 United States-Mexico-Canada Agreement).[44]

It should be noted, incidentally, that respondent states can sometimes bring counterclaims against investors.[45] This helps balance things. The system could certainly be more symmetrical than it currently is. Some scholars have proposed amending the treaties to include obligations that foreign investors must honor. If an investor breached its obligations, the host state would be entitled to take it to an arbitral tribunal. The consent of the investor would be needed, of course. To this end, domestic law could require acceptance of treaty-based arbitration as a condition for the admission of foreign investments. Alternatively, the contract between the host state and the investor could provide for symmetrical treaty-based arbitration.[46] Proposals along these lines deserve serious consideration, though we should not lose sight of the fact that states can already use their own domestic institutions to ensure that foreign investors comply with their duties under national (an even international) law.[47]

Second, the available evidence indicates that investors are not successful in a large percentage of cases.[48] The amount of damages they are awarded when they win, moreover, is often much lower than they had originally claimed.[49] It is hard to use

44 See USMCA, Chapter 14, Annex 14-D, on Mexico-United States Investment Disputes.

45 See, for instance, *Saluka Investments B.V.* v. *The Czech Republic*, UNCITRAL, Decision on Jurisdiction over the Czech Republic's Counterclaim, 7 May 2004; and *Urbaser S.A and Consorcio de Aguas Bilbao Bizkaia, Bilbao Biskaia Ur Partzuergoa* v. *The Argentine Republic*, ICSID Case No. ARB/07/26, Award, 8 December 2016.

46 For more details, see Gustavo Laborde, "The Case for Host State Claims in Investment Arbitration," 1 *Journal of International Dispute Settlement*, 97 (2010); and Gabriel Bottini, "Extending Responsibilities in International Investment Law," E15Initiative. Geneva: International Centre for Trade and Sustainable Development (ICTSD) and World Economic Forum, 2015, www.e15initiative.org/.

47 On this issue, see The Honorable Charles N. Brower and Sadie Blanchard, "What's in a Meme? The Truth about Investor-State Arbitration: Why It Need Not, and Must Not, Be Repossessed by States," 52 *Columbia Journal of Transnational Law*, 689 (2014), pp. 709–716. As they argue, "as sovereigns, host states have many tools at their disposal for responding to investor breaches, including civil and criminal penalties, legal actions for breach of contract, and political pressure. The very nature of the relationship means that the foreign investor will typically have assets in the host state, guaranteeing enforcement leverage," p. 712.

48 According to the statistics gathered by the United Nations Conference on Trade and Development (UNCTAD), as of December 31, 2019, of all the known treaty-based investor-state arbitration proceedings, 36.5 percent were decided in favor of the state, 29.4% were decided in favor of the investor, 2.1 percent were decided in favor of neither party (liability was found but no damages were awarded), 20.6 percent were settled, and 11.4 percent were discontinued. See UNCTAD statistics, available on its website at www.investmentpolicyhub.unctad.org/investment-dispute-settlement.

49 See Susan D. Franck, *Arbitration Costs. Myths and Realities in Investment Treaty Arbitration* (New York: Oxford University Press, 2019), pp. 140–179. Franck has conducted a thorough empirical study covering all publicly available investment treaty arbitral awards as of January 1, 2012. She has measured, among other things, the relative success of investors, which is a function of the proportionate difference between amounts requested and awarded. According to her findings, the mean investor success rate for all cases (which included cases where respondents both won and lost) was 18 percent,

the available data to endorse the proposition that investor-state arbitration is structurally biased in favor of investors. In her careful empirical study, Susan Franck has observed a low investor success in arbitration proceedings, prompting her to conclude that states should not seek to avoid arbitration as a matter of principle. The risk for states is certainly smaller "than sensationalist stories on Twitter or in the popular press may suggest."[50] In the same vein, Alec Stone Sweet and Florian Grisel note that "the extant empirical research provides no support for the claim that awards on liability in [investor-state arbitration] are biased in favor of investors."[51]

Of course, it is possible to be critical of particular awards, on the grounds that they embrace too broad a conception of the kinds of governmental measures that should trigger compensation. But the judgments of domestic courts on this matter are also contested. The constitutional jurisprudence on regulatory takings and legitimate expectations, in particular, is often controversial, and judges disagree among themselves.[52] The European Court of Human Rights is also internally divided. In a recent case, for example, it examined a Hungarian law introducing a state-managed system of schoolbook distribution.[53] The state monopoly established by the new law meant the end of the free market that had developed in that sector for many years. The companies that had been operating consequently suffered a sudden loss of clientele. The European Court, taking into account the circumstances of the case, concluded that the right to property had been breached and compensation consequently needed to be paid to the affected companies. The judgment was not unanimous, however: one judge filed a concurring opinion, and another dissented. Similarly, the European Court has held that states enjoy wide discretion when enacting statutes fixing the maximum amount of rent tenants must pay landlords for leasing their apartments or houses. This discretion is not unlimited, however: the rent specified by the statutes cannot be "extremely low." The judges have disagreed when applying this standard in particular instances. They were unanimous that the rent was too low in a case against Malta, but they were divided (by twelve votes to five) in an earlier case concerning Austria.[54] These examples illustrate the complexity of this branch of human rights jurisprudence. Investor-state arbitration case law is no different in this regard.

and the median was 2 percent. As much as 75 percent of investors recovered less than 30 percent of their request (p. 172). Focusing on the subset where investors won and obtained damages, the mean investor success rate was 35 percent, and the median was 28.7 percent. Even after prevailing on the merits, 75 percent of investors were awarded less than half of their request (p. 173).

50 Franck, *Arbitration Costs*, p. 176.

51 Alec Stone Sweet and Florian Grisel, *The Evolution of International Arbitration. Judicialization, Governance, Legitimacy* (Oxford: Oxford University Press, 2017), p. 247.

52 For a comparative view, see Gregory S. Alexander, *The Global Debate Over Constitutional Property. Lessons for American Takings Jurisprudence* (Chicago: The University of Chicago Press, 2006).

53 *Könyv-Tár Kft and Others* v. *Hungary*, no. 21623/13, Judgment of 16 October 2018.

54 See *Edwards* v. *Malta*, no. 17647/04, Judgment of 24 October 2006, and *Mellacher and Others* v. *Austria*, nos. 10522/83, 11011/84 and 11070/84, Judgment of 19 December 1989.

A different way of questioning the objectivity of investment arbitration relates to the types of jurists that are appointed in arbitration. If those jurists are experts in investment law, it may be claimed, they will be biased in favor of investors. This criticism is not persuasive, however. Of course, experts in investment law generally adhere to the values that this area of the law tries to realize, in the same way that experts in human rights law are usually committed to the rights enshrined in the pertinent legal texts. But this does not mean that those experts will necessarily disregard any other values or considerations that are relevant. It is only a bad human rights lawyer that is insensitive to the important public interests that a government may invoke in justification of a measure that restricts human rights. Similarly, it is a bad expert in investment law that is deaf to any talk about considerations that may justify measures that negatively affect the interests of investors (such as the need to protect public health and the environment, for instance). So the question is whether arbitrators are good jurists. The mere fact that they are specialized in investment law does not entail that they are skewed in favor of investors. Of course, there is much to be said in favor of interdisciplinary bodies.[55] It would be advisable, for example, for arbitral tribunals to include jurists with some constitutional legal background, in order to draw from common constitutional traditions when construing investment treaties. But this does not mean that arbitral tribunals are currently biased just because experts on investment law get appointed to adjudicate the cases.

There is certainly room for improvements, to better guarantee objectivity. With regard to ICSID, for example, Antonio R. Parra has observed that the preponderance of developing countries that are parties to disputes "has not been reflected in the proportion of developing country nationals among members of ICSID arbitral tribunals."[56] "In large measure," he explains, "parties to the proceedings have been responsible for the imbalances as most of the arbitrators have been their appointees." But an imbalance also exists among the arbitrators designated by the Chairman of the Administrative Council. In this connection, Parra urges states to take seriously the power they possess under the ICSID Convention to designate four experts each to be included in the Panel of Arbitrators, from which the Chairman must generally draw his or her appointees. As it happens, not all states have made the pertinent designations. To better safeguard impartiality, moreover, Parra proposes that the Chairman of the Administrative Council should formally delegate to the Secretary-General of ICSID the appointments task. Given that the President of the World Bank is *ex officio* Chairman of the Administrative Council, his or her involvement may raise a conflict of interest in the occasional cases where the

[55] On the connection between the specific legal backgrounds of arbitrators and the basic categories they will use to understand the point and nature of investment law, see Anthea Roberts, "Clash of Paradigms: Actors and Analogies Shaping the Investment Treaty System," 107 *The American Journal of International Law*, 45 (2013).

[56] Antonio R. Parra, *The History of ICSID* (Oxford: Oxford University Press, 2017), p. 288.

Bank is helping finance the investment project under dispute, or in cases where the measures taken by the host government were connected to programs urged by the Bank.[57]

Another issue that has raised concerns has to do with the fact that arbitrators sometimes work as counsel or experts in other arbitration cases. This "double-hatting" or "role confusion" entails the risk that arbitrators will decide on an issue in a particular way so as to help a party they represent in another dispute. There is also the danger that counsel will appoint an arbitrator in one case with the expectation that their roles as counsel and arbitrator will be reversed in a future dispute. Ethical rules on conflicts of interest should be strictly enforced in these instances. Whether arbitrators should generally abstain from acting as counsel or experts in other cases that are not related to the controversies they are being asked to adjudicate is a more delicate matter. The argument has been made, for example, that relatively young lawyers who seek to become full-time arbitrators cannot afford to stop working as counsel in arbitration cases at the beginning of their careers, when they only get a few appointments as arbitrators. If enlarging and diversifying the pool of arbitrators is desirable in order to enhance the legitimacy of the system, prohibiting arbitrators from working as lawyers in arbitral procedures may turn out to be counterproductive. It would ultimately favor well-established arbitrators. In any event, double-hatting does raise legitimate worries on impartiality grounds, and adjustments are necessary. The UNCITRAL (United Nations Commission on International Trade Law) has tackled this issue in recent years, in the context of its program to study and suggest reforms to improve investor-state arbitration.[58]

So the arbitral system should be improved in various respects to reinforce objectivity. While there is no strong reason to believe that investor-state arbitration is structurally tilted toward the interests of foreign investors, nuanced and constructive criticisms are justified. The defense of investor-state arbitration in its current form, therefore, can only be a qualified one.

Suppose, however, that when all is said and done, the critics turn out to be right that arbitration is structurally biased in favor of foreign investors. In that scenario, the domestic judiciary would be authorized to step in. Courts would have to hold the investment regime to be incompatible with the constitution, on account of the discriminating effect produced by arbitral adjudication.

A judicial response of this sort would be similar in spirit to the approach some national courts in Europe have followed when assessing the extent to which European Union law may prevail over national law. The German Constitutional Court, for example, has accepted the primacy of European Union law when it comes to fundamental rights, so long as the level of protection that rights are

57 Ibid., pp. 295–296.

58 See "Possible reform of investor-State dispute settlement (ISDS). Ensuring independence and impartiality on the part of arbitrators and decision-makers in ISDS. Note by the Secretariat," UN Doc A/CN.9/WG.III/WP.151, 30 August 2018, pp. 6–9.

accorded by European Union courts is substantially similar to (not lower than) the level of protection that the German Constitution secures.[59] By the same token, the national judiciaries could assert that the investment treaty regime is acceptable as long as the level of protection granted to foreign investors is generally equivalent to (*not higher than*) the level of protection that the national constitution extends to local investors. If this condition turned out not to be satisfied, the regime would not pass the constitutional test, and governments should be bound by courts to reshape it accordingly.

7.5 CONCLUSION

The investment treaty regime needs to be justified against constitutional norms guaranteeing equality. One justification invokes the goal of attracting foreign capital, but this approach is problematic for both empirical and normative reasons. An alternative theory based on the need to secure effective parity between foreign and local investors is more convincing. This theory presupposes, however, that the domestic legal system is sufficiently protective of the rights of investors. As we have seen, doctrinal consequences follow from embracing this theory: arbitrators need to pay attention to the common constitutional traditions of liberal democracies when construing the principles contained in investment treaties. At this juncture, the objection advanced by critics of investment treaty arbitration, to the effect that it exhibits a pro-investor structural bias, is of great relevance. If they are right on this point, the investment regime as a whole cannot survive constitutional scrutiny. There are reasons to undermine the force of the objection, however, even if institutional reforms may be necessary to enhance the legitimacy of the system.

59 See the "*Solange II*" decision, BVerfG 73, 339, Judgment of 22 October 1986, 2 BvR 197/83. For an overview of the strategies deployed by national judiciaries to accommodate the primacy of European Union law with domestic constitutional commitments to fundamental rights, see Paul Craig and Gráinne de Búrca, *EU Law. Text, Cases, and Materials* (Oxford: Oxford University Press, 2015), pp. 266–315; and Robert Schütze, *European Constitutional Law* (Cambridge: Cambridge University Press, 2015), pp. 127–134. For a normative assessment of the interactions between national and supranational courts in Europe from a dialogical perspective, see Aida Torres Pérez, *Conflicts of Rights in the European Union. A Theory of Supranational Adjudication* (Oxford: Oxford University Press, 2009).

8

Adjudicative Coherence and Democratic Checks on Arbitral Jurisprudence

In the previous chapter, we have touched on the role of arbitrators in the development of investment law. We must now dwell more deeply on this issue. We must bear in mind that the principles commonly contained in investment treaties are rather abstract. The principle that secures "fair and equitable treatment," for example, is particularly open-ended. We need case law to clarify the meaning and scope of provisions of this sort. No international court has been set up to do the job, however. Only marginally does the International Court of Justice intervene in investment cases. No specialized investment tribunal, moreover, has been created on the global stage. As we will see, some treaties have recently established investment tribunals, but their jurisdiction is limited to the few countries that have subscribed those treaties.

Arbitration has consequently come to occupy the central lawmaking position in the investment domain. There is pressure, indeed, for arbitrators to understand their task to include the elaboration of legal doctrines to operationalize the abstract principles embodied in the treaties. Arbitrators cannot confine their attention to the particular disputes they handle. They have to look beyond. For purposes of formulating rules to implement the treaties, they are to take into account the decisions made in past cases, and they must be aware that future tribunals will examine their own awards. How good is the arbitral regime to generate a consistent body of rulings, however?

Insofar as arbitrators produce case law that has a significant impact on the evolution of investment law, we need to think about the mechanisms the political branches can employ to exercise appropriate checks. At the domestic level, courts do not decide cases in a political vacuum. They are part of a broader system that encompasses popularly elected institutions with the ability to exert some measure of control. What devices can the democratic governments use to check the jurisprudence emanating from the arbitral process? These and other related themes are the subject of this chapter.

8.1 A CULTURE OF PRECEDENT

If we need investor-state arbitrators to form a consistent body of precedents, let us inquire into the conditions that must be met for this endeavor to be successfully carried out. As we discussed in Chapter 4, certain requirements must be satisfied before a system of precedents can emerge from an array of decisions. How do these conditions play out in the investment context?

The first requirement, we noted, refers to reason-giving: adjudicators must state the grounds for their decisions. This condition is complied with to a very large extent in the investment domain. Arbitrators dealing with investment claims are expected to provide reasons. Arbitral awards issued under the ICSID Convention, in particular, must do so, a requirement that cannot be derogated from by the contending parties.[1] This is not surprising. Arbitral decisions in this setting are apt to have an enormous economic and political impact on an entire country. Citizens are entitled to know why the arbitrators decided the way they did.[2]

The second condition for the development of a system of precedents is publicity. Investor-state arbitration is working well enough in this regard. The vast majority of ICSID awards are published. Although the Centre cannot publish an award without the consent of the parties, the latter usually give their consent.[3] In addition, the Centre must include in its publications excerpts of the legal reasoning of arbitral decisions.[4] A party, moreover, is free to publicize an award on its own (unless the parties have agreed to keep the award confidential).

A similar trend toward publicity can be observed in arbitrations conducted under the UNCITRAL (United Nations Commission on International Trade Law) Arbitration Rules. The 2013 UNCITRAL Rules on Transparency in Treaty-based Investor-State Arbitration lay down the general principle that awards (as well as other relevant documents) are to be made available to the public, subject to exceptions affecting confidential or protected information. Hearings for the presentation of evidence or for oral argument, moreover, must generally be public.[5] To facilitate the wide application of these Rules, the General Assembly of the United Nations adopted the 2014 Convention on Transparency in Treaty-based Investor-State Arbitration. The states that subscribe to this Convention commit themselves to the employment of the UNCITRAL Rules on Transparency in a whole range of investment disputes.

1 See articles 48(3) and 52(1)(e) of the ICSID Convention.

2 See Guillermo Aguilar Alvarez and W. Michael Reisman, "How Well Are Investment Awards Reasoned?," in Guillermo Aguilar Alvarez and W. Michael Reisman (eds.), *The Reasons Requirement in International Investment Arbitration. Critical Case Studies* (Leiden: Martinus Nijhoff Publishers, 2008), p. 2.

3 See article 48(5) of the ICSID Convention.

4 See Rule 48(4) of the ICSID Arbitration Rules.

5 See articles 3 and 7 of the 2013 UNCITRAL Rules on Transparency in Treaty-based Investor-State Arbitration, effective April 1, 2014.

There is actually another feature of investment arbitration that connects with publicity: nonparties are increasingly allowed to participate in the proceedings, to supplement the arguments advanced by the parties.[6] Thus, the treaty partners are sometimes permitted to intervene. Because the interpretation of the treaty reached by arbitrators will matter in future cases, the states have an interest in making their own interpretive contributions. Moreover, other actors – typically, NGOs – are enabled to file *amicus curiae* briefs. The ICSID Arbitration Rules, in particular, explicitly provide that an arbitral tribunal can allow a person or entity that is not a party to the dispute to file a written submission. The tribunal must take into account, among other things, the extent to which the submission would assist the tribunal in the determination of a factual or legal issue related to the proceeding by bringing a perspective, particular knowledge or insight that is different from that of the disputing parties, and the extent to which the non-disputing party has a significant interest in the proceeding.[7] A similar provision is included in the 2013 UNCITRAL Rules on Transparency in Treaty-based Investor-State Arbitration.[8]

The third condition for the emergence of a system of precedents, as you will recall, relates to the incentives arbitrators need to have in order to look beyond the specific dispute they are handling to connect their rulings to past holdings and to think about the consequences of their own decisions for future cases. At the domestic level, as we saw, arbitrators generally lack incentives to move in this direction. Things are different in the investment terrain, however.

To begin with, the legitimacy of the investment regime depends, among other factors, on adjudicative consistency. A degree of uniformity in the application of the relevant norms is critical to preserve legal certainty. Investors, of course, are interested in being able to rely on a relatively clear jurisprudence specifying the terms of the protections they enjoy under the treaties. But states also need clarity as to which measures can survive arbitral scrutiny. Governments will otherwise experience "regulatory chill": they will abstain from enacting certain measures that are actually in conformity with the treaties for fear of the financial consequences of an unfavorable award.[9] Equality in the application of the law also matters. Arbitrators need to be consistent in order to avoid the risk of treating investors covered by the same international agreement differently depending on their nationality. With respect to agreements signed by rich capital-exporting nations and less developed capital-importing nations, in particular, it is crucial to guarantee that the level of protection

[6] On the evolution of investor-state arbitration with regard to the participation of non-disputing parties, see Eric De Brabandere, *Investment Treaty Arbitration as Public International Law. Procedural Aspects and Implications* (Cambridge: Cambridge University Press, 2014), pp. 160–174.

[7] See Rule 37(2) of the ICSID Arbitration Rules.

[8] See article 4 of the 2013 UNCITRAL Rules on Transparency in Treaty-based Investor-State Arbitration.

[9] For a discussion of this problem, see Jonathan Bonnitcha, *Substantive Protection under Investment Treaties. A Legal and Economic Analysis* (Cambridge: Cambridge University Press, 2014), pp. 113–133.

foreign investors get when they come from the poorer country is not lower than that of investors coming from the richer country.[10]

Arbitrators are generally aware of the importance of achieving a certain level of uniformity. As Andrés Rigo Sureda points out, since "arbitral tribunals themselves have found that legal stability and respect for the expectations of the investors are part of the treatment guaranteed by the treaties," it would be strange if arbitrators were not worried about the legal stability and predictability of their own jurisprudence.[11] In practice, arbitrators regularly take into account the awards rendered in earlier cases, even if the latter arose under a different international instrument than the one that applies to the instant case. A culture of precedent has thus developed.[12] The arbitral tribunal in the *Saipem* v. *Bangladesh* case, for example, reflected this culture when it wrote that a tribunal must pay due consideration to previous decisions even if it is not bound by them. "Subject to compelling contrary grounds," it asserted, the tribunal "has a duty to adopt solutions established in a series of consistent cases." Indeed, "subject to the specifics of a given treaty and of the circumstances of the actual case, it has a duty to seek to contribute to the harmonious development of investment law and thereby to meet the legitimate expectations of the community of States and investors towards certainty of the rule of law."[13]

In spite of this culture of precedent, the arbitral arrangements are not conducive to a high level of consistency. This brings us to the fourth requirement that must be satisfied for a system of precedents to develop adequately: as we discussed in Chapter 4, there must exist a central body of a permanent kind in charge of settling interpretive disagreements among a plurality of adjudicators.

No such body has been established in the arbitral forum. Under the ICSID Convention, arbitral awards can be reviewed by an annulment committee.[14] The grounds for attacking the awards, however, are very narrow, basically limited to jurisdictional and procedural irregularities, so it is not possible for the committee to

10 The claim has been made, in this regard, that arbitrators tend to follow more expansive doctrines favoring investors when the latter come from Western-capital exporting states than when they come from other countries. See Gus Van Harten, "Arbitrator Behaviour in Asymmetrical Adjudication (Part Two): An Examination of Hypotheses of Bias in Investment Treaty Arbitration," 53 *Osgoode Hall Law Journal*, 540 (2016).

11 Andrés Rigo Sureda, *Investment Treaty Arbitration. Judging Under Uncertainty* (Cambridge: Cambridge University Press, 2012), p. 114.

12 See Gabrielle Kaufmann-Kohler, "Arbitral Precedent: Dream, Necessity or Excuse?," 23 *Arbitration International*, 357 (2007), pp. 368–373; and Stephan W. Schill, *The Multilateralization of International Investment Law* (Cambridge: Cambridge University Press, 2009), pp. 321–347. For a more critical approach, see Irene M. Ten Cate, "The Costs of Consistency: Precedent in Investment Treaty Arbitration," 51 *Columbia Journal of Transnational Law* 418 (2013).

13 *Saipem S.p.A* v. *The People's Republic of Bangladesh*, ICSID Case No. ARB/05/07, Decision on Jurisdiction and Recommendation on Provisional Measures, 21 March 2007, para. 67.

14 See article 52 of the ICSID Convention.

play a significant role in resolving interpretive controversies among arbitrators.[15] An annulment committee can thus opine that the award was wrong as a matter of law and yet uphold it, if none of those limited grounds apply. In one case, for example, the committee explicitly said that the award under review contained "manifest errors of law," in spite of which the award could not be annulled on that basis.[16] The committee, moreover, is not a permanent body. Its members are selected *ad hoc* for each particular case.[17] Although proposals have been considered within ICSID to set up a standing appeals facility, they have not been implemented.[18]

Because of this institutional weakness, there is stronger need for adjudicative practices to develop professional norms aimed at producing consistency. As Mirjan Damaška observed in his comparative study of legal systems, cultural norms of *stare decisis* are particularly necessary in countries that lack a centralized bureaucratic judiciary.[19] Jurisdictions pertaining to the common law tradition, for example, have had to rely on the doctrine of *stare decisis* to a larger extent than civil law nations, on account of their comparatively low degree of bureaucratization. In the arbitral context, the *ad hoc* character of arbitral tribunals can drive participants to insist on professional norms of *stare decisis*. In the *Glamis* case, for instance, the arbitrators wrote:

> The fact that any particular tribunal need not live with the challenge of applying its reasoning in the case before it to a host of different future disputes (the challenge faced by standing adjudicative bodies) does not mean such a tribunal can ignore that challenge. A case-specific mandate is not license to ignore systemic implications. To the contrary, it arguably makes it all the more important that each tribunal renders its case-specific decision with sensitivity to the position of future tribunals and an awareness of other systemic implications.[20]

So arbitrators are aware that consistency in adjudication is a key element of legitimation. All things considered, however, the arbitral regime is ill-equipped to carry out the rule-formulation task. Arbitration's radically decentralized nature militates against it.

15 The grounds for judicial review of awards are: (a) the tribunal was not properly constituted; (b) the tribunal has manifestly exceeded its powers; (c) there was corruption on the part of a member of the tribunal; (d) there has been a serious departure from a fundamental rule of procedure; and (e) the award has failed to state the reasons on which it is based.

16 See *CMS Gas Transmission Company* v. *The Republic of Argentina*, ICSID Case No. ARB/01/8 (Annulment Proceeding), Decision of the ad hoc Committee on the Application for Annulment of the Argentine Republic, 25 September 2007, para. 158.

17 The Chairman of the Administrative Council appoints an *ad hoc* committee of three persons from the Panel of Arbitrators. The latter are designated in advance by the States and the Chairman. See articles 13 and 52 of the ICSID Convention.

18 See ICSID Secretariat, "Possible Improvements of the Framework for ICSID Arbitration," Discussion Paper, October 22, 2004.

19 Mirjan R. Damaška, *The Faces of Justice and State Authority. A Comparative Approach to the Legal Process* (New Haven: Yale University Press, 1986), pp. 36–37.

20 *Glamis Gold, Ltd.* v. *The United States of America*, UNCITRAL, Award, 8 June 2009, para. 6.

Indeed, great contradictions between different awards have sometimes arisen concerning the same facts.[21] More generally, arbitrators have given contrasting answers to many important legal questions. Consider the legitimate expectations doctrine, which is commonly taken to be part of the fair and equitable treatment standard. Which types of expectations deserve protection? Only those that rest on the specific rights the investor has acquired under domestic law? Or also the expectations that rest on the specific representations made to the investor by governmental officials? Or also the expectations that rest on the regulatory framework in force in the host state at the time the investor made the investment? Or also the expectations that rest on the business plans of the investors? Jonathan Bonnitcha has usefully classified the available arbitral awards in different groups, in light of these distinctions.[22] As he shows, there is no agreement on a single theory.

Profound disparities have also arisen with regard to jurisdictional matters. Which investments, for example, are covered by the ICSID Convention and the relevant treaty? Must the investment make a contribution to the economic development of the country? What is the impact of so-called umbrella clauses? Do they elevate any contract breach to a violation of the treaty? What is the scope of most-favored-nation clauses? Are their effects limited to the substantive standards of protection, or do they extend to procedural requirements? Under what conditions are corporations covered by the investment treaties, if they have been created with the specific purpose of triggering the application of a particular treaty? And what is the nature of investment treaty provisions as they apply to contracts concluded by the host government and a foreign investor? Do they operate as mandatory rules, or as default rules?[23] Questions of this sort should be settled through relatively crisp rulings. Such rulings must be sensitive, of course, to the textual variation that investment treaties display. Different treaties may include distinctly worded clauses dealing with these issues. But we need consistent background principles to determine how such clauses ought to be interpreted and applied. Arbitrators have failed to furnish a coherent set of answers in this connection.

Not surprisingly, a 2018 Report of the UNCITRAL Working Group on Investor-State Dispute Settlement Reform included inconsistency of arbitral outcomes as

[21] A famous instance concerned an American investor who first lost his arbitration against the Czech Republic, based on a BIT between the Czech Republic and the United States, but later won the same dispute using his Dutch holding company in a parallel procedure, invoking the BIT between the Czech Republic and The Netherlands. The language of the two treaties was very similar, and yet the arbitrators reached contradictory conclusions for the same set of facts. Compare *Ronald S. Lauder v. The Czech Republic*, UNCITRAL, Final Award, 3 September 2001, and *CME Czech Republic B. V. v. The Czech Republic*, UNCITRAL, Partial Award, 13 September 2001.

[22] Bonnitcha, *Substantive Protection under Investment Treaties*, pp. 167–194.

[23] For an illuminating review of arbitral jurisprudence on this important issue, which tends to be neglected in the literature, see Julian Arato, "The Logic of Contract in the World of Investment Treaties," 58 *William & Mary Law Review*, 351 (2016).

one of the problematic aspects of arbitration. It registered the broad view among participants that the mechanisms in place to achieve consistency are insufficient.[24]

This lack of uniformity is especially striking if we take into account that arbitrators constitute a small legal elite group. As Alec Stone Sweet and Florian Grisel explain, fewer than twenty presiding arbitrators have produced most final awards in this area, a circumstance that "favours the development of a more consistent arbitral case law."[25] In the same vein, Moshe Hirsch observes a connection between jurisprudential coherence and the social cohesion of the arbitral community, at the heart of which is a group of frequent arbitrators.[26] Sergio Puig, in turn, explains the centrality of this small group as a function of time: those arbitrators who were appointed earlier on have an advantage. "Once members of the profession work together or know about others' appointments, this information is passed on and translates into a proportionately greater number of appointments."[27] All this means that, if the field becomes less elitist in the future, as one should hope, the degree of consistency of arbitral decisions may turn out to be even lower than it currently is.

In light of all these considerations, and as we will discuss later in the chapter, there is much to be said for the creation of permanent investment tribunals in order to overcome the limitations of arbitration in terms of adjudicative consistency and rule-formulation.

8.2 DEMOCRATIC CHECKS ON ARBITRATORS

Let us now look at the democratic checks on arbitral jurisprudence. In the domestic arena, our reasonable faith in the objectivity of courts does not lead us to insulate them completely from the political branches. For reasons we explored in Chapter 4, having to do with the role of courts in the lawmaking process, we want courts to be subject to some form of control by institutions that are accountable to the people. The same should be true of arbitration here. In so far as arbitral tribunals in the investment field generate case law, even if the degree of consistency of their rulings is low, mechanisms should be available for the political branches to reorient its contents. What avenues are open for the democratic institutions to express their inputs?

At the domestic level, courts are basically subject to two kinds of democratic checks, as we saw. One operates through the appointment process: the political

24 See "Report of Working Group III (Investor-State Dispute Settlement Reform) on the work of its thirty-fifth session (New York, 23–27 April 2018)," UN Doc A/CN.9/935, 14 May 2018, pp. 5–8.

25 Alec Stone Sweet and Florian Grisel, *The Evolution of International Arbitration. Judicialization, Governance, Legitimacy* (Oxford: Oxford University Press, 2017), p. 72.

26 Moshe Hirsch, "The Sociology of International Investment Law," in Zachary Douglas, Joost Pauwelyn and Jorge E. Viñuales (eds.), *The Foundations of International Investment Law. Bringing Theory into Practice* (Oxford: Oxford University Press, 2014), p. 165.

27 Sergio Puig, "Social Capital in the Arbitration Market," 25 *The European Journal of International Law*, 387 (2014), p. 421.

branches have a say when it comes to recruiting judges. The other check is more abstract: the political branches can step in and clarify the interpretation that needs to be given to the relevant body of law, and they can also change the law. Let us see how things play out in the domain of investment treaty arbitration.[28]

8.2.1 *Appointing Arbitrators*

As is true of arbitration in general, the parties to an investment dispute choose the arbitrators. If a tripartite tribunal is formed, the investor will appoint an arbitrator, the host state will appoint another, and the two co-arbitrators or the contending parties will jointly select the chairperson. The governments have therefore a partial say. This is not a good way, however, for the political branches to activate checks on the case law produced by arbitrators.

The reason, obviously, is that there is no congruence between the states that have concluded the underlying investment treaty, on the one hand, and the states that are entitled to select arbitrators in a particular case, on the other. Only the respondent state in a given instance has the chance to influence the composition of the tribunal. The other treaty partners are excluded. The home state, in particular, plays no part. This is actually regarded as an advantage. One of the virtues of investment arbitration is that a dispute between an investor and the host state need not poison the political relationships between the latter and the home state. Home states are not generally expected to get involved.[29] Only rarely do they intervene in arbitral proceedings to advance their interpretive positions on the legal issues under discussion, sometimes in disagreement with the arguments made by their own nationals.[30] In general, however, home governments are out of the picture, so as not to politicize the difference between the investor and the host state. The less politicized the arbitral atmosphere, the more smoothly the dispute will be handled.

The fact that the arbitral tribunal is not a permanent body, moreover, makes it difficult for states to transcend their interest in winning the particular case and think more generally about the direction arbitral jurisprudence ought to take. At the domestic level, the political branches need to think in rather abstract terms when designating judges. They are choosing the persons who will be shaping the law in

[28] For a general study of the variety of mechanisms of control that are available in the investment field, drawing on economic contract theory and principal-agent theory, see Anne van Aaken, "Control Mechanisms in International Investment Law," in Douglas, Pauwelyn, and Viñuales (eds.), *The Foundations of International Investment Law*, pp. 409–435. See, also, Andreas Kulick (ed.), *Reassertion of Control over the Investment Treaty Regime* (Cambridge: Cambridge University Press, 2017).

[29] As already mentioned, the ICSID Convention provides that the investor waives his right to diplomatic protection if he chooses to initiate arbitration proceedings. Only if the arbitral award is not abided and complied with by the host state may the home state give that kind of protection. See article 27 of the ICSID Convention.

[30] See, for instance, the submission of the United States in *Gami Investments, Inc.* v. *Mexico*, UNCITRAL; and Canada's submission in *Mondev International Ltd.* v. *United States of America*, ICSID Case No. ARB(AF)/99/2.

a general way, as they go about deciding hundreds or thousands of cases over time as members of a permanent court. In the investment field, on the other hand, the *ad hoc* nature of arbitral tribunals makes it hard for the disputants to pay attention to general principles. The respondent state will be prone to select an arbitrator that is as friendly as possible to its own position in the instant case. If the state is entitled to name one of the arbitrators, it is small wonder that it will take into account the chances that its nominee will help produce a favorable award.

For these reasons, it is not feasible to rely on the way arbitrators are selected to channel the interpretive views of the political branches. When states enter the arbitral picture wearing the hat of a litigant, no interesting democratic inputs on the character of arbitral jurisprudence are to be expected. In order to institute democratic checks, we need to look elsewhere: to procedures where the states, wearing a different hat than that of litigants in specific cases, can express in a more abstract way what they think about the rules and principles pertaining to foreign investment.

8.2.2 *State-to-State Arbitration*

One possibility, which is very underdeveloped in practice, is for the democratic governments to express their points of view in state-to-state arbitral procedures.[31] When states conclude an investment treaty, they can insert a clause that remits to arbitration any interpretive dispute that may arise among them in connection to the treaty. An arbitral tribunal can thus be asked to rule on a general interpretive question that elicits controversy. The tribunal's ruling will be abstract, and may bind arbitrators charged with hearing specific investor-state disputes. So arbitration will proceed on two different levels: a general level (state-to-state arbitration) and a more specific level (investor-state arbitration).

State-to-state arbitration is potentially useful, not only to clarify the interpretation of the treaty in response to the contradictory views of different arbitrators in specific cases, but also in order to confirm or qualify the more coherent doctrines the latter may have created. Presumably, the tribunal that adjudicates the state-to-state dispute will fix an interpretation of the treaty that is within the range of readings advanced by the states.

The abstract nature of the legal inquiry in state-to-state arbitration brings with it some advantages.[32] Consistency in the application of the law is one of them. Because the tribunal dealing with the abstract procedure is asked to lay down a general rule

[31] For an interesting defense of this type of procedure, see Anthea Roberts, "State-to-State Investment Treaty Arbitration: A Hybrid Theory of Interdependent Rights and Shared Interpretive Authority," 55 *Harvard International Law Journal*, 1 (2014). See, also, Andreas Kulick, "State-State Investment Arbitration as a Means of Reassertion of Control: From Antagonism to Dialogue," in Kulick (ed.), *Reassertion of Control over the Investment Treaty Regime*, pp. 128–152.

[32] The arguments here are similar to those that may be offered in the domestic sphere to support the establishment of procedures of abstract review of legislation under the Constitution. See Victor

that is expected to bind arbitrators in future cases, investors are ensured equal treatment under the treaty (no matter their nationality).

In addition to consistency, abstraction generates a higher level of objectivity. A tribunal asked to rule in the abstract does not know how exactly its holding will favor or disfavor particular investors or particular states in specific controversies that will erupt in the future – under a relatively stable treaty. When construing the treaty, the tribunal may be more or less friendly to states as a class, or to investors as a class, but not to a specific state in one case, or to a specific company in another. Abstraction is a veil of ignorance technique. It is true that the tribunal may be asked to rule on a question that is relevant for a pending case. In order to reinforce objectivity, a possible strategy is for the ruling to be granted prospective effects only.[33]

Another virtue of state-to-state arbitration is that it facilitates a systematic approach to legal problems. As Owen Fiss has argued in the constitutional context, courts should take into account the interests of the many people who are affected by a judgment. With regard to welfare rights, for example, Fiss has written:

> Because it lays down a rule for a nation and invokes the authority of the Constitution, the Court necessarily must concern itself with the fate of millions of people, all of whom touch the welfare system in a myriad of ways: some on welfare, some wanting welfare, some being denied welfare, some dispensing welfare, some creating and administering welfare, some paying for it. Accordingly the Court's perspective must be systematic, not anecdotal: The Court should focus not on the plight of four or five or even twenty families but should consider the welfare system as a whole – a complex network embracing millions of people and a host of bureaucratic and political institutions.[34]

Similar problems may arise in the investment domain. Suppose an investor argues that the restriction placed by the government on his property rights in order to protect the environment was not justified, since the state could have acted differently to reach its goals. Other investors make the same argument. Suppose, however, that the state could have acted differently in a handful of cases only, but not in all the cases altogether, for it lacks the necessary resources. The accumulation of unconnected judgments rendered in different specific cases may lead to a suboptimal outcome. A systematic look at the problem is necessary. An avenue to explore in this connection is for a state to submit a request for declaratory relief, in order to have a tribunal in a state-to-state procedure assess the general impact of a governmental measure and determine its conformity with the treaty.[35]

Ferreres Comella, *Constitutional Courts and Democratic Values. A European Perspective* (New Haven: Yale University Press, 2009), pp. 66–70.

33 See Roberts, "State-to-State Investment Treaty Arbitration," pp. 63–66.

34 Owen Fiss, "Reason v. Passion," in Owen Fiss, *The Law As It Could Be* (New York: New York University Press, 2003), pp. 218–219.

35 On this possibility, see Roberts, "State-to-State Investment Treaty Arbitration," p. 68, footnote 310.

So there are a number of strengths to state-to-state arbitration. Of course, the types of experts entrusted with the resolution of an abstract interpretive question may be different from those charged with the task of deciding particular disputes between investors and governments.[36] A controversy involving the construction of a bridge, for example, may call for arbitrators who are familiar with certain factual complexities that are not present when an interpretive issue is framed in the abstract. The general interpretive problems that the treaty poses may be better dealt with by experts in public international law and constitutional law, whereas the issues that arise in a specific dispute may be more appropriately tackled by jurists with a strong background in commercial law or administrative law.

8.2.3 *Treaty Amendments, Interpretive Notes, and New Treaties*

In addition to the mechanism just described, states may participate in the interpretive process in a more direct way: they may amend the relevant treaty to clarify and specify the norms they meant to embody in it. As masters of the treaty, the states are empowered to make the necessary modifications and adjustments to express their will, if they disagree with the content the arbitrators have ascribed to the original terms.[37]

An alternative, less cumbersome possibility is this: some treaties provide for the establishment of a commission comprising representatives of the states, endowed with the power to issue interpretive notes. Such notes are binding on arbitrators. The Free Trade Commission under NAFTA (North American Free Trade Agreement) is a prominent example.[38] On July 31, 2001, the Commission issued a note clarifying the scope of the fair and equitable treatment standard, thus responding to the interpretations reached by arbitrators in a number of cases.[39] The Commission asserted that such standard does not "require treatment in addition to or beyond that which is required by the customary international law minimum standard of treatment of aliens." The categorically binding character of such interpretive notes has sometimes been questioned, however.[40]

36 Ibid., p. 62.

37 For a defense of the interpretive role of states in the investment field, see Anthea Roberts, "Power and Persuasion in Investment Treaty Interpretation: The Dual Role of States," 104 *The American Journal of International Law*, 179 (2010); and Eleni Methymaki and Antonios Tzanakopoulos, "Masters of Puppets? Reassertion of Control through Joint Investment Treaty Interpretation," in Kulick (ed.), *Reassertion of Control over the Investment Treaty Regime*, pp. 155–181.

38 See NAFTA, article 1131. The same arrangement figures in the new 2018 treaty modifying NAFTA. See USMCA, article 14.D.10.

39 See *Metalclad Corporation* v. *The United Mexican States*, ICSID Case No. ARB (AF)/97/1, Award, 30 August 2000; and *Pope & Talbot Inc.* v. *The Government of Canada*, UNCITRAL, Award on the Merits of Phase 2, 10 April 2001.

40 Thus, in *Pope & Talbot Inc.* v. *The Government of Canada*, UNCITRAL, Award in Respect of Damages, 31 May 2002, the arbitrators reasoned that the binding character of the notes issued by the Commission depends on whether they actually establish an interpretation of the treaty as opposed to

Similarly, the CETA (the Comprehensive Economic and Trade Agreement between Canada and the European Union) enables a Joint Committee representing the contracting parties to issue binding interpretations. The treaty explicitly empowers the Joint Committee to indicate the specific date from which the binding interpretation will produce effects.[41] Interestingly, when the Court of Justice of the European Union reviewed the validity of the CETA against European Union legal principles, it reasoned that judicial independence would be infringed if such interpretive decisions were to produce effects on disputes that had already been dealt with or were pending. The Court thus held that the CETA must not be interpreted as permitting the European Union to consent to interpretive decisions of the Joint Committee that would produce such retroactive effects.[42]

Some treaties empower investor-state arbitrators to certify interpretive questions to the treaty parties. Under NAFTA, for example, arbitrators must refer questions to the Free Trade Commission when certain specific issues covered by NAFTA arise.[43] The same procedure is stipulated in the new 2018 treaty (USMCA) updating NAFTA.[44]

The ASEAN-Australia-New Zealand Free Trade Agreement also provides that an investor-state tribunal "shall, on its own account or at the request of a disputing party, request a joint interpretation of any provision of this Agreement that is in issue in a dispute."[45] The joint decision of the treaty parties declaring their interpretation is binding on the tribunal. If the treaty parties are unable to reach an interpretive agreement, the arbitral tribunal decides the issue on its own account.

In the same vein, the 2012 United States Model BIT stipulates that, when the respondent state asserts certain kinds of defenses, the arbitral tribunal shall request the interpretation of the treaty partners on the issue (if the respondent state asks for it). If the partners agree on a joint decision declaring their interpretation on the matter, the arbitral tribunal must adjudicate the controversy accordingly. If they fail to issue a joint interpretive decision, the arbitral tribunal decides the issue on its own authority.[46]

It is worth noticing the similarity between these mechanisms enabling arbitrators to obtain the "authentic" interpretation of the treaty, and the *référé législatif* that the French revolutionaries created in 1790 to make sure judges would not interpret the law on their own but would instead ask parliament to clarify any doubts. In both cases, the point of the procedure is to cabin the interpretive discretion of adjudicators. The French *référé législatif* was finally abolished in 1804, through a reform

an amendment of it. Arbitrators cannot accept as an "interpretation" whatever the Commission says (para. 23).

41 See article 8.31.3 of the CETA.

42 Opinion 1/17, 30 April 2019, paras. 236 and 237.

43 See article 1132 of NAFTA.

44 See article 14.D.10 of USMCA.

45 See 2009 ASEAN Australia-New Zealand Free Trade Agreement, chapter 11, article 27(2).

46 See article 31 of the 2012 United States Model BIT.

driven to a significant extent by the belief that parliament performs its functions better when it legislates in the abstract than when it speaks its mind in the context of a specific case, under the pressures exerted by the parties whose interests are implicated. The Court of Justice of the European Union echoed similar worries when it examined the temporal effects of the Joint Committee's interpretive decisions under the CETA. As already mentioned, the Court held that the effects of such interpretive decisions must be prospective only, in order to safeguard the right to an impartial adjudication of claims.

Now, for all these checks to operate, a consensus has to be reached between the treaty partners concerning the way the abstract principles they wrote in the treaty should be read and implemented. That consensus is easier to work out, of course, if the treaty is bilateral than if it is multilateral.

The experience with the WTO (World Trade Organization), for example, illustrates how difficult it is to change the rules of a system that is based on a multilateral instrument. Since unanimity is needed to modify many of the provisions contained in the WTO treaties, amendment is hard to achieve.[47] It is also possible for the Ministerial Conference and the General Council to adopt authoritative interpretations of provisions of the WTO agreements. Such interpretive decisions, however, require a three-fourths majority of the members of the organization.[48] In practice, only in very extreme situations can this mechanism be used to correct the interpretation reached by the dispute resolution bodies.[49] Consequently, as Federico Ortino points out, "the level of dialectic between the political and the judicial branches in the WTO is very low."[50]

In contrast, political checks on arbitral jurisprudence are easier to activate when the underlying treaty is bilateral. Since most investment treaties are concluded bilaterally for an initial period of ten years, "national policy makers can modify or adapt international disciplines on the basis of the rich jurisprudence now available."[51]

An interesting development has taken place in this connection. In the past, powerful capital-exporting nations encouraged weaker capital-importing countries to ratify international treaties that were very protective of investors. At present, however, the contrast between the two groups of states is less stark. More often than was the case in the past, states find themselves in a dual position: they are both

47 See article X of the WTO agreement.

48 See article IX of the WTO agreement.

49 See Pieter Jan Kuijper, "The Court and the Appellate Body: Between Constitutionalism and Dispute Settlement," in Sanford E. Gaines, Birgitte Egelund Olsen and Karsten Engsig Sørensen (eds.), *Liberalising Trade in the EU and the WTO. A Legal Comparison* (Cambridge: Cambridge University Press, 2012), p. 107.

50 Federico Ortino, "Non-Discriminatory Treatment in Investment Disputes," in Pierre-Marie Dupuy, Francesco Francioni and Ernst-Ulrich Petersmann (eds.), *Human Rights in International Investment Law and Arbitration* (Oxford: Oxford University Press, 2009), p. 365, footnote 71.

51 Ibid., p. 365.

exporters and importers of capital. While they are interested in protecting their nationals investing abroad, they are also interested in safeguarding their governmental capacity to regulate matters in the public interest when they receive outside investments. Actually, different social groups within these countries may lobby the government in different directions, depending on the interests and values they want to advance. While corporations that usually invest abroad will favor very protective investment rules, environmental associations will press in the opposite direction, in favor of recognizing a wide regulatory space for public authorities. All this has led to the introduction of some qualifications in the new investment agreements.[52] As M. Sornarajah puts it, "states which devised swords now had to devise shields."[53] Of course the higher the number and diversity of countries that conclude a particular international agreement to protect investors, the more balanced that agreement will be in terms of the combination of swords and shields.

The evolution in the United States concerning its Model BIT is revealing of current trends. The 2004 and 2012 Models are more nuanced than the earlier 1983 Model. A better balance is now struck between investor protection and the governmental right to regulate the market to serve public interests. Thus, the Preamble to the 2012 Model announces that investments need to be protected "in a manner consistent with the protection of health, safety, and the environment, and the promotion of internationally recognized labor rights." Within the framework of the treaty, the state parties recognize "that it is inappropriate to encourage investment by weakening or reducing the protections afforded in domestic environmental laws."[54] It is further stipulated that "nothing in this Treaty shall be construed to prevent a Party from adopting, maintaining, or enforcing any measure otherwise consistent with this Treaty that it considers appropriate to ensure that investment activity in its territory is undertaken in a manner sensitive to environmental concerns." Similarly, the state parties "reaffirm their respective obligations as members of the International Labor Organization," and recognize that "it is inappropriate to encourage investment by weakening or reducing the protections afforded in domestic labor laws."[55] With regard to indirect expropriations, the 2012 Model BIT prescribes that "except in rare circumstances, non-discriminatory regulatory actions by a Party that are designed and applied to protect legitimate public welfare objectives, such as public health, safety, and the environment, do not constitute indirect expropriations."[56]

[52] On this trend, see José E. Alvarez, *The Public International Law Regime Governing International Investment* (The Hague: Hague Academy of International Law, 2011), pp. 143–176. For a skeptical view on the success of the new "balanced treaties" in preserving governmental regulatory space while protecting foreign investors, see M. Sornarajah, *Resistance and Change in the International Law on Foreign Investment* (Cambridge: Cambridge University Press, 2015), pp. 348–365.

[53] Sornarajah, *Resistance and Change in the International Law on Foreign Investment*, p. 305.

[54] See article 12 of the 2012 United States Model BIT.

[55] See article 13 of the 2012 United States Model BIT.

[56] See Annex B of the 2012 United States Model BIT.

So a range of options is available for states to cabin the interpretive powers of arbitrators and to move the law forward in new directions, as this brief comparative survey reveals.

It is important to point out that the checks the political institutions can bring to bear on arbitral jurisprudence, and the changes they are entitled to make with regard to the terms of the underlying treaties, are not to be justified on the grounds that states are absolutely free to decide which benefits to extend to foreign investors. Of course, if the protections that investors are afforded under the treaties were understood to be mere devices governments design to encourage capital flows, it would follow that states are free to change their minds and eliminate or reduce the protections that were originally provided in those treaties. Investors would have no "rights" under this scheme. They would simply be the beneficiaries of an instrumentalist strategy.

As we saw in the previous chapter, however, investment treaties are best justified against constitutional equality norms if they are understood to guarantee that foreigners will enjoy certain basic rights (to private property and due process, for example), on roughly equal terms with domestic investors. This being so, the legitimacy of the political checks that can be put in motion to respond to arbitral jurisprudence cannot rest on the idea that investors have no rights. The legitimacy of such checks is to be conceived in a different way. At this juncture, we can take a page from dialogical constitutional theories developed at the domestic level. Because of the relatively abstract character of the constitutional clauses carrying rights, there is reasonable disagreement about their meaning and impact. For democratic reasons, courts should not be alone in the interpretive enterprise. The political institutions ought to have a say. The latter are authorized to reorient judicial doctrines through the appointment process or by means of constitutional amendments. An interbranch dialogue develops, and the political institutions can ultimately prevail.[57] This does not imply, however, that fundamental rights are arbitrarily given and taken away by the political branches. Democratic institutions are expected to participate in the process of constitutional construction to work out in good faith the specific content of abstract rights widely believed to be morally valuable. When there is reasonable contestation over the meaning and consequences of norms safeguarding rights, courts should not be the only relevant voice. The same theory of interpretive dialogue should be extended to the investment legal realm, to make sense of the checks that political institutions can exercise. If those mechanisms of control are in place, it is because democratic governments must have a significant input in the process through which the rights of investors are gradually constructed and refined, not because there is no intrinsic normative value in investment protection.

[57] For a classical exposition of this theory of constitutional dialogue, see Alexander M. Bickel, *The Least Dangerous Branch: The Supreme Court at the Bar of Politics* (Indianapolis: Bobbs-Merrill, 1962).

8.3 TOWARD PERMANENT INVESTMENT TRIBUNALS?

Given the issues and problems we have discussed in this chapter, would it not be better to institute standing international tribunals specialized in investment matters? Some proposals have been made in this direction, and there is much to be said in their support.[58] The United Nations Conference on Trade and Development (UNCTAD) issued a report in 2013 portraying a multilateral investment court as a good institutional arrangement to overcome the defects of existing investor-state dispute-resolution mechanisms. It pointed out, however, that this solution would be difficult to implement in practice since it would require the coordinated action of a large number of states.[59] UNCITRAL has also been discussing the option of building standing tribunals to improve the current regime.[60]

The European Union, for its part, has spearheaded an international campaign to create permanent tribunals. In the course of its negotiations with the United States concerning the Transatlantic Trade and Investment Partnership (TTIP), the European Commission made a proposal to set up a standing body to settle investor-state disputes arising under the treaty.[61] Permanent tribunals already figure in the CETA (the Comprehensive Economic and Trade Agreement between Canada and the European Union), as well as in the 2018 European Union-Singapore Investment Protection Agreement, and the 2019 European Union-Vietnam Investment Protection Agreement.

The institutional scheme adopted in these agreements recently signed by the European Union is two-tiered. It comprises a first instance tribunal and an appeals tribunal. The members of the first instance tribunal are elected by a joint committee representing the governments. The investors have no role in the appointment

58 For an early defense of permanent investment courts, see Gus Van Harten, *Investment Treaty Arbitration and Public Law* (Oxford: Oxford University Press, 2007), pp. 180–184. A comprehensive discussion of various proposals to create standing tribunals is provided in Gabrielle Kaufmann-Kohler and Michele Potestà, "Can the Mauritius Convention serve as a model for the reform of investor-State arbitration in connection with the introduction of a permanent investment tribunal or an appeal mechanism?," 3 June 2016, research paper prepared for UNCITRAL (the United Nations Commission on International Trade Law) within the framework of a research project of the Geneva Center of International Dispute Settlement, available at www.uncitral.org. For a very detailed plan to create a multilateral investment court, see Marc Bungenberg and August Reinisch, *From Bilateral Arbitral Tribunals and Investment Courts to a Multilateral Investment Court. Options Regarding the Institutionalization of Investor-State Dispute Settlement. Special Issue of the European Yearbook of International Economic Law* (Berlin: Springer, 2020).

59 See "Reform of investor-state dispute settlement: in search of a roadmap," IIA Issues Note No. 2, June 2013.

60 See "Report of Working Group III (Investor-State Dispute Settlement Reform) on the work of its resumed thirty-eighth session," UN Doc A/CN.9/1004/Add.1, 28 January 2020.

61 For a description and assessment of the European Commission's proposal, see Ingo Venzke, "Investor-State Dispute Settlement in TTIP from the Perspective of a Public Law Theory of International Adjudication," 17 *The Journal of World Investment & Trade*, 374 (2016). An influential voice in favor of the establishment of standing tribunals is Joseph Weiler: "European Hypocrisy: TTIP and ISDS," *EJIL: Talk! Blog of the European Journal of International Law*, January 21, 2015, available at www.ejiltalk.org

process. Cases are heard in divisions of three. The adjudicators sit for a fixed period of time, and receive a monthly retainer fee and specific fees for each case they adjudicate, although the possibility is expressly contemplated of transforming those fees into a regular salary in the future.[62] As far as nationality is concerned, the composition of the tribunal is mixed. In the case of the CETA, for example, one third of the members of the tribunal must be nationals of Canada, another third must be nationals of a member state of the European Union, and the rest must be nationals of third countries.[63] The appeals tribunal is structured in a similar way, for it is also a permanent body whose members are selected by the states. Its authority to review arbitral awards is relatively broad: in addition to the grounds that already exist under the ICSID Convention, awards can be challenged for errors in the application or interpretation of the relevant law, and for manifest errors in the establishment of the facts.

Apart from these bilateral tribunals, it is possible to envisage the inception of a global permanent court with jurisdiction to adjudicate investor-state disputes connected to a plurality of investment treaties. A single tribunal could thus centralize the interpretation of a large multiplicity of substantive treaties. To this end, the United Nations could draft a multilateral convention, the effect of which would be to automatically modify (for the state signatories) the procedural aspects of a whole range of investment treaties, in order to introduce a standing adjudicative body.[64] There is precedent for this strategy: the United Nations Convention on Transparency in Treaty-based Investor-State Arbitration of 2014, which was already mentioned, is designed to facilitate the application of the UNCITRAL Transparency Rules to the roughly 3000 investment treaties that were concluded before such Rules were adopted. Through this technique, states can easily subject themselves to the Rules, without bearing the burden of amending each treaty on a case-by-case basis. A similar strategy has been proposed to give birth to a global investment tribunal.

The European Union has also taken the initiative in this regard. In March 2018, the European Commission was given the mandate by the Council of the European Union to negotiate a Multilateral Investment Court. Actually, the bilateral treaties the European Union has recently signed setting up bilateral investment court systems express the parties' intention to transfer the latter to a multilateral system in the future. The CETA, for instance, provides that

> the Parties shall pursue with other trading partners the establishment of a multilateral investment tribunal and appellate mechanism for the resolution of investment disputes. Upon establishment of such a multilateral mechanism, the

62 See, for example, CETA, article 8.27.15.

63 See CETA, article 8.27.2.

64 See Kaufmann-Kohler and Potestà, "Can the Mauritius Convention serve as a model for the reform of investor-State arbitration in connection with the introduction of a permanent investment tribunal or an appeal mechanism?".

> CETA Joint Committee shall adopt a decision providing that investment disputes under this Section will be decided pursuant to the multilateral mechanism and make appropriate transitional arrangements.[65]

It is debatable, however, whether this transformation is likely to take place. Stephan Schill has plausibly argued that as more bilateral courts are formed, bilateralism will get entrenched, and it will therefore be more difficult for a multilateral tribunal to supersede them at a later stage.[66]

A less radical alternative, which the United States embraces as a possibility for the future, centers on the establishment of a permanent body with jurisdiction to review arbitral awards. In this model, investor-state arbitration of the classical kind would be maintained for first-instance decisions. The latter, however, could be appealed to a standing tribunal authorized to quash the awards on relatively broad legal grounds.[67]

Yet another possibility draws inspiration from the preliminary reference procedure that is one of the hallmarks of the judicial architecture of the European Union. A permanent tribunal comprising experts in investment law could be instituted tasked with answering interpretive doubts raised by arbitral tribunals. Consistency would be achieved through the body of jurisprudence developed by that tribunal in the course of providing guidance to arbitrators.[68]

There are a number of advantages to permanent tribunals, whatever their specific configuration. In the first place, governments can channel their interpretive inputs when making the judicial appointments. Instead of selecting arbitrators once a particular dispute has erupted, the governments make their appointments in advance, in light of the more general professional backgrounds and legal philosophies of the candidates. It is also easier for the governments to secure a diversified composition of the tribunal, in terms of gender, age, ethnicity, and professional and academic training, for example, since they can coordinate their appointment proposals to reach that goal. In addition, the permanent character of the tribunal facilitates the production of a coherent jurisprudence, which serves the values of equality and legal certainty.

Are investors unduly disadvantaged under such a system, insofar as they do not participate in the process to select the adjudicators? Is there a risk that the new

65 See CETA, article 8.29.

66 Stephan W. Schill, "The European Commission's Proposal of an 'Investment Court System' for TTIP: Stepping Stone or Stumbling Block for Multilateralizing International Investment Law?," 20 *ASIL Insights*, April 22, 2016, available at www.asil.org.

67 See article 28(10) of the 2012 United States Model BIT. The United States-Chile Free Trade Agreement of 2003, for example, contemplates the possibility that a multilateral agreement may establish such an appellate body in the future. See article 10.19(10).

68 For a detailed proposal to reform the ICSID system along these lines, see Katharina Diel-Gligor, *Towards Consistency in International Investment Jurisprudence. A Preliminary Ruling System for ICSID Arbitration* (Leiden: Brill Nijhoff, 2017), pp. 333–451.

arrangements will have an unacceptable pro-state bias?[69] Not really. The governments make the appointments with several goals in mind. They wish to preserve their own regulatory capacity when they receive foreign investments, but they also wish to protect their national investors abroad. They understand, moreover, that foreign investors should be treated fairly, not only for intrinsic reasons having to do with equality, but also in order to reap the economic benefits that encouraging investments may bring about. Because the governments have to strike a balance between these different ends, they are likely to appoint jurists who are not extremists one way or the other. Classical forms of arbitration seek to achieve the same balance in a different manner: the two co-arbitrators that are unilaterally appointed may be sympathetic to the interests of the respective sides, but these partial sympathies cancel each other out; the president's contribution becomes critical to secure objectivity. Setting up a permanent court is probably a more straightforward strategy to achieve the necessary equilibrium, but this does not mean that the traditional modality of investor-state arbitration is biased in favor of investors, as we saw earlier. Critics who insist that a permanent tribunal will be too friendly to the states are actually undermining the case in support of the classical forms of arbitration, since they are implicitly conceding that the latter are indeed skewed toward investors.

The experience with the WTO (World Trade Organization) dispute resolution mechanisms is instructive in this regard. As Michael Waibel explains, because the WTO panelists are appointed by the common agreement of the contending states (or by the WTO Secretariat), they are less ideologically polarized than investment arbitrators dealing with investor-state disputes are. The members of the permanent WTO Appellate Body, in turn, are selected by governmental consensus. Such members also exhibit a lower degree of polarization than arbitrators do. While the latter may attach more or less importance to investor protection depending on whether they have been nominated by the investor or by the host state, the members of the WTO dispute resolution bodies cannot easily be separated into "pro-trade" or "protectionist" ideologies.[70]

Indeed, in other international settings, it is also the case that political branches are empowered to select the members of permanent tribunals, and there is no reason to believe that the jurisprudence emanating from such tribunals is generally titled in favor of governments. In the case of the European Court of Human Rights, for example, only the governments (together with the Parliamentary Assembly of the

69 Some observers have answered in the affirmative. Nikos Lavranos, for example, has written that "obviously, there is a high risk that States will create a pro-State biased body, which will not gain the trust of investors." See Nikos Lavranos, "How the European Commission and the EU Member States Are Reasserting Their Control over Their Investment Treaties and ISDS Rules," in Kulick (ed.), *Reassertion of Control over the Investment Treaty Regime*, p. 323.

70 Michael Waibel, "Arbitrator Selection. Towards Greater State Control," in Kulick (ed.), *Reassertion of Control Over the Investment Treaty Regime*, pp. 347–350. For a detailed analysis of this contrast, see Joost Pauwelyn, "The Rule of Law without the Rule of Lawyers? Why Investment Arbitrators are from Mars, Trade Adjudicators from Venus," 109 *The American Journal of International Law*, 761 (2015).

Council of Europe) have a say when it comes to designating the judges. The Court is a permanent institution whose members serve for a period of time (nine years). The persons who claim to be victims of human rights violations play no part in the selection of judges. Similarly, the members of the Iran-United States Claims Tribunal established in 1981 (following the hostage crisis) as a standing body to resolve various commercial claims between the United States, Iran and their respective nationals, are picked directly or indirectly by the governments. The tribunal consists of nine members, three appointed by each government, and three (third-country) members appointed by the six government-appointed members. The private parties that bring claims do not participate in the designations. These tribunals have performed quite well in dealing with human rights and private law rights, respectively. The fact that the governments have been responsible for recruiting the adjudicators has not resulted in a low level of protection of the relevant individual interests. The same should be true of standing investment tribunals.[71]

All things considered, there are sound grounds to favor the establishment of permanent investment tribunals. If we wish to facilitate democratic control, enhance diversity, and ensure a high degree of adjudicative consistency, a standing adjudicative body seems preferable.[72]

8.4 CONCLUSION

One of the noteworthy features of the investment treaty regime is that, in the absence of international courts hearing investment cases, arbitrators are expected to supply a consistent string of rulings to specify the very broad principles protecting foreign investors. The legitimacy of the system depends, among other things, on arbitration's ability to achieve consistency in the application of the relevant norms, in the service of legal certainty and equality. Arbitrators are conscious of their role in the construction of the law, and a culture of precedent has accordingly materialized. The radically horizontal character of existing arbitral arrangements, however, makes it difficult for arbitration to deliver the needed legal coherence. With regard to democratic checks on arbitral case law, treaty amendments and interpretive notes appear to be the most suitable avenues for the political branches to register their

[71] In order to alleviate potential concerns about pro-state biases, Bungenberg and Reinisch, *From Bilateral Arbitral Tribunals and Investment Courts to a Multilateral Investment Court*, p. 60, suggest that the investor and the respondent state could be allowed to appoint judges *ad hoc*, to be added to the permanent members of the court. This is an interesting proposal, which injects an arbitral element into an institution that is basically judicial in nature. But objectivity does not really require empowering the contending parties to make such designations.

[72] It is important, of course, to design permanent tribunals in such a way that states are prevented from stopping the tribunal's activity by failing to participate in judicial appointments. Although international courts have not generally faced this problem, the risks exists. Witness, for example, the recent crisis with the Appellate Body of the WTO, prompted by the United States' decision to block new appointments.

inputs in the interpretive process and for them to adjust the investment regime in the direction they deem right.

There is much to be said, we have concluded, for the constitution of permanent tribunals dealing with investment matters. It is very unlikely, however, that a global investment court will be built in the coming years. Permanent tribunals will probably be created under some specific treaties, but the replacement of arbitration will be a long and fragmentary process. For a long while, therefore, we will need to be thinking about the best ways to secure the coherence of arbitral jurisprudence and to open the latter to the scrutiny of democratic institutions.

9

Investment Treaty Arbitration, Regional Integration, and Fragmentation of International Law

The investment treaty regime we have studied so far is not detached from the rest of international law. It is part of a broad landscape that encompasses various institutional arrangements and branches of the law. In the first place, in some parts of the world supranational organizations have been created that help link the countries of a region in a fairly strong manner. Secondly, international law includes specific branches dealing with issues that may have implications for investment law. Human rights law is particularly important in this regard. States must respect the rights of investors, but they must do so in a way that complies with human rights standards (involving, for example, public health, the environment, fair labor standards, or the rights of indigenous peoples). How is this systemic coherence to be achieved? These are the themes we will explore in this chapter.

9.1 INVESTMENT TREATY ARBITRATION AND REGIONAL INTEGRATION

If a group of states constitute a regional organization whose goal is the establishment of a common market where goods, services, capital, and persons can move without discrimination on grounds of nationality, is it possible for two such member states to enter a bilateral treaty to protect investments?

This question has arisen with great force in the context of the European Union. The argument has been advanced that investment treaties between European Union member states contravene the principle that bans discrimination on grounds of nationality, which is a core principle of the Union. The Treaty on the Functioning of the European Union is quite explicit when it declares that, within the scope of application of the Treaties, "any discrimination on grounds of nationality shall be prohibited."[1] It seems to follow that it is not acceptable for two member states to grant the nationals of each other more rights than they extend to the citizens of other member states. Only a multilateral investment treaty ratified by all members would

[1] See article 18 of the Treaty on the Functioning of the European Union.

neutralize the objection based on equality. The Court of Justice of the European Union has not addressed this issue, however. In the *Achmea* case, the Court left unanswered the specific question that the German Supreme Court had raised concerning the compatibility of a BIT (concluded in 1991 between The Netherlands and the Czech and Slovak Federative Republic) with the prohibition of discrimination on grounds of nationality.[2]

A further question such investment treaties pose concerns their impact on the judicial architecture of the European Union. The Treaty on the Functioning of the European Union provides that "Member States undertake not to submit a dispute concerning the interpretation or application of the Treaties to any method of settlement other than those provided for therein."[3] This exclusivity clause certainly implies that the Court of Justice of the European Union has exclusive jurisdiction to settle disputes between member states, insofar as European Union law (totally or partially) governs such disputes. The clause does not imply the further consequence, however, that a controversy between an investor from a member state and the host government of another member state may only be adjudicated by European Union courts. The exclusivity clause does not automatically rule out investor-state arbitration.[4]

The worry, however, is that the centrality of the Court of Justice of the European Union as the supreme interpreter of European Union law will be undermined if arbitrators adjudicate such investment disputes. The reason is that arbitrators are not empowered to use the preliminary reference procedure to ask questions to the Court regarding European Union law. In the *Achmea* case, the Court insisted on its traditional position that arbitrators are not authorized to raise preliminary questions. The Court also noted that national judges can only exercise very limited checks on arbitral awards (if at all) when reviewing their validity. So national judges have limited opportunities to refer preliminary questions to the Court concerning the legal issues arbitrators may have dealt with. The Court therefore concluded that intra-European Union BITs are not in conformity with European Union law, since they jeopardize the full effectiveness of European Union law.

As discussed in Chapter 3, however, there is a sound argument that arbitrators ought to be permitted to use the preliminary reference mechanism. The Court should reconsider its case law, therefore, or the European Union treaties should be

2 See Judgment of 6 March 2018, C-284/16, *Achmea* case. In his Opinion delivered on 19 September 2017, Advocate General Melchior Wathelet had argued that intra-European Union BITs do not breach the principle of nondiscrimination on grounds of nationality. To support his conclusion, he relied on the Court's earlier case law upholding bilateral agreements between member states on double taxation (paras. 66–80).

3 See article 344 of the Treaty on the Functioning of the European Union.

4 Arbitral tribunals in several cases have so held. See, for example, *Eureko B.V. v. The Slovak Republic*, UNCITRAL, PCA case No. 2008–13, Award on Jurisdiction, Arbitrability and Suspension, 26 October 2010; and *Electrabel S.A v. The Republic of Hungary*, ICSID Case No. ARB/07/19, Decision on Jurisdiction, Applicable Law and Liability, 30 November 2012.

amended, in order to better link arbitration and European Union law. The centrality of the Court, and the effectiveness of European Union law, would then be preserved.

Beyond all these technical details, a deeper issue concerns the rationale of investor-state arbitration in the context of a supranational organization like the European Union. Is it really necessary to organize this type of arbitration when the relevant states have gathered together to give birth to a supranational political community? This question goes to the very foundations of international investment law.

As discussed in Chapter 7, there are good reasons to believe that foreign investors may sometimes need specific protection through international investment treaties, given the potential biases of local authorities. Is the situation different when investors operate in a supranational space like the European Union?

One might argue that the citizens who elect the members of the legislative assembly of a member state of the European Union are a fragment of a larger people that is committed to the well-functioning operation of the supranational organization. The Italian legislature, for example, is elected by a group of citizens (Italians) that are part of a more extensive group (Europeans) that do things together within the framework of the European Union. Spanish citizens, say, should therefore be less suspicious of what Italians do through their laws, since both Spaniards and Italians share a common identity as European citizens. This identity is based on the common values the Union is founded upon. Moreover, there is a supranational legislature (the European Union legislature) that constrains what national parliaments may do. This contributes to the trust among citizens coming from different countries. The question, of course, is whether this is sufficient. Are investment treaties still necessary, to overcome the limitations of the European Union project as far as biases against outsiders goes?

Similarly, when it comes to adjudicative procedures, one might contend that domestic courts are to be trusted when the rights of European Union investors are at stake. State courts do not work in isolation. They are part of a judicial network headed by a supranational (neutral) institution: the Court of Justice of the European Union. The members of this central court are nationals of the various countries that belong to the Union. Local biases are transcended in that body. Again, is this sufficient? Isn't international arbitration a more reliable method in comparison to adjudication by state judiciaries, no matter how strongly connected the latter may be to the Court of Justice of the European Union?

In the *Achmea* case, the Court of Justice recalled that the Union is based "on the fundamental premiss that each Member State shares with all the other Member States, and recognizes that they share with it, a set of common values." This justifies "the existence of mutual trust between the Member States that those values will be recognized."[5]

[5] See *Achmea* case, para. 34.

In spite of all the progress that has been made in Europe, however, it may be claimed that there is still room for arbitration to play a role to better protect foreign investors. Member states vary in terms of the reliability of their political and judicial structures. Maybe the Court of Justice of the European Union has gone too fast, when it has forced member states to dismantle the existing intra-European Union BITs? In this context, we discern again the tension between the "external strategies" and the "internal strategies" we discussed in Chapter 5. Because the construction of the European Union as a federal polity is incomplete, we may need to resort to external strategies to transcend national favoritism. But the more we rely on such strategies, the more we reinforce the expectation that national favoritism is at work in the domestic arena, in spite of the European project. There is no easy way out of this dilemma.

9.2 INVESTMENT TREATY ARBITRATION AND THE FRAGMENTATION OF INTERNATIONAL LAW

We now proceed to investigate the interactions between investment law and other branches of international law that safeguard basic values, including norms protecting the environment, public health, fair labor standards, and the rights of indigenous communities. "Human rights" is a broad category that can be understood to encompass many of these other values investment law must cohere with. The problems that arise in this context illustrate the "fragmentation" of international law, a phenomenon that has been closely studied and debated in recent years. It will be useful to say a few words about fragmentation to better understand the potential frictions between investment law and human rights law.

The fragmentation of international law has many faces. One of them relates to the legal system. International law is made up of a collection of rules and principles that are not organized in as structured a way as domestic law is.[6] Domestic legal systems normally include a constitution that occupies the top of the normative hierarchy. This constitution specifies, among other things, which organs have the power to create and modify legal rules. In the field of international law, in contrast, we encounter no such thing.

It is true that the United Nations Charter (which includes the Statute of the International Court of Justice) can be regarded as a sort of constitution of the world community, to the extent that it structures a set of international institutions holding legislative, administrative and judicial powers.[7] The Charter contains some rules that are relevant to the construction of a legal system – such as the rule prescribing

[6] See, generally, International Law Commission, United Nations, "Fragmentation of International Law: Difficulties Arising from the Diversification and Expansion of International Law." Report of the Study Group of the International Law Commission, finalized by Martti Koskenniemi, UN Doc A/CN.4/L.682, 13 April 2006.

[7] On the constitutional nature of the United Nations Charter, see Bardo Fassbender, *The United Nations Charter as the Constitution of the International Community* (Leiden: Martinus Nijhoff Publishers, 2009). There has been debate about the extent to which international law has undergone

that the obligations the Charter imposes on states have primacy over obligations arising from any other treaty (article 103 of the Charter). In addition, article 38 of the Statute of the International Court of Justice lists the sources of law that the Court is required to apply to adjudicate legal disputes: treaties, customs, and general principles. The Statute, however, does not establish any hierarchy between these sources, and experts disagree about how conflicts between different norms are to be resolved. No clear rule of priority applies when customs and treaties collide, or when contradictions emerge between different treaties.

The 1969 Vienna Convention on the Law of Treaties, for its part, lays down several criteria to resolve conflicts between treaties, but important problems are left without clear solutions. Things are relatively easy when the normative collision involves treaties with identical parties. There is a general presumption that the later treaty prevails over the earlier one. But what happens when the treaties in conflict have no identical parties? In the simplest situation, if A concludes a treaty with B, and A later concludes a treaty with C, which treaty is to be honored by A, if an incompatibility arises? Scholars have spent decades trying to work out a generally accepted set of criteria to answer this question, but no consensus has emerged.[8] Not surprisingly, the Vienna Convention supplies no plain answer to the problem.[9] According to Jan Klabbers, the fairly accepted proposition, at the end of the day, is this: "When confronted with conflicting treaty obligations, a state must simply pick and choose which one to honour, and compensate the party which loses out."[10]

International law is also fragmented from an institutional point of view. The United Nations, as the heart of the international community, has authority to deal with a wide variety of matters. But it is surrounded by a large number of institutions operating in specialized sectors (trade, finance, investment, labor, crimes, etc . . .). The General Assembly of the United Nations cannot effectively check and override the decisions of the specialized institutions, for it has no power to issue binding instructions. It can only make recommendations. We should recall that, at the domestic level, the "generalist" political branches can usually intervene to guide and counteract the policies implemented by administrative agencies. The fact that no such thing is possible on the international plane is problematic from

a process of "constitutionalization." For international law to acquire a constitutional status, it seems necessary for it to include some special rules that regulate and constrain the production of "ordinary" international law. The structure of the lawmaking process, moreover, must observe certain principles, such as separation of powers and democratic norms, and its products must respect fundamental rights. For a good discussion of the international landscape from a constitutional perspective, see Jeffrey L. Dunoff and Joel P. Trachtman, "A Functional Approach to International Constitutionalization," in Jeffrey L. Dunoff and Joel P. Trachtman (eds.), *Ruling the World? Constitutionalism, International Law, and Global Governance* (Cambridge: Cambridge University Press, 2009), pp. 3–35.

8 For a description of the diverse positions held by scholars, both before and after the Vienna Convention on the Law of Treaties was adopted, see Jan Klabbers, *Treaty Conflict and the European Union* (Cambridge: Cambridge University Press, 2009), pp. 49–112.

9 See International Law Commission, "Fragmentation of International Law," p. 118.

10 Klabbers, *Treaty Conflict and the European Union*, p. 227.

a democratic standpoint. As Armin von Bogdandy and Ingo Venzke explain, "the principle of democratic generality requires a thematic openness of the democratic process, one that makes it possible to take all perspectives into account." "This requirement rests on an understanding of the individual as a multidimensional human being who cannot be split into functional logics."[11] We thus need institutions capable of integrating the different specialized perspectives on international issues.

International fragmentation has repercussions, of course, on the internal organization of states. Different national officers (regulators, judges, legislators) are prone to interact with their national counterparts in specialized international forums, dealing with specific matters. These gatherings are sometimes rather informal and produce nonbinding law. Other times they are conducted through a stable institutional framework, and the force of the agreements reached is stronger. Anne-Marie Slaughter has written about the emergence of a "disaggregated state" to refer to this phenomenon.[12] There is still a unitary state that speaks with one voice, through ambassadors and ministers of foreign affairs at traditional conferences, but the state also speaks, and increasingly so, through the more specialized voices of experts that meet in global settings.

Given the legal and institutional fragmentation just described, it is not surprising that one of the key operating principles of international law directs adjudicators to seek a "harmonic interpretation" or "systemic integration" of the different branches of international law. Jurists must resort to interpretive devices to counteract the dangers of fragmentation. The values animating the diverse legal regimes are to be integrated into a consistent normative scheme. As the Study Group of the International Law Commission concluded, without the principle of systemic integration "it would be impossible to give expression to, and to keep alive, any sense of the common good of humankind, not reducible to the good of any particular institution or regime."[13]

The adjudicators in charge of resolving controversies under a specific regime of international law, such as investment law, are accordingly urged to read the applicable treaties consistently with other regimes, within the general framework of public international law.[14] Article 31(3)(c) of the 1969 Vienna Convention on the Law of Treaties is the master rule in this regard: it provides that in the interpretation of a treaty, there shall be taken into account "any relevant rules of international law

11 Armin von Bogdandy and Ingo Venzke, *In Whose Name? A Public Law Theory of International Adjudication* (Oxford: Oxford University Press, 2014), p. 134.

12 Anne-Marie Slaughter, *A New World Order* (Princeton: Princeton University Press, 2004).

13 International Law Commission, "Fragmentation of International Law," p. 244.

14 On this call for systemic coherence, see Pierre-Marie Dupuy, "Unification Rather than Fragmentation of International Law? The Case of International Investment Law and Human Rights Law," in Pierre-Marie Dupuy, Francesco Francioni and Ernst-Ulrich Petersmann (eds.), *Human Rights in International Investment Law and Arbitration* (Oxford: Oxford University Press, 2009), pp. 45–62; and Bruno Simma, "Foreign Investment Arbitration: A Place for Human Rights?", in Dupuy, Francioni and Petersmann (eds.), *Human Rights in International Investment Law and Arbitration*, pp. 573–596.

applicable in the relations between the parties." This article invites judges to develop a systematic style of interpretation. The plurality of values that international law preserves can thus be properly accommodated. Values must be construed in light of each other, and reasonable balances are to be struck. In this connection, the principle of proportionality, which can be regarded as a general principle of international law, becomes a critical tool when confronting clashes between relevant rights and interests.[15]

9.3 DO HUMAN RIGHTS CONVENTIONS HAVE A HIGHER NORMATIVE RANK THAN INVESTMENT TREATIES?

It is sometimes contended, however, that the solution to the conflicts between investment treaties and human rights conventions does not require a complex harmonic accommodation. The solution is easier, it is asserted: human rights conventions are to prevail over investment agreements, since they occupy a higher rank in the international normative hierarchy.[16] What arguments can be adduced in support of this hierarchical theory?

It may be claimed that human rights conventions explicitly recognize "rights," while investment treaties simply impose obligations on states and incorporate no explicit reference to the rights of investors. This linguistic contrast, however, is a superficial one. We must dig deeper to determine whether normative differences are really at work.

In defense of the hierarchical theory, it may be argued that human rights conventions embody rights that are linked to human dignity and thus have an intrinsic value, whereas investment treaties are of an instrumental character. This distinction may be connected to a further distinction some scholars have drawn between "fundamental rights" recognized by "constitutional international law," on the one hand, and "ordinary rights" granted by "ordinary international law," on the other.[17]

The contrast between human rights and the rights of foreign investors, however, is not a sharp one. As we discussed in Chapter 7, investment treaties are not to be primarily regarded as instruments to promote foreign investment, but as instruments to secure structural parity between foreign and national investors. To this end, the treaties embody norms guaranteeing foreign investors that they will not be

[15] On the status of the principle of proportionality as a general principle of international law within the meaning of article 38 of the Statute of the International Court of Justice, see Gebhard Bücheler, *Proportionality in Investor-State Arbitration* (Oxford: Oxford University Press, 2015), pp. 28–83. As Bücheler argues, the principle of proportionality is common to the major legal systems of the world, and is transposable to international law. The principle is actually employed when tribunals have to pass judgment on the legality of countermeasures, for example, or when a state invokes its right to self-defense. It figures prominently, moreover, in the jurisprudence of the WTO dispute resolution bodies.

[16] See, for instance, M. Sornarajah, *Resistance and Change in the International Law on Foreign Investment* (Cambridge: Cambridge University Press, 2015), p. 234.

[17] On this distinction, see Jan Klabbers, Anne Peters, and Geir Ulfstein, *The Constitutionalization of International Law* (Oxford: Oxford University Press, 2009), pp. 168–171.

expropriated without compensation, will not be treated arbitrarily, will not be denied the protection of judicial authorities, etc ... All these guarantees have an intrinsic value. They mirror fundamental rights often enshrined in national constitutions. Because of this connection, I argued, arbitrators should pay attention to the common constitutional traditions of well-functioning legal systems. By the same token, investment protections and international human rights overlap to a significant extent.[18] As Bruno Simma observes, "the ultimate concern at the basis of both areas of international law is one and the same: the protection of the individual against the power of the State."[19]

It is important to observe at this juncture that the typical BIT does not require the host state to open its economy to foreign capital. The more common practice, as Kenneth Vandevelde explains, is for the treaty to grant a right to establishment in accordance with the law of the host state. This means that the latter can lay down substantial restrictions on the establishment of foreign investments.[20] The central purpose of this kind of BIT, therefore, is to preserve the rights of investors, once the investment has been accepted in accordance with domestic law.

Furthermore, we should bear in mind that investment treaties typically apply, not only to future investments, but also to investments that have already been made. Actually, as Joost Pauwelyn has explained, one of the core objectives historically pursued by many BITs was safeguarding investment stocks committed long before the BITs were signed.[21] With respect to such assets, the treaties cannot achieve the purpose of encouraging capital flows. Their purpose is purely protective of the rights of investors. To be sure, a collateral effect of safeguarding current investments is that a signal is being sent to future investors that their investments will be held secure. But this collateral effect should not obscure the protective nature of the treaties, when they are applied to assets that had been invested long before the treaties were concluded.

In support of the hierarchical theory, it may be contended that the scope of protection of human rights conventions is different and wider than that of investment treaties. Human rights conventions protect any person within the jurisdiction of the state, whereas investment treaties only cover foreign investors (who are

18 Regarding property rights, for example, José Alvarez notes that they are included in twenty-one multilateral human rights treaties. See José E. Alvarez, *The Boundaries of Investment Arbitration. The Use of Trade and European Human Rights Law in Investor-State Disputes* (Huntington: Juris, 2018), p. 209.

19 Bruno Simma, "Foreign Investment Arbitration: A Place for Human Rights?," 60 *International & Comparative Law Quarterly*, 573 (2011), p. 576

20 Kenneth J. Vandevelde, "The Liberal Vision of the International Law on Foreign Investment," in C. L. Lim (ed.), *Alternative Visions of the International Law on Foreign Investment. Essays in Honour of Muthucumaraswamy Sornarajah* (New York: Cambridge University Press, 2016), p. 62.

21 Joost Pauwelyn, "Rational Design or Accidental Evolution? The Emergence of International Investment Law," in Zachary Douglas, Joost Pauwelyn, and Jorge E. Viñuales (eds.), *The Foundations of International Investment Law. Bringing Theory into Practice* (Oxford: Oxford University Press, 2014), pp. 40–41.

nationals of the relevant state parties). This difference, however, is not a profound one. It is true that the scope of application of investment treaties is technically narrower than that of human rights conventions. But this does not mean that these international instruments are detached from one another. We can view investment treaties as tools to strengthen from a specific angle the international guarantee of rights which human rights conventions seek to secure more broadly. As already mentioned, there is significant normative overlap. In the *Yukos* case, for example, similar issues concerning basic rights were handled in parallel proceedings by the European Court of Human Rights and investor-state arbitrators. Both the Court and the arbitral tribunal concluded that Russia had breached the rights of investors in that case.[22]

There are also mutually reinforcing ties between treaties in other contexts. Consider environmental protection. The government's adoption of stringent environmental regulations may certainly impinge upon the economic interests of investors. Doctrines need to be crafted specifying and qualifying the rights of investors in light of the imperative need to protect the environment. Sometimes, however, a harmonic relationship arises. Imagine the case of an investor who complains that the domestic authorities are not properly implementing the applicable environmental laws, as a result of which the investor is being harmed by the illegal antienvironmental activity of other businesses. Because the latter are not being stopped from damaging the environment, the value of the investor's property declines. Or take the case of companies that have invested in the renewable energies sector. If the domestic government wrongs them through an unwarranted regulatory change, the public interest in preserving the environment suffers as well. In situations of this sort, investment law and environmental law push in the same direction.[23]

All things considered, the hierarchical theory is not convincing. We cannot avoid the intellectual challenge of working out normative schemes to properly balance investment protections with human rights and other values. No easy hierarchy will do the job. In this regard, the Inter-American Court of Human Rights went too quickly in the *Sawhoyamaxa Indigenous Community* v. *Paraguay* case, when it seemed to suggest that the American Convention on Human Rights has a higher authority than the BIT between Paraguay and Germany, on the ground that the former "stands in a class of its own." The Convention is special, the Court argued, in that it "generates rights for individual human beings" and "does not depend entirely on reciprocity among States."[24] This statement was not really necessary to justify the Court's main holding in the case, since the Court also said, quite reasonably, that

22 See OAO *Neftyanaya Kompaniya Yukos* v. *Russia*, no. 14902/04, Judgment of 20 September 2011, and *Yukos Universal Limited (Isle of Man)* v. *The Russian Federation*, UNCITRAL, PCA Case No. 2005–04/AA 227, Final Award, 18 July 2014.

23 For a systematic analysis of both the frictions and mutually supportive links between international investment law and environmental law, see Jorge E. Viñuales, *Foreign Investment and the Environment in International Law* (Cambridge: Cambridge University Press, 2012).

24 Judgment of March 29, 2006, Series C No. 146, para. 140.

land restitution to indigenous people counts as a public interest justifying nationalization of property held by foreign investors. There was thus no collision between the Convention and the BIT. But the Court appeared to gesture toward an implausible hierarchical theory.[25]

9.4 IN SEARCH OF JURISPRUDENTIAL DIALOGUES AND INSTITUTIONAL COORDINATION

The fact that there is no hierarchy in favor of human rights conventions does not mean, of course, that arbitrators are not to take human rights very seriously when adjudicating differences between states and investors.

Arbitral practices are evolving in the right direction in this regard. For a long while, investment law and human rights law have been rather isolated from each other. They have been practiced by distinct epistemic communities, whose members have followed different career paths and have generated their own specific networks, conferences, courses, and journals. The normative contrasts between these two branches of international law are not as profound as they are sometimes said to be, as we have just seen, but such differences have been magnified as a result of the "socio-cultural distance" that has separated the two groups of experts, as Moshe Hirsch has pointed out.[26] The interactions between these legal communities are likely to increase in the future, especially as a result of the higher level of visibility that investor-state arbitration has reached in recent years. In this context, the growing number of instances where arbitrators refer to human rights documents is to be welcomed.

Arbitrators should certainly observe human rights norms, from which investment law cannot be unhooked. Arguments based on human rights can easily enter the conversation that develops before an arbitral tribunal. The host government, as well as the organizations that participate in the proceedings as *amicus curiae*, can appeal to human rights by way of justification of the public measures called into question by investors.

In a notable investor-state controversy triggered by a tobacco plain packaging law enacted by Uruguay, for example, the arbitral tribunal accorded great weight to the fundamental right to health when reasoning its way to the conclusion that such law did not breach the investment treaty invoked by the investors.[27]

It is critical to notice that the fact that the jurisdiction of an international tribunal is limited to the particular types of disputes that arise under a specific treaty does not

[25] For a criticism of the Court's judgment in this regard, see Pedro Nikken, "Balancing of Human Rights and Investment Law in the Inter-American System of Human Rights," in Dupuy, Francioni and Petersmann (eds.), *Human Rights in International Investment Law and Arbitration*, pp. 265–270.

[26] Moshe Hirsch, "The Sociology of International Investment Law," in Douglas, Pauwelyn and Viñuales (eds.), *The Foundations of International Investment Law.*, pp. 152–158.

[27] See *Philip Morris Brands Sàrl, Philip Morris Products S.A. and Abal Hermanos S.A.* v. *Oriental Republic of Uruguay*, ICSID Case No. ARB/10/7, Award, July 2016.

mean that the tribunal is only licensed to apply such treaty. The scope of the applicable law is broader.[28] As the WTO Appellate Body has held, international treaty provisions cannot be interpreted in a vacuum. The WTO agreements cannot be read "in clinical isolation from public international law," since they are part of a broad international legal order.[29] Similarly, arbitrators should be attentive to human rights norms, even if the latter are not explicitly referred to in the investment treaties.[30]

Of course arbitrators need to pay attention to the specific text of the investment treaty they are called upon to adjudicate. They must be careful when identifying the broader domain of applicable law that the investment treaty can be regarded to be part of. Arbitrators should also keep clear from rules of other branches of law that are fundamentally different and do not serve as useful analogies to construe investment principles.[31] Basic human rights, however, pertain to general international law. They are thus basic normative components of the law that applies to investment disputes.

If arbitrators do not take rights seriously into account, contradictions and tensions will emerge. If arbitrators fail to preserve human rights that clearly bear on a dispute, a domestic court may later refuse enforcement of the award, if legal grounds can be invoked to block its execution – such as public policy grounds. In the context of ICSID, local courts cannot deny enforcement of awards, as explained in Chapter 6, but problems may still arise. If the courts execute an ICSID award that is defective from a human rights perspective, the enforcement state could be sued for human rights violations before a regional court (such as the Inter-American Court of Human Rights, or the European Court of Human Rights, for example).

So we need jurisprudential coordination between investment law and human rights law. This coordination could be reinforced if procedures were available for arbitral tribunals to refer interpretive questions to human rights adjudicative bodies and agencies concerned with the protection of basic interests, such as the World Health Organization and the International Labour Organization. This connects with similar calls for institutional interactions of this kind in other spheres of international law. Several Presidents of the International Court of Justice, for example, in presenting annual reports of the Court to the General Assembly of the United Nations, have suggested the introduction of preliminary reference procedures that would allow the Court to answer interpretive questions regarding general

28 International Law Commission, "Fragmentation of International Law," pp. 28–29.

29 WTO Appellate Body Report, *United States-Standards for Reformulated and Conventional Gasoline*, AB-1996–1, WT/DS2/AB/R, adopted on 29 April 1996, p.17.

30 See Francesco Francioni, "Access to Justice, Denial of Justice, and International Investment Law," in Dupuy, Francioni and Petersmann (eds.), *Human Rights in International Investment Law and Arbitration*, pp. 71–77; and Clara Reiner and Christoph Schreuer, "Human Rights and International Investment Arbitration," in Dupuy, Francioni and Petersmann (eds.), *Human Rights in International Investment Law and Arbitration*, pp. 89–94.

31 Arbitrators need to exercise caution and rigor when borrowing norms from WTO law or the European Convention on Human Rights, for example. On this matter, see the detailed discussion in Álvarez, *The Boundaries of Investment Arbitration*.

international law raised by other courts and tribunals.[32] A procedure of this sort could be extended to other domains.

In the context of the WTO, for instance, the panel that decided the *Thailand-Cigarettes* case first consulted with the World Health Organization. The panel asked the latter to present its conclusions on certain technical issues, including the health effects of tobacco consumption.[33] Scholars have applauded this landmark case, which "opened the door to inter-organizational cooperation."[34]

Mechanisms of this type would certainly help enhance the consistency of adjudication in a world of fragmented jurisdictions. Thinking about the best procedures to enable investor-state arbitrators (and, in the future, investment courts) to interact with human rights bodies and other specialized institutions should be one of the important items on the agenda of future reforms.

9.5 CONCLUSION

The discussion in this chapter brings us to the conclusion that the legitimacy of investor-state arbitration does not only depend on the ability of arbitrators to produce a sufficiently consistent case law that the democratic branches can interact with and ultimately check. It also depends on the degree of coherence that obtains between the arbitral case law and the fundamental norms that govern other branches of international law, including human rights law. Although investment treaties are not hierarchically inferior to human rights conventions, they have to be read in the light of the latter to secure harmonic outcomes. The growing number of arbitral awards containing references to human rights norms is a welcome development. International investment law cannot be hermetically sealed from other departments of the law.

This chapter closes our discussion of investment treaty arbitration. We now shift to state-to-state arbitration.

[32] Henry G. Schermers and Niels M. Blokker, *International Institutional Law* (Leiden: Martinus Nijhoff Publishers, 2011), p. 497.

[33] WTO Panel Report, *Thailand-Restrictions on the Importation of and Internal Taxes on Cigarettes*, WT/DS/10/R, adopted on 7 November 1990.

[34] Valentina Sara Vadi, "Reconciling Public Health and Investor Rights: The Case of Tobacco," in Dupuy, Francioni and Petersmann, *Human Rights in International Investment Law and Arbitration*, p. 464.

PART III

State-to-State Arbitration

10

The Arbitral Foundations of International Adjudication

When states are involved in a dispute in the international sphere, they can take different paths to resolve it in a peaceful way. Among other things, they can try to negotiate an agreement, resort to arbitration, or send the case to an international court.

In this chapter and the next, we will study the differences between arbitration and judicial adjudication in this field and will explore the potential advantages of arbitration.

10.1 HISTORICAL OVERVIEW

It will be useful to first say a few words on the history of state-to-state arbitration, given the important part it played in the early stages of international law.[1] From a historical point of view, arbitration came first. The establishment of standing courts to resolve controversies between states was a later phenomenon: only in 1922 was the Permanent Court of International Justice inaugurated, under the aegis of the League of Nations. This tribunal was later replaced by the International Court of Justice (ICJ) when the United Nations was formed in 1945.

In ancient Greece, for example, it was typical for disputes between two cities to be referred to a neutral city, which would be in charge of appointing the arbitrators.[2] Most often, the arbitral tribunal comprised three persons, who would hear the arguments of the contending parties before issuing a reasoned decision. The

[1] For the history of state-to-state arbitration, see Jackson H. Ralston, *International Arbitration from Athens to Locarno* (Stanford: Stanford University Press, 1929); John Collier and Vaughan Lowe, *The Settlement of Disputes in International Law. Institutions and Procedures* (Oxford: Oxford University Press, 1999), pp. 31–39; J. G. Merrills, *International Dispute Settlement* (Cambridge: Cambridge University Press, 2017), pp. 88–92; Christine Gray and Benedict Kingsbury, "Inter-State Arbitration since 1945: Overview and Evaluation," in Mark W. Janis (ed.), *International Courts for the Twenty-First Century* (Dordrecht: Martinus Nijhoff Publishers, 1992), pp. 55–83; and Cornelis G. Roelofsen, "International Arbitration and Courts," in Bardo Fassbender and Anne Peters (eds.), *The Oxford Handbook of the History of International Law* (Oxford: Oxford University Press, 2012), pp. 145–169.

[2] Ralston, *International Arbitration from Athens to Locarno*, pp. 153–168.

award was usually deposited in the temples or at public places, so that citizens would have access to it. Similarly, political communities governed by the Roman Empire often arbitrated their disputes under the direction of the central authorities.[3]

In the Middle Ages, and in later periods, arbitration continued to be employed by states to settle their disagreements. The Pope, in particular, was often asked to intervene. In the context of medieval Christendom, his authority could hardly be contested. The efficacy of his pronouncements was reinforced by the fact that the relevant treaty often provided for excommunication as a sanction for failure to comply with the Pope's decision.[4] A famous controversy that was composed in this way was the dispute between Spain and Portugal regarding their territories in the New World. Pope Alexander VI issued an award tracing an imaginary line from one pole to the other to fix the division. In addition to the Pope, emperors and monarchs were also appointed as arbitrators. Typically, the awards made by these prominent figures were not reasoned. The Pope spoke *ex cathedra*, so he did not need to state the grounds for his decisions. The emperors and monarchs, in turn, did not deliver reasoned awards either, since they did not want that "the sufficiency of their reasoning should be called into question by people of lesser dignity in their eyes," as Jackson Ralston nicely put it in his classic study on international arbitration.[5]

The modern era of arbitration dates from the signing in 1794 of the Jay Treaty, the Treaty of Amity, Commerce and Navigation between the United States and Great Britain whose purpose was to resolve the many disputes that were still alive after Great Britain's formal recognition of American independence. Arbitration adopted a completely new form. Instead of selecting Popes, emperors or monarchs to adjudicate disputes, tribunals comprising experts in international law were set up. Arbitrators were tasked with the responsibility to decide cases in accordance with the rules of international law. The awards, moreover, were expected to be reasoned.

A clear separation was thus established between political and legal means of settling controversies. Arbitration developed and flourished as a dispute resolution mechanism of a legal nature. It took a while, however, for states to accept that a commission of jurists, not the head of a state, would rule on a disagreement. States were prone to think that referring a controversy to someone who was not the head of a state was offensive to their dignity.[6] In spite of this traditional inertia, the form of arbitration that finally became standard relied on independent legal experts. Such was the method chosen to adjust the *Alabama* controversy in 1871–1872, for example, a famous dispute concerning Great Britain's neutrality during the American civil war. The United States claimed that Britain had breached neutrality by not preventing vessels built in British yards from helping the southern states during the war. By way of the Washington Treaty of 1871, the United States and Great Britain agreed to

[3] Ibid., pp. 168–173.
[4] Ibid., p. 188.
[5] Ibid., p. 92.
[6] Ibid., p. 54.

establish an arbitral tribunal to adjudicate the controversy. The tribunal laid down a reasoned award based on the law. It found that Britain had indeed violated its obligations as a neutral and ordered the payment of around fifteen million dollars by way of compensation. Britain duly complied: the full sum was satisfied in British Treasury Bonds, and the American receipt was framed and hung in 10 Downing Street.[7] In some exceptional cases, states went so far as to choose domestic institutions (the Royal Geographic Society, for example, or domestic courts), to arbitrate international disputes.[8]

In the modern period, the promotion of arbitration was connected to international campaigns striving for peace among nations. It figured prominently on the agenda of the first peace conference convened at The Hague in 1899 on the initiative of the Russian Minister of Foreign Affairs. A Convention for the Pacific Settlement of International Disputes was concluded at the conference. By means of the Convention, the contracting powers agreed "to use their best efforts to insure the pacific settlement of international differences" in order to obviate recourse to force in the relations between states.[9] They declared arbitration to be the most effective and equitable way of resolving disagreements of a legal nature when diplomacy failed.[10] The Permanent Court of Arbitration was created at that time as the first global institution to oversee proceedings to resolve disputes. Among other things, it provided rosters of qualified arbitrators the contending parties could choose from.

The Convention was revised in 1907 at a second peace conference at The Hague. Shortly afterward, the Peace Palace was built (with the financial backing of Andrew Carnegie) to house the Permanent Court of Arbitration. The 1907 Convention (like the 1899 Convention) reflected the modern conception of arbitration. It defined arbitration as "the settlement of disputes between states by judges of their own choice and on the basis of respect for law."[11] The arbitrators, moreover, were required to reason their awards.[12] And the awards had to be read out in public sitting.[13]

It is worthy of note that British and American figures were among the historical leaders of the arbitration movement. As already mentioned, the origins of modern arbitration go back to the Jay Treaty of 1794. Decades later, international arbitration was strongly advocated by British and American lawyers and politicians. Randal Cremer, an influential British peace activist, devoted lots of energy to the cause of international arbitration, and was awarded the Nobel Peace Prize in 1903 in recognition of his efforts. President Theodor Roosevelt (in 1906) and secretary of state

7 Mark Weston Janis, *International Law* (New York: Wolters Kluwer, 2016), p. 124.
8 Ralston, *International Arbitration from Athens to Locarno*, p. 55.
9 See article 1 of the 1899 Convention for the Pacific Settlement of International Disputes.
10 See article 16.
11 See article 37 of the 1907 Convention for the Pacific Settlement of International Disputes.
12 See article 79.
13 See article 80.

Elihu Root (in 1912) also received the Peace Prize in large measure to celebrate their endorsement of international arbitration.[14]

Latin American countries, for their part, contributed significantly to international arbitration as well. Many conferences were held in the region to work for its promotion. Actually, they sought to enshrine state-to-state arbitration as a specific governing principle of American international law.[15]

So modern international arbitration was shaped by a combination of social, political, and diplomatic movements of various kinds that sought to stop the use of force in international relations. In practice, of course, the progressive development of arbitration did not eliminate violence altogether. European countries went to war in 1914, dashing the hopes of earlier generations. The United States, in turn, also refused to arbitrate important disputes, such as the grievances that led to the Spanish-American War of 1898.[16]

In spite of these failures, arbitration was included in a number of international agreements adopted later in the twentieth century, such as the 1928 Geneva General Act for the Pacific Settlement of International Disputes, the 1948 American Treaty on Pacific Settlement (Pact of Bogotá), and the 1957 European Convention for the Peaceful Settlement of Disputes, among others.

As we will discuss, arbitrators have exerted a considerable influence on the evolution of international law. Their decisions have relied on legal rules and principles whose specific content they have helped to define. In general, arbitrators have not searched for compromises between the positions of the contending parties. They have tried, instead, to identify the right legal answer to the issues raised in the cases.[17] The impact of arbitrators on the evolution of international law would not have been so relevant, had they simply tried to work out compromises between the positions advanced by the parties. It is interesting to observe, in this connection, that decisions *ex aequo et bono* have been rare in international adjudication.[18]

Of course the establishment of the Permanent Court of International Justice in 1922 and the International Court of Justice in 1945 eroded the preeminence arbitration had had in the past, since a new forum was opened up for the adjudication of disputes among states. Arbitration continued to be used nevertheless. Just to mention a couple of examples, Chile and Argentina agreed in 1971 to arbitrate the *Beagle Channel*

14 Mark Mazower, *Governing the World. The History of an Idea* (New York: The Penguin Press, 2012), pp. 81–93.

15 On the Latin-American initiatives in this field, see Ralston, *International Arbitration from Athens to Locarno*, pp. 141–149.

16 Janis, *International Law*, p. 127.

17 Hersch Lauterpacht insisted on this idea in his classic study, *Private Law Sources and Analogies of International Law (With Special Reference to International Arbitration)* (Hamden, Connecticut: Archon Books, 1970; first published in 1927), pp. 63–67.

18 Thus, although article 38(2) of the Statute of the ICJ grants the Court the power to decide a case *ex aequo et bono*, if the parties agree thereto, this option has never been chosen. See Andreas Zimmermann and Christian J. Tams (eds.), *The Statute of the International Court of Justice. A Commentary* (Oxford: Oxford University Press, 2019), p. 886.

dispute over the possession of certain islands. Interestingly, the arbitral procedure unfolded under the auspices of United Kingdom's Queen Elizabeth II. The arbitrators were all judges of the International Court of Justice. The tribunal ruled that the islands belonged to Chile, but Argentina rejected the ruling, which brought the two countries to the brink of war. After Pope John Paul II's mediation, an agreement was finally reached, which the Argentine people approved in a national referendum. Similarly, in 1986 and 1990, New Zealand and France resorted to arbitration to settle disputes regarding the sinking in a New Zealand port of the *Rainbow Warrior*, a Greenpeace vessel that had been used to protest French nuclear testing.

With all this historical background, let us now discuss the contrast between arbitration and litigation regarding disputes between states.

10.2 THE PRINCIPLE OF CONSENSUALITY IN INTERNATIONAL ADJUDICATION

The first idea to bear in mind when we enter the international scene is that the distinction between arbitration and litigation in court cannot be understood in the same way that distinction is drawn in the domestic sphere.

As we saw in Chapter 1, one of the crucial differences between arbitrators and courts at the domestic level has to do with consent. Courts, it will be recalled, are part of the machinery of the state. They exercise *potestas* – public power. This means, in particular, that for a court to be able to decide a controversy it is not necessary for the contending parties to agree to its jurisdiction. In contrast, arbitrators are not part of the state, and are accordingly not in a position to exercise public power. If they get the authority to issue a binding decision for the parties to comply with, this is because the parties have consented to that authority through the pertinent contractual instruments.

This foundational difference between arbitration and judicial adjudication disappears when we move to the international stage: the authority of both arbitral tribunals and courts is based on the consent of the states in dispute. Indeed, no international court has been instituted to settle controversies between states whose jurisdiction is detached from the consent of the parties. There exists no court endowed with "compulsory jurisdiction," if this expression is understood in a strict sense. The authority of an international court always derives from the joint agreement of the contending states.

Consider the International Court of Justice. The Security Council of the United Nations can take measures with respect to political conflicts that may endanger international peace and security, and is empowered to recommend the parties involved to refer the legal aspects of the disputes to the International Court of Justice.[19] The Court cannot adjudicate a controversy, however, unless the parties agree.[20] States can register their consent in different ways and at different moments.

19 See article 36(3) of the Charter of the United Nations.

20 See Zimmermann and Tams (eds.), *The Statute of the International Court of Justice. A Commentary*, pp. 199–203.

After a controversy arises, for example, the disputants may decide to refer the case to the Court through a special agreement. Alternatively, when a state institutes an action in Court, the respondent may accept the Court's jurisdiction, whether explicitly or implicitly. Another possibility is for states to consent to the Court's authority in advance. They can do so in a specific treaty, so that the Court is empowered to adjust any future difference arising under the treaty. Or they may confer jurisdiction on the Court by means of a more general treaty covering any dispute that may emerge in the future. Yet another possibility is for states to subscribe the so-called "optional clause": they can make a declaration to the effect that they consent to subject to the Court any future disputes that may involve any other state that has also subscribed the clause.[21]

The important point is that, one way or another, whether before or after the dispute has crystallized, the agreement of the relevant states is required for the Court to be empowered to adjudicate a controversy. Such consent, however, is not so easy to get. In general, states are inclined to circumscribe their consent to the adjudication of disputes that arise in connection with specific treaties, rather than become parties to general treaties on the peaceful settlement of disputes. And only about one third of the countries in the world have made declarations to accept the Court's jurisdiction.[22] Of the five permanent members of the Security Council, in particular, Russia (or the former Soviet Union) and China have never made such declaration, whereas France (in 1974) and the United States (in 1985) withdrew the one they had previously made. Only the United Kingdom has a declaration currently in force. Such declarations, moreover, usually include important reservations limiting their scope. Given the principle of consensuality, it is possible for a state to file a reservation in order to shield an act against international judicial review.[23]

Consent, of course, is also required in state-to-state arbitration. For arbitrators to be enabled to settle a controversy between two states, it is necessary for such states to have granted the arbitrators the relevant authority. States register their consent in advance or, most frequently, once the dispute has erupted. In practice, arbitration is usually grounded in a special agreement concluded by the parties after the controversy has arisen (even if the parties were already under a previous treaty commitment to arbitrate potential disputes).[24]

So, we can say, international courts have an arbitral foundation. Their authority flows from the consent of the parties, as is typically the case with arbitral tribunals. There are still important contrasts between international courts and arbitral tribunals, of course. Basically, courts are permanent bodies whose members are appointed by

[21] See article 36(2) of the Statute of the ICJ.

[22] More precisely, as of 1 April 2020, 74 states of a total of 193 United Nations member states have filed such declarations. See www.icj-cij.org/en/declarations.

[23] See, for instance, *Fisheries Jurisdiction (Spain v. Canada)*, Jurisdiction of the Court, Judgment, I.C.J. Reports 1998, p. 432.

[24] Gray and Kingsbury, "Inter-State Arbitration since 1945: Overview and Evaluation," p. 61.

political institutions, whereas arbitrators decide on an *ad hoc* basis and are selected by the contending parties. These differences are significant enough to raise the question about the potential strengths and weaknesses of arbitration in comparison to judicial adjudication. But a key difference that we noticed in the domestic arena (which has to do with the relevance or irrelevance of consent) vanishes when we enter the international domain.

Before we discuss the respective pros and cons of arbitration and judicial adjudication, we should first reflect on the principle of consensuality and the technical limitations and imperfections of international law that result from it.

10.3 THE NORMATIVE RELEVANCE OF STATE CONSENT IN INTERNATIONAL LAW

The big question is this: Why aren't things at the international level similar to the ways they are domestically? That is, why aren't there international courts whose jurisdiction does not stem from the consent of the parties to the controversy? Isn't international law primitive, to the extent that it has not transcended the arbitral foundations of adjudication? What normative values are being served by the current system?

In order to justify the existing legal arrangements, the principle of state sovereignty is often invoked. Because states are sovereign, it is argued, they can only acquire those obligations they have freely consented to. They can do so through a treaty, which establishes the reciprocal rights and obligations of the parties. They can also consent to a practice that eventually gives birth to a custom that has binding force. According to this theory, the principle of state sovereignty generates an additional consequence: not only is state consent necessary to create international norms imposing substantive obligations. Consent is also required to establish the jurisdiction of international courts. Due to their sovereignty, states can only be brought to a court if they have accepted its adjudicative authority. As James Crawford puts it, one of the "corollaries" of the sovereignty and equality of states, according to the prevailing constitutional doctrine of the law of nations, is that "the jurisdiction of international tribunals depends on the consent of the parties."[25]

This theory, however, is not persuasive. It cannot be the case that consent is the only source of international obligations. Powerful objections have been raised against the consent theory. This is not the place to discuss them in detail. It will be sufficient to mention some of them briefly.[26]

25 James Crawford, *Brownlie's Principles of Public International Law* (Oxford: Oxford University Press, 2012), p. 447.

26 For a thorough analysis of the limitations of the consent theory in different areas of international law, see Christian Tomuschat, "Obligations Arising for States Without or Against their Will," *Collected Courses of The Hague Academy of International Law*, Volume 241 (Dordrecht: Martinus Nijhoff Publishers, 1993), pp. 195–374. See, also, Martti Koskenniemi, *From Apology to Utopia. The Structure of International Legal Argument* (Cambridge: Cambridge University Press, 2005, originally published

First, it is commonly accepted that international treaties are binding on the states that have concluded them. The *pacta sunt servanda* principle prescribes that agreements must be honored by the relevant parties. Now, what is the foundation of this principle? We cannot say that it is located in consent, since this answer would generate an infinite regress problem. Why should parties honor the agreement that stipulates that agreements have to be honored? We must instead maintain that the *pacta sunt servanda* principle is valid as a matter of justice: it would indeed be unfair for a party not to comply with the obligations it has freely assumed through a treaty.

We need rules, moreover, defining the conditions under which an international treaty is valid. The duty to observe treaties only extends to those that are actually valid. Such rules, of course, must be external to the particular treaty whose validity is at stake. The rules may derive from customary norms, or they may be linked to unwritten general principles of law. It is true that the 1969 Vienna Convention on the Law of Treaties lays down rules on the validity of treaties, but the Convention is itself a treaty whose validity has to rest on external rules, and whose binding force, as a treaty, only extends to the states that have subscribed it. So the Vienna Convention alone cannot do all the work to sustain a legal framework that permits treaties to exist and gain force.

Second, international customs are considered to be binding when a general opinion emerges among states to the effect that a certain practice ought to be followed as a matter of law. Customs may be global, regional or local, so the states engaged in the practice can vary. Now, what criteria should the relevant states use to determine which practices ought to be followed? These criteria need to be external to state consent. It cannot be the case that states believe that a practice should be followed simply on the grounds that they so believe. Their opinion must refer to ideas of justice and fairness that are independent of their own consent.

How many states, moreover, must agree before a custom emerges? If consent were the only source of obligation, no custom could be created unless all the states in the relevant field agreed. But the unanimity requirement makes the development of international law very difficult. It seems more reasonable to take the view that it is sufficient for most states to agree on the binding character of a practice. This proposition, however, is at odds with the notion that a state is only bound by obligations it has consented to. A state, moreover, should not be allowed to be exempted from a custom on the grounds that it has withdrawn the consent it once expressed.

in Helsinki: Lakimiesliiton Kustannus, 1989). Koskenniemi distinguishes two patterns of justification that figure in arguments in international law. One pattern is "ascending," in that it centers on actual state behavior and assigns a key role to consent. The other is "descending," in that it begins with ideal notions of justice and fairness. While the ascending arguments run the risk of ultimately legitimating whatever states do ("apology"), the descending arguments run the opposite risk of postulating principles and rules that are disconnected from actual international practices ("utopia"). Not surprisingly, scholars and practitioners combine the two types of arguments, so the legal theories they produce are internally unstable, Koskenniemi observes.

The theory of consent regarding customs is also problematic when applied to new states. Should a state that comes into existence freely disregard any custom it does not wish to follow, in virtue of the fact that it did not have the opportunity to give its consent to the customs that were formed in the past? It is one thing for the many new states that have been brought to life after decolonization to help produce novel customs or qualify the existing ones through new practices.[27] It is quite another for a single new state to pick and choose which customary norms to abide by.

Third, it would be very counterintuitive to hold the view that a state is free to engage in aggression or genocide, for example, simply because that state refuses to recognize the norms that prohibit such conduct. The International Court of Justice has explicitly endorsed the category of peremptory norms of international law (*ius cogens*), which states cannot derogate from. Article 53 of the Vienna Convention on the Law of Treaties defines a peremptory norm of general international law as "a norm accepted and recognized by the international community of States as a whole as a norm from which no derogation is permitted and which can be modified only by a subsequent norm of general international law having the same character." The specific content of this normative category is contested, but it is common ground that it includes, at least, rules that prohibit aggression, slavery, genocide, apartheid, and torture.[28]

Actually, the Charter of the United Nations announces in article 2 certain principles (including sovereign equality, the duty to settle international disputes by peaceful means, and the duty to refrain from the threat or use of force against the territorial integrity or political independence of any state) that are binding on all states, regardless of their membership in the United Nations. Indeed, article 2(6) provides that "the Organization shall ensure that states which are not Members of the United Nations act in accordance with these Principles so far as may be necessary for the maintenance of international peace and security." This is one of the key features some scholars have highlighted in making their case that the Charter operates as the constitution of the international community.[29] Hans Kelsen had already drawn attention to the revolutionary character of the Charter in this regard. Writing a few years after it was adopted, Kelsen asserted: "From the point of view of existing international law, the attempt of the Charter to apply to states which are not contracting parties to it must be characterized as revolutionary. Whether it will be considered a violation of the old, or as the beginning of a new international law, remains to be seen."[30]

The centrality of consent is also problematic when it comes to global public goods, which can only be produced if all states cooperate. In many contexts, failure

27 On the reluctance of new states to accept existing norms of customary law and their preference for treaties as sources of rules, see Pierre-Marie Depuy and Yann Kerbrat, *Droit international public* (Paris: Dalloz, 2010), p. 295.

28 Crawford, *Brownlie's Principles of Public International Law*, pp. 594–597.

29 See Bardo Fassbender, *The United Nations Charter as the Constitution of the International Community* (Leiden: Martinus Nijhoff Publishers, 2009), pp. 109–115.

30 Hans Kelsen, *The Law of the United Nations. A Critical Analysis of Its Fundamental Problems* (London: Stevens & Sons Limited, 1950), p. 110.

to generate the relevant public good entails the infliction of unjust harms on others.[31] Preserving the planet against the risks of climate change is an obvious example. Rules need to be established to reduce the level of pollution of the atmosphere and mechanisms must be created to force all states to cooperate. Free riders will predictably invoke the consent theory – they will argue that they cannot be enjoined to respect limits they have not agreed upon. But this position is untenable, since others are made to suffer harms in an unjustified way.

Fourth, states wield power over the population that lives in their territory. For this power to be exercised in a legitimate manner, certain conditions need to be met. There are basic human rights, for example, that states must respect for the exertion of governmental power to be legitimate. If so, we have weighty reasons to envisage rules of international law that condition the exercise of state powers to a sufficiently high level of compliance with human rights standards. Whether a given state consents to such rules should be irrelevant, for such rules would establish the preconditions for legitimate state authority.[32]

Finally, there is a deeper problem with consent theory. The states whose consent is necessary must already exist, and the territorial and personal scope of their authority must be defined. We need rules of international law to determine whether or not a particular state exists, and to specify who is subject to its jurisdiction. We cannot maintain that each state is individually free to reject such rules. Without rules of this kind, the very possibility of valid consent is logically impossible. At the domestic level, freedom of contract presupposes a set of background rules identifying the persons who are capable of consenting. International law also needs background rules of this sort.[33] The principle declaring that states are "equal" in sovereignty, moreover, is a constitutional norm of the system whose validity cannot

31 See Mattias Kumm, "Sovereignty and the Right to Be Left Alone: Subsidiarity, Justice-Sensitive Externalities, and the Proper Domain of the Consent Requirement in International Law," 79 *Law and Contemporary Problems*, 239 (2016). According to Kumm, not all the negative externalities caused by states are justice-sensitive. Only those externalities that are justice-sensitive are relevant, in order to justify the existence of rules of international law that bind states without their consent.

32 Thus, Allen Buchanan, *Justice, Legitimacy, and Self-Determination* (Oxford: Oxford University Press, 2004), argues that we all have a natural duty to help ensure that everybody has access to just institutions of government that secure human rights. State governments facilitate compliance with this natural duty if they contribute to a system of international law that forces states to honor such rights. For a slightly different argument to reach similar conclusions, see Ronald Dworkin, "A New Philosophy for International Law," 41 *Philosophy & Public Affairs*, 2 (2013).

33 This claim is endorsed even by "realist" scholars who portray international relations as power struggles between states. Hans J. Morgenthau, for example, in his classic study, *Politics Among Nations: The Struggle for Power and Peace* (New York: McGraw-Hill, 2005, 7th ed., revised by Kenneth W. Thompson and W. David Clinton), asserts that some rules of international law "do not owe their existence to the consent of the members of the international community" (p. 318). He refers, in particular, to those rules that are "the logical precondition for the existence of a multiple-state system, such as the rules delimiting the jurisdiction of individual states." According to Morgenthau, "rules of this kind are binding upon all states, regardless of their consent." As he rightly notes, "their binding force does not affect the sovereignty of individual nations." "Indeed, it makes sovereignty as a legal concept possible."

hinge on individual consent. As Christian Tomuschat argues, "to assert that the principle of sovereign equality has been accepted by an individual State is a contention that has no real meaning, since sovereign equality is the core element of the constitutional framework which no State, acting individually, can reject."[34]

These and other objections that can be marshaled against the consent theory are powerful enough to open up space for the emergence of obligations that bind states regardless of their consent.[35] At the domestic level, it would be weird to imagine a legal system that made contractual consent the source of all legal obligations. There is room for freedom of contract in national legal orders, of course, but the law also sets out a large number of obligations that are not rooted in individual consent. Tort law, criminal law, tax law, for example, have no basis on contractual agreements. Actually, in past decades the field of private law has witnessed an expansion of nonvoluntary rights and duties.[36] International law would appear to be too idiosyncratic, if all the obligations it prescribed were taken to rest on the principle of consensuality.

In light of all this, sovereignty is not to be understood as a normative concept that is external and prior to international law. Sovereignty must instead be read to amount to the specific bundle of rights and duties states possess under international law. A state is sovereign in that it is not subject to the national law of any other state: it is only bound by international law. But there is no prelegal sphere of sovereignty that international law must recognize. As Bardo Fassbender argues, following in the footsteps of Hans Kelsen, the specific rights and duties that states hold "constitute" sovereignty; they do not "flow" from sovereignty as an external concept. Accordingly, sovereignty is neither "natural" nor static: "In a process that has placed ever more constraints on the freedom of action of states, its substance has changed, and will further change in the future."[37]

We should not lose sight of the fact that in actual practice the principle of consensuality has often been sacrificed in the name of competing values and interests, including the protection of minorities, human rights, political stability, and economic development.[38] The world has often been a better place as a result of such departures from the consent principle.

34 Tomuschat, "Obligations Arising for States Without or Against their Will," pp. 292–293.

35 It is important to note that the objections against the consent theory are compatible with a theory of international justice such as that of John Rawls, which derives the basic organizing principles from the hypothetical agreements that communities of the right kind ("decent peoples") would reach under a veil of ignorance. See John Rawls, *The Law of Peoples* (Cambridge, Massachusetts: Harvard University Press, 1999). The principles Rawls's theory generates impose a number of duties on states, including the duty of nonintervention, the duty to honor human rights, restrictions on the conduct of war, and the duty to assist other peoples living in unfavorable conditions that prevent their having a just or decent regime.

36 P. S. Atiyah, *The Rise and Fall of Freedom of Contract* (Oxford: Oxford University Press, 1979), p. 716.

37 Bardo Fassbender, "Sovereignty and Constitutionalism in International Law," in Neil Walker (ed.), *Sovereignty in Transition* (Oxford: Hart Publishing, 2003), p. 129.

38 For the view that states have never been as sovereign as most standard accounts of international law suggest, see Stephen D. Krasner, *Sovereignty. Organized Hypocrisy* (Princeton: Princeton University Press, 1999).

10.4 TOWARD COMPULSORY JURISDICTION?

Given the defects of the consent theory, it is reasonable to work in the direction of creating international courts with compulsory jurisdiction to adjudicate disputes between states. If the source of international law cannot be purely contractual, the foundation of international adjudication need not be exclusively arbitral.

Among other things, the introduction of a system of compulsory jurisdiction would level the playing field among states when controversies arise. Weak states would not need the consent of strong states to institute judicial actions against them. The authority of an international court could be invoked without having to negotiate the consent of the other party. Actually, as J. G. Merrills explains, the major difficulty in practice is to persuade states to accept the jurisdiction of the International Court of Justice, or of an arbitral tribunal. "Once that hurdle has been surmounted, the question of enforcement [of the judicial or arbitral decision] will normally not arise."[39]

International law has its own normative resources to endorse a strong criticism of the practical consequences that result from the consensual basis of the jurisdiction of courts. The Charter of the United Nations provides that members of the organization "shall settle their international disputes by peaceful means in such a manner that international peace and security, and justice, are not endangered."[40] It further specifies that "the parties to any dispute, the continuance of which is likely to endanger the maintenance of international peace and security, shall, first of all, seek a solution by negotiation, enquiry, mediation, conciliation, arbitration, judicial settlement, resort to regional agencies or arrangements, or other peaceful means of their own choice."[41] So states are under the duty to resolve their disputes in a peaceful manner, and a menu of possibilities is offered to them. There is an important mismatch, however, between this duty and the rules through which the duty is operationalized. The absence of courts endowed with compulsory jurisdiction makes it less likely that states will comply with that duty. Indeed, if no court exists in the background vested with compulsory jurisdiction to hear disputes, states are less pressed to work out peaceful and reasonable solutions to their differences.

In the domestic sphere, it would be considered very primitive for individuals to have to negotiate agreements with other individuals in order to subject the latter to adjudicative processes. The law introduces a measure of legal equality when it gives the weak party the right to go to court, no matter what the stronger party may prefer in this regard. And it is a basic principle of justice that no one can be a judge in his own cause. International law deviates from these general principles of equality and impartiality animating domestic legal systems. To this extent, international law exhibits notable imperfections. Instead of glossing over such

[39] Merrills, *International Dispute Settlement*, p. 121.
[40] Article 2(3) of the Charter of the United Nations.
[41] Article 33(1) of the Charter of the United Nations.

imperfections, we should be critical of them. We should struggle to bring international law closer to municipal law in this respect. As Hersch Lauterpacht wrote, "the more international law approaches the standards of municipal law, the more it approximates to those standards of morals and order which are the ultimate foundation of all law."[42]

To be sure, consent has sometimes played a critical role in the formation of federal states. The political units that at some point in history decided to get together and constitute a federation can be said to have consented, among other things, to the jurisdiction of the federal courts empowered to resolve controversies among them. The situation, however, is different from the one we encounter on the international plane. In the federal setting, consent may have been at work at the foundational moment, but its relevance tends to decline as the federation matures. Thus, the right to secession is not commonly accepted to be part of the constitutional rules of a federal polity. In the international context, in contrast, the force of the principle of consensuality in adjudication extends over time. States remain free to opt out of treaties setting up adjudicative bodies. The imperfections of international adjudication resulting from the principle of consensuality cannot be underplayed by pointing to the birth logic of federations by way of analogy.[43]

One of the objections traditionally advanced against the establishment of international compulsory jurisdiction points to the deficient character of substantive international law. The absence of a global legislative institution of the kind we find at the state level has been thought to militate against the idea of compulsory jurisdiction. But the objection is not persuasive. As Hans Kelsen eloquently argued in his writings, as well as in the Oliver Wendell Holmes Lectures that he delivered at the Harvard Law School in 1940–1941, the evolution of domestic legal systems indicates that courts precede legislation. "The obligation to submit to the decision of the courts long precedes legislation, the conscious creation of law by a central organ." "Within the individual states courts have for centuries applied a legal order which could not be changed by any legislator, but which developed, exactly like present-day international law, out of customs and agreements; and in this legal system custom was for the most part formed by the practice of the courts themselves." He concluded that "we have no reason to assume that international law will necessarily develop differently from national law."[44] In any event, international law

[42] Hersch Lauterpacht, *The Function of Law in the International Community* (Hamden, Connecticut: Archon Books, 1966; originally published by Oxford University Press, 1933), p. 432.

[43] The relevance of consent in federations is, of course, an intricate issue requiring a full-length treatment that cannot be offered here. For some thoughts on this matter, see Victor Ferreres Comella, "Does Brexit Normalize Secession?," 53 *Texas International Law Journal*, 139 (2018).

[44] Hans Kelsen, *Law and Peace in International Relations. The Oliver Wendell Holmes Lectures, 1940–41* (Cambridge, Massachusetts: Harvard University Press, 1942), p. 161. For an exposition of Kelsen's view on this matter, see Jochen von Bernstorff, *The Public International Law Theory of Hans Kelsen. Believing in Universal Law* (Cambridge: Cambridge University Press, 2010), pp. 191–224.

has nowadays reached a high level of complexity and density, so that the nonexistence of courts with compulsory jurisdiction appears to be particularly dysfunctional.

Actually, a great anomaly of international law is that while the International Court of Justice's adjudicative function rests on consent, the Court produces case law that is of cardinal importance for the development of international normativity ultimately binding on all states. There is thus an incongruity between the narrow basis of the Court's authority to settle a particular dispute, on the one hand, and the universal reach of the norms that emerge from the Court's jurisprudence, on the other. Indeed, an international tribunal's authority to originate norms is at odds with the traditional conception of adjudication rooted in consent. As Armin von Bogdandy and Ingo Venzke point out, traditionally the emphasis has been placed on the dispute-settlement function of international courts. From this perspective, they write, "the legitimacy of international adjudication has rested firmly on the parties' consent: consent to the court's jurisdiction, to the law to be applied, and in some situations even to the judges or arbitrators who are called upon to apply the law." But if we shift our attention to the role of courts in shaping the law, the consent theory runs into problems. "Drawing attention to international courts' lawmaking function challenges this classic narrative of legitimacy."[45]

So a variety of considerations should move us to favor the establishment of international adjudicative bodies armed with compulsory jurisdiction. Such bodies can only be formed through state action, of course. States are the relevant actors when it comes to building and maintaining institutions at the international level. As Bardo Fassbender explains, "international law does not protect the right to existence of any particular organization."[46] But this does not mean that, in the future, all states will have to agree before courts with compulsory jurisdiction can be brought to life. A broad coalition of states could succeed in creating such a court. This is not likely to happen any time soon, but it is not to be excluded in a distant future. It will certainly necessitate a legal revolution, since the current legal order undoubtedly links adjudication to the consent of the contending parties.[47] And difficulties will certainly arise when attempting to enforce judgments against recalcitrant parties. When disputants have previously agreed to refer their differences to a court, they are rather willing to accept and comply with its judgments. In a future scenario where a court can exert compulsory jurisdiction, in contrast, enforcement of its decisions is likely to encounter significant obstacles.

45 Armin von Bogdandy and Ingo Venzke, "The Spell of Precedents: Lawmaking by International Courts and Tribunals," in Cesare P. R. Romano, Karen J. Alter, and Yuval Shany (eds.), *The Oxford Handbook of International Adjudication* (Oxford: Oxford University Press, 2013), p. 519.

46 Bardo Fassbender, "The State's Unabandoned Claim to Be the Center of the Legal Universe," 16 *I. CON, International Journal of Constitutional Law*, 1207 (2018), p. 1210.

47 The establishment of a better system of international law to achieve justice may require taking steps that violate positive law. On this issue, Allen Buchanan, *Justice, Legitimacy, and Self-Determination* (Oxford: Oxford University Press, 2004), pp. 273–294.

Meanwhile, more modestly, an organization with a potentially global reach could be created, membership of which would require subjection to the jurisdiction of its court. When the United Nations was designed, for example, it would have been possible to stipulate that the states joining the organization would have to accept the jurisdiction of the International Court of Justice automatically. Actually, at the San Francisco Conference, the majority of the Committee of Jurists that submitted a draft of a Statute of an International Court of Justice was in favor of this rule.[48] The adoption of such a rule was not politically feasible, it turned out, but it would have been a move in the right direction, as Hans Kelsen and others suggested.[49]

Actually, some organizations already link membership to the submission to the authority of a specific court. At the global level, the Word Trade Organization requires states to accept the dispute resolution mechanisms it sets up. In the regional sphere, the Council of Europe makes acceptance of the jurisdiction of the European Court of Human Rights a condition for membership. The European Union also obliges member states to refer their disputes to European Union courts. It actually goes further and requires member states to join the European Convention on Human Rights and thus be subject to the jurisdiction of the European Court of Human Rights as an external tribunal. The Inter-American Court of Human Rights, for its part, has held that countries must exit the entire Inter-American system if they want to withdraw from the jurisdiction of the Court. That is, as far as the jurisdiction of the Court is concerned, states are free not to opt in, but once they have made the decision to opt in, they can only opt out if they leave the whole organization.[50]

It should also be mentioned that the International Court of Justice, by way of exception, has a limited compulsory power to adjudicate certain issues, though only of a marginal kind. The most relevant example concerns the ability of the Court to accept the request of a third state to intervene in the proceedings when it has an interest of a legal nature which may be affected by the decision in the case.[51] For the Court to allow a state to intervene, it is not necessary for the parties to the dispute to agree. Thus, while the dispute between A and B can only be adjudicated by the Court on the basis of their joint consent, the differences between these two states and a third-party intervener C, in contrast, can sometimes be decided by the Court even in the absence of consent by A and B. In practice, however, the Court has rarely extended intervention.[52]

48 Kelsen, *The Law of the United Nations*, pp. 522–523.

49 Hans Kelsen, *Peace Through Law* (Chapel Hill: The University of North Carolina Press, 1944), pp. 3–67.

50 See Karen Alter, *The New Terrain of International Law. Courts, Politics, Rights* (Princeton: Princeton University Press, 2014), p. 150. In this book, Alter offers an overview of current trends towards the formation of courts that possess "compulsory jurisdiction." This expression has to be understood in the limited sense that a state that wishes to join a given organization is bound to accept the authority of that organization's court to adjudicate disputes arising within its framework.

51 See article 62 of the Statute of the ICJ.

52 See Zimmermann and Tams (eds.), *The Statute of the International Court of Justice. A Commentary*, pp. 1686–1740.

Another indirect way in which the Court can address disputes that the parties have not consented to refer to it is through its advisory jurisdiction. The Security Council and the General Assembly (as well as other organs and specialized agencies) can request the Court to issue an advisory opinion on a legal question.[53] Such question may turn out to be related to an ongoing dispute between two states. Actually, the impact of the advisory opinion on the dispute may be such that the Court accepts that the states affected are entitled to appoint a judge *ad hoc*.[54] When the Court acts in this capacity, it does not settle the underlying controversy through a binding decision. Nevertheless, the Court makes its authoritative voice heard, and this may have practical consequences.

If more radical changes were introduced in the international field, and courts were finally instituted whose authority did not derive from the consent of the disputants, the distinction between arbitration and courts we are familiar with at the domestic level would reappear in the international arena. States could undertake to arbitrate a dispute, but they would do so under the shadow of courts, whose jurisdiction could be invoked by a contending party without the consent of the other. The fact that no such transformation has occurred shows the rudimentary nature of international law as a constitutional order, in spite of all the progress that has been made since the creation of the United Nations in 1945.

10.5 CONCLUSION

Arbitration has historically played a significant part in the adjustment of differences between states in the international sphere, since permanent courts were not created until the twentieth century. When courts were finally instituted, the arbitral foundations of state-to-state adjudication were not transcended. The consent of the disputants was still required for a court to be conferred the authority to settle a controversy through a binding decision. This requirement could make sense if all international obligations placed on states were grounded in individual consent. But, as we have seen, international law encompasses a set of rules and principles whose force cannot depend on the consent of each state. There is thus normative space for developing the argument in support of the establishment of international courts endowed with compulsory jurisdiction. The creation of such courts will not happen any time soon. It will take the political struggles and mobilizations of future generations working at the global stage to achieve that goal. Meanwhile, we should not validate and normalize the absence of compulsory jurisdiction. If we stand on the platform provided by national constitutional orders,

53 See article 65 of the Statute of the ICJ. See, for example, *Legal Consequences of the Construction of a Wall in the Occupied Palestinian Territory*, Advisory Opinion, I.C.J. Reports 2004, p. 136.

54 See, for instance, *Western Sahara, Order of 22 May 1975*, I.C.J. Reports 1975, p. 6. Morocco's application to appoint a judge *ad hoc* was allowed.

committed as they are to the rule of law and to the right of access to independent courts, we cannot help being critical of the imperfections of state-to-state adjudication. It is paradoxical that the same states that are internally committed to the rule of law and the fundamental right to judicial protection have been unable to project these values onto the international scene.

11

The Virtues and Limitations of State-to-State Arbitration

In the previous chapter, we have observed that the consent of the states involved in a dispute is necessary for courts and arbitral tribunals to get jurisdiction to settle it. So states have to make a decision whether to jointly agree to arbitration or to jointly agree to judicial adjudication, if they wish to have a third party resolve the controversy. What considerations may lead them to prefer one dispute resolution mechanism to the other? In this final chapter, we will explore the potential virtues of international arbitration, as well as its downsides and shortcomings.

It is important to note that international law gives states freedom to choose the means to settle controversies in a peaceful manner. As already mentioned, article 33 of the Charter of the United Nations includes a non-exhaustive list of procedures to resolve disputes, which states are free to draw from. Arbitration is one of them. In addition, article 95 of the Charter reinforces this idea when it provides that "nothing in the present Charter shall prevent Members of the United Nations from entrusting the solution of their differences to other tribunals [different from the International Court of Justice] by virtue of agreements already in existence or which may be concluded in the future."[1] The "Manila Declaration," adopted by the General Assembly of the United Nations in 1982, later reaffirmed the "principle of free choice of means" to settle international disputes.[2]

11.1 THE ADVANTAGES OF INTERNATIONAL ARBITRATION

What are the potential advantages of arbitration as a method to resolve controversies between states? They are basically the same advantages we have encountered earlier in the book when discussing arbitration in other spheres.

[1] This provision, however, is in some tension with article 36(3) of the Charter, which states that in making recommendations regarding procedures to settle disputes, the Security Council should "take into consideration that legal disputes should as a general rule be referred by the parties to the International Court of Justice." On this tension, see Hans Kelsen, *The Law of the United Nations. A Critical Analysis of Its Fundamental Problems* (London: Stevens & Sons Limited, 1950), p. 477.

[2] See first part, para. 3, of the Manila Declaration on the Peaceful Settlement of International Disputes, UN Doc A/RES/37/10, 68th plenary meeting, 15 November 1982.

The first strength of state-to-state arbitration is connected to specialization and expertise. The International Court of Justice may lack a sufficient number of judges who are experts in the particular branch of the law that needs to be applied to a given dispute. Most judges on the Court have a generalist background in international law. States may prefer to select a group of more specialized jurists to settle a complex controversy. It is worthy of note that the Court can form permanent chambers to deal with certain categories of cases.[3] A Chamber for Environmental Matters was thus created in 1993. No state ever requested that a case be adjudicated by it, however, so the Court decided in 2006 not to hold elections for a bench for the Chamber.

It makes sense, for example, that the World Health Organization Framework Convention on Tobacco Control refers to arbitration any future disputes concerning the interpretation and application of the Convention.[4] This international instrument covers a very specific technical field, so it is advisable to rely on specialized experts to resolve any controversies that may arise under it. Taxation is another area where international treaties invite specialization. Arbitration is in a better position than the International Court of Justice to offer specialized expertise in taxes.[5]

It is possible, of course, to create specialized permanent courts. Actually, two tribunals of that kind have been instituted with a global reach. One is the International Tribunal for the Law of the Sea. The other is the Appellate Body of the World Trade Organization, which has many features of a court. To a large extent, the establishment of these permanent tribunals is to be explained by the need to put adjudicative functions in the hands of specialized jurists. The judges of the International Court of Justice may be too generalist and thus insufficiently equipped to deal with controversies that emerge in specific branches of international law.

So if the controversy does not pertain to these two particular areas (law of the sea, international trade), and the disputants are of the view that the International Court of Justice is too generalist, they may be inclined to resort to arbitration. Only in this way will they manage to have specialized experts resolve the controversy.

It is worth noticing that since 1984 states have availed themselves of the possibility to submit a dispute to an *ad hoc* chamber of the International Court of Justice.[6] The composition of the chamber changes depending on the case. The parties may express their points of view to the President of the Court as to which judges should be selected. The Court decides on the appointments through a secret ballot. In practice, the choices of the parties are respected. As Pierre-Marie Dupuy and Yann Kerbrat explain, if the Court did not follow the suggestions of the parties, the latter

3 See article 26(1) of the Statute of the ICJ.

4 See article 27 of the Framework Convention on Tobacco Control.

5 On the need to strengthen international arbitration in this area, through international procedures that taxpayers should be enabled to trigger, see William W. Park, *Arbitration of International Business Disputes. Studies in Law and Practice* (Oxford: Oxford University Press, 2006), pp. 609–624.

6 See article 26(2) of the Statute of the ICJ. The Rules of the Court were amended in 1972 and 1979 to allow the parties to have a say in the composition of the chamber.

would then prefer to resort to an arbitral forum.[7] Actually, the first time this procedure was used, in a controversy between the United States and Canada, the disputants made it clear that if the composition of the chamber was not the one they wanted, they would withdraw the case and refer the dispute to an arbitral tribunal. Six cases have so far been dealt with by these *ad hoc* chambers. According to Eric Posner, the Court works better when it acts in this way, as an arbitration panel.[8]

It is also worth observing that some judges of the Court have occasionally been hired as arbitrators in different types of procedures, including state-to-state and investor-state arbitration. This reminds us of a similar practice we encountered at the domestic level. As we saw in Chapter 1, the laws in a number of countries allow sitting judges to arbitrate disputes. In recent years, however, the ever-increasing workload of the International Court of Justice has prompted a revision of the rules on the matter. As Abdulqawi Yusuf, President of the Court, explained in his 2018 speech before the United Nations General Assembly, under the new rules judges will only be authorized to arbitrate state-to-state disputes, not other kinds of controversies, and only if the circumstances of the particular case warrant it. Judges, moreover, will only be permitted to participate in one arbitration procedure at a time, and will have to decline to arbitrate if the state that nominates them is a party in a case pending before the Court, even if there is no connection between the two disputes.[9]

The second strength of arbitration has to do with the procedures that are employed to adjudicate controversies. As was mentioned in earlier chapters, arbitration offers flexibility: the parties can shape the procedures to be followed in each case in light of the particular type of dispute they confront. The same is true of state-to-state arbitration.[10] The International Court of Justice, in contrast, conducts procedures that were designed in advance in general terms, without having in mind the variety of controversies that might emerge between states.

One important aspect of procedural flexibility concerns the size of the arbitral tribunal. In litigation, the dispute will be heard by the fifteen judges of the International Court of Justice (unless the contending states request an *ad hoc* chamber to decide the case, as explained earlier). In arbitration, in contrast, the parties can select a small tribunal, typically comprising three or five members. According to Sir Robert Jennings, the deliberations among arbitrators are usually deeper and more fluent than those that unfold among judges of a full Court. Arbitrators tend to work as a team and take responsibility for drafting the award together.[11] The arbitral decision may also be delivered earlier than a judicial opinion would, as a result of this

7 Pierre-Marie Dupuy and Yann Kerbrat, *Droit international public* (Paris: Dalloz, 2010), p. 639.
8 Eric A. Posner, *The Perils of Global Legalism* (Chicago: The University of Chicago Press, 2009), p. 141.
9 See "Speech by H.E. Mr. Abdulqawi A, Yusuf, President of the International Court of Justice, on the Occasion of the Seventy-Third Session of the United Nations General Assembly," 25 October 2018, pp. 11–12, available at www.icj-cij.org/files/press-releases.
10 The arbitral procedures that are used in practice are often borrowed from the Hague Convention of 1907.
11 Sir Robert Jennings, "The Differences Between Conducting a Case in the ICJ and in an ad hoc Arbitration Tribunal – An Inside View," in Nisuke Ando, Edward McWhinney, and Rüdiger Wolfrum

cooperative spirit. On the other hand, a small arbitral tribunal is not as representative of world legal opinion as the Court is. This limitation is important when thinking about the legitimate sources of international case law, as we will see later.

The third advantage of arbitration is that the long-term relationship between the contending parties may suffer less if they refer the dispute to arbitrators than if they have recourse to a court. As we observed in Chapter 1, the social meaning of filing a lawsuit in court may be different than that of arbitrating a dispute. Arbitration, moreover, requires a certain degree of cooperation between the parties. Similar considerations apply in the international arena. The political relationship between two states is less likely to be damaged if arbitral proceedings are instituted, than if one of them sues the other before the International Court of Justice. According to James Crawford, one of the factors that explain state reluctance to resort to the Court is "the political fact that hauling another state before the Court is often regarded as unfriendly."[12]

In this connection, the confidentiality of arbitral proceedings may prove helpful. As is true in other settings, the default rule in arbitration is that hearings are confidential, while the opposite rule applies to the International Court of Justice.[13] As Christine Gray and Benedict Kingsbury explain, confidentiality makes states feel free when deciding which positions to take in their pleadings and oral arguments, without getting into the domestic political difficulties that the publicity of proceedings might give rise to.[14] The positions and arguments that states articulate in a confidential context tend toward reasonableness and moderation, thus reducing the risk of polarizing the international conflict. This observation is in keeping with the claim many theorists have made about the need for states to conduct diplomatic negotiations in secret in order to adjust differences. Democratic norms of transparency require final agreements to be made public and justified with good reasons, but the procedure leading to such agreements should not be fully open. A space is to be carved out for confidential talks to take place. As Hans Morgenthau wrote, "no government that wants to stay in power or simply retain the respect of its people can afford to give up publicly part of what it had declared at the outset to be just and necessary, to retreat from a position initially held, to concede at least a partial justice of the other side's claims."[15] Constitutional theorists, too, have emphasized the

(eds.), *Liber Amicorum Judge Shigeru Oda* (The Hague: Kluwer Law International, 2002), pp. 898–899.

12 James Crawford, *Brownlie's Principles of Public International Law* (Oxford: Oxford University Press, 2012), p. 732.

13 Article 46 of the Statute of the ICJ provides that "the hearing in Court shall be public, unless the Court shall decide otherwise, or unless the parties demand that the public be not admitted." In practice, the exception is rarely applied. See Andreas Zimmermann and Christian J. Tams (eds.), *The Statute of the International Court of Justice. A Commentary* (Oxford: Oxford University Press, 2019), pp. 1330–1342.

14 Christine Gray and Benedict Kingsbury, "Inter-State Arbitration since 1945: Overview and Evaluation," in Mark W. Janis (ed.), *International Courts for the Twenty-First Century* (Dordrecht: Martinus Nijhoff Publishers, 1992), pp. 63–64.

15 Hans J. Morgenthau, *Politics Among Nations: The Struggle for Power and Peace* (New York: McGraw-Hill, 2005, 7th ed., revised by Kenneth W. Thompson and W. David Clinton), pp. 552–553.

advisability of combining confidentiality and publicity at different stages of the process leading to the enactment of a constitution.[16]

There is yet another advantage to arbitration, which is specific to international law. It has to do with the fact that the International Court of Justice can only adjudicate disputes between states. The Statute of the Court is very clear when it provides that "only states may be parties in cases before the Court."[17] It follows that when the controversy involves an international organization, the Court has no jurisdiction to resolve it. Not even an entity like the European Union is conferred standing.[18] Only indirectly may the Court be asked to speak when a dispute arises between an international organization and a state: an advisory opinion can sometimes be requested.[19] But this is an imperfect alternative to the Court's contentious jurisdiction.

The fact that only differences between states may be adjudicated by the Court is increasingly dysfunctional, given the number and importance of international organizations. This limitation has been the object of sharp criticism.[20] In 1995, the President of the Court, Sir Robert Jennings, considered it an "extraordinary anomaly."[21] This feature of the Court was already criticized by some observers at the foundational moment. Hans Kelsen, for example, raised powerful objections against it.[22] More recently, Antonio Cassese has insisted on the need to reform the system and open up the contentious jurisdiction of the Court to intergovernmental organizations, "which should be allowed to submit to the Court disputes between two or more organizations or a dispute between one of them and a state (be it a member state or otherwise)."[23]

As a result of this limitation of the Court's jurisdiction, arbitration needs to be resorted to when international organizations are parties to disputes. The World Health Organization Framework Convention on Tobacco Control serves as an example, once more. Since regional economic integration organizations can become parties to the Convention, arbitration is the method that has been established to settle disputes that may arise under it. The Court is not available for these purposes, since its jurisdiction is confined to disputes between states.

16 For a discussion of this issue, see Jon Elster, "Clearing and Strengthening the Channels of Constitution Making," in Tom Ginsburg (ed.), *Comparative Constitutional Design* (New York: Cambridge University Press, 2012), pp. 15–30.

17 See article 34(1) of the Statute of the ICJ.

18 Crawford, *Brownlie's Principles of Public International Law*, p. 718, footnote 3.

19 Henry G. Schermers and Niels M. Blokker, *International Institutional Law* (Leiden: Martinus Nijhoff Publishers, 2011), p. 862.

20 For references to critics, see Zimmermann and Tams (eds.), *The Statute of the International Court of Justice. A Commentary*, pp. 673–676.

21 Cited in ibid., p. 683.

22 Kelsen, *The Law of the United Nations*, pp. 485–487.

23 Antonio Cassese, "The International Court of Justice: It is High Time to Restyle the Respected Old Lady," in Antonio Cassese (ed.), *Realizing Utopia. The Future of International Law* (Oxford: Oxford University Press, 2012), p. 244.

Of course, it is possible for a treaty to institute a specific court with the authority to resolve differences that affect states and international organizations alike. Thus, both the International Tribunal for the Law of the Sea and the World Trade Organization Appellate Body are empowered to adjudicate disputes that involve international organizations.[24] If no such specific court has been created in a given field, however, arbitration is the only option on the table.

11.2 THE SHORTCOMINGS OF ARBITRATION

The advantages discussed so far are the main strengths that arbitration exhibits on the international scene. There are some drawbacks to arbitration, however. In the first place, international arbitration shares some of the downsides of domestic arbitration when the parties fail to agree on the appointment of arbitrators. At the domestic level, arbitral centers may be given the authority to nominate arbitrators, and in many countries courts can ultimately be reached to overcome the impasse. In the international arena, likewise, nominating institutions need to be resorted to. Possible candidates, among others, are the Secretary-General of the United Nations, the International Court of Justice, the Permanent Court of Arbitration, or another state. There is no judiciary in the background, however, whose assistance may be requested, unless the parties have so provided.[25]

Secondly, there is a minor disadvantage that arbitration exhibits, in terms of finality. While it is not possible to challenge the decision of an international court on the ground that the court has overstepped the limits of its authority, it is possible to contest an arbitral award on such ground. The parties, however, very rarely bestow upon the International Court of Justice the power to review arbitral awards.[26] As a result, nullity claims are handled diplomatically, which entails the risk that a party will refuse to recognize the validity of the award on the basis of legally worthless objections, thus depriving the award of legal force. As J. G. Merrills observes, "this is a serious practical weakness of inter-state arbitration."[27]

[24] See article 20(2) of Annex VI, as well as Annex IX, of the 1982 United Nations Convention on the Law of the Sea; and article 1 of Annex 2 of the WTO Agreement: Understanding on Rules and Procedures Governing the Settlement of Disputes.

[25] Interestingly, the 1971 Montreal Convention for the Suppression of Unlawful Acts against the Safety of Civil Aviation provides in article 14 that disputes that cannot be settled by negotiation shall be referred to arbitration, and if the parties cannot agree on the organization of the arbitration, the disputes may then be brought to the International Court of Justice.

[26] Sometimes they do. The International Court of Justice, for instance, in the *Case concerning the Arbitral Award made by the King of Spain on 23 December 1906*, Judgment of 18 November 1960, I.C.J. Reports 1960, p. 192, had to decide whether Nicaragua was right when it claimed that an arbitral award issued by the King of Spain in 1906 was invalid because the arbitrator had not observed the terms of the 1894 Treaty establishing its authority. In another case, *Arbitral Award of 31 July 1989*, Judgment, I. C.J. Reports 1991, p. 53, the Court was asked to review an arbitral award challenged by Guinea-Bissau.

[27] J. G. Merrills, *International Dispute Settlement* (Cambridge: Cambridge University Press, 2017), p. 122. It is worth mentioning that proposals were made at the second Hague Conference of 1907 in order to

Thirdly, when it comes to enforcement, an arbitral award is less protected than decisions of the International Court of Justice. The Charter of the United Nations grants the Security Council the authority to intervene in order to make recommendations or take measures to prompt a state to comply with a judgment of the Court. Although this mechanism has never been used effectively, it is there to cover the Court's decisions, not arbitral awards.[28]

Finally, international arbitration generates costs that the contending states must bear. The disputants have to pay the arbitrators, as well as the administrative staff tasked with managing the proceedings, for their services. The costs of running the International Court of Justice, in contrast, are charged to the United Nations budget.[29]

In spite of these downsides, arbitration incorporates a number of advantages (notably, in terms of the expertise and competence of arbitrators, procedural flexibility, and promotion of friendly relationships among states) that account for its attractiveness as a mechanism to compose controversies.

11.3 THE ARBITRABILITY OF *IUS COGENS*

An interesting question is whether states should be allowed to submit to arbitration those disputes that are governed by peremptory rules of international law (*ius cogens*).

By way of background, we need to note that the position of states when they negotiate treaties is (formally, at least) horizontal. Similarly to private individuals who interact with each other and reach agreements to pursue their respective interests, states meet on the international stage and conclude treaties to serve their interests. International law here operates as a "law of coordinated entities," as Hersch Lauterpach emphasized. Its function is similar to that of private law in the domestic field.[30] It is true that while individuals carry private interests, governments serve public interests. When different governments transact in the international domain, however, the public interests each of them speaks for are placed on the same plane.

establish a permanent court of arbitral justice with the authority to decide cases of alleged nullity of arbitral awards. According to Hersch Lauterpacht, the proposals failed because of Germany's opposition. See *Private Law Sources and Analogies of International Law (With Special Reference to International Arbitration)* (Hamden, Connecticut: Archon Books, 1970; first published in 1927), p. 209.

28 See article 94(2) of the United Nations Charter. The Security Council has never taken formal action in the rare instances brought before it. Nicaragua once requested the Security Council to ensure United States' compliance with a decision by the Court, but the United States exercised its veto power as a permanent member of the Security Council. For a discussion of article 94(2), see Zimmermann and Tams (eds.), *The Statute of the International Court of Justice. A Commentary*, pp. 252–263. It bears mentioning that, under the Covenant of the League of Nations, arbitral awards were treated similarly to decisions of the Permanent Court of International Justice: in the event of a failure to carry out an arbitral award or a judicial decision, the Council of the League had the power to propose what steps were to be taken to secure compliance. (See article 13 of the Covenant of the League of Nations.)

29 See article 33 of the Statute of the ICJ.

30 Lauterpacht, *Private Law Sources and Analogies of International Law*, p. 305.

The relationship is horizontal. As Lauterpacht put it, "however public and collectivistic may be the character of the State's activities on the international arena when judged from the point of view of persons composing the State, it is, from the point of view of the members of the international community, distinctly individualistic."[31]

By means of treaties, then, states channel the interests they represent, which they can dispose of as they see fit. They cannot, however, dispose of the interests of other states, or the interests of the international community as a whole. There are, indeed, peremptory rules of international law that must be respected by states, as already noted. International treaties, in particular, must observe such rules. Otherwise, the pertinent clauses are null and void.[32]

The question concerning arbitrability is thus similar to the question we confronted in Chapter 3, when we discussed the issue whether mandatory law in the private sphere is arbitrable. May arbitrators adjudicate disputes governed by mandatory rules (which the parties cannot contract around)? The tendency in most legal systems, as we saw, favors arbitrability of mandatory law in a number of fields. I argued, however, that arbitrability can only be justified if the forum and procedures chosen by the parties are reliable, in terms of the factual and legal accuracy of the decisions made through them. To this end, establishing some measure of judicial review of awards to control for violations of basic mandatory rules is warranted.

In the case of international law, a similar conclusion ought to be reached. Under current arrangements, the states cannot be sued before the International Court of Justice (or any other tribunal) without their consent, as we have repeatedly stressed. This means that, if a dispute were regarded not to be arbitrable because peremptory norms applied, the consequence would not necessarily be that the Court would hear the dispute. In the absence of consent to the Court's jurisdiction, the conflict would not be adjudicated at all. The Court has made clear that the fact that a dispute concerns the observance of a peremptory norm of international law is not a sufficient basis to establish the Court's jurisdiction.[33] This being so, arbitrability should not be barred. If arbitrators were disabled from ruling on controversies governed by *ius cogens*, an adjudicative gap would emerge.

Even if, in a distant future, the international legal regime were profoundly transformed and international courts were conferred compulsory jurisdiction to settle disputes between states, it would not be reasonable to automatically exclude the arbitration of *ius cogens* norms. Assuming the arbitral procedures were designed

31 Ibid., p. 82.

32 See article 53 of the Vienna Convention on the Law of Treaties.

33 See *Armed Activities on the Territory of the Congo (New Application: 2002) (Democratic Republic of the Congo v. Rwanda), Jurisdiction and Admissibility*, Judgment, I.C.J. Reports 2006, p. 6, para. 64. It should also be noted that article 66 of the Vienna Convention on the Law of Treaties provides that a party to a dispute concerning the application or interpretation of peremptory rules may unilaterally submit the dispute to the International Court of Justice for its resolution. This procedure has never been used so far. An important number of states (France, among them), has not ratified the Vienna Convention because it disagrees with this provision. Dupuy and Kerbrat, *Droit international public*, p. 323.

in the right way, there should be no reason to fear arbitrators would tend toward under-enforcement of such norms. Antonio Cassese, for example, has argued that the notion of *ius cogens* is so open-ended that states should be legally bound to submit to third-party adjudication those controversies that turn on its application. Although he prefers the International Court of Justice to adjudicate the issues so that a consistent body of case law can be produced, he is not against arbitrability. Whoever invokes *ius cogens* to support a legal claim, he writes, "must be prepared to submit to arbitral or judicial determination."[34]

The other side of the coin, of course, is that states cannot set aside peremptory norms when the go for arbitration. It is true that arbitration affords states great flexibility when it comes to specifying the law to be applied. While the International Court of Justice must decide in accordance with the sources of law listed in article 38 of its Statute (unless, of course, the parties ask the Court to decide the case *ex aequo et bono*), the parties in arbitration are free to determine the norms that adjudicators must use. There is a limit to this liberty, however: the application of peremptory rules of international law cannot be excluded by the parties. Consistently with this, making it possible for arbitral awards to be impugned before the Court for failure to properly apply *ius cogens* norms would be a reasonable institutional arrangement to set up. Judicial review could be limited, in that the Court might be authorized to control for clear mistakes only, as is often the case with domestic and international commercial arbitration. But a measure of judicial scrutiny would be appropriate.

11.4 ARBITRATION AND THE PRODUCTION OF CASE LAW

As we discussed in earlier chapters, a critical question concerns arbitration's contribution to the production of rules through case law. Courts, as we saw, do not limit themselves to resolving disputes in accordance with the law. They perform an additional function: they produce rulings that help clarify the meaning of the law and fill in the gaps. Arbitrators, in contrast, play a more modest part in the lawmaking process.

How does this idea fare in the international context? Interestingly, the role of case law is even more consequential in international law than in many areas of domestic law. Given the absence of a global legislature, international law is made up of many different pieces that result from the interactions among states. There are thousands of treaties, but no clear system of rules has been adopted stipulating which one prevails in the event of a conflict, as noted earlier in the book. Adjudicative organs are needed to contribute to putting some order on this front. Customs and general principles are also a source of international law, but

[34] Antonio Cassese, "For an Enhanced Role of *Ius Cogens*," in Cassese (ed.), *Realizing Utopia. The Future of International Law*, p. 169.

their content is not easy to ascertain. Guidance is to be provided through case law.

A fruitful dialogue between arbitrators and judges has developed over the years as part of the international lawmaking process. As was mentioned in Chapter 10, arbitrators deciding disputes between states have played a significant part in the evolution of international law, especially before courts were instituted. Their awards have not, of course, created any binding precedents. Nor have they been able to generate a consistent body of rules. The decentralized character of arbitration militates against this.[35] The International Court of Justice, however, has benefited from the legal constructions advanced by arbitrators. The general principles of law, in particular, were initially worked out by arbitrators. Among their relevant contributions, Pierre-Marie Dupuy and Yann Kerbrat mention precedents regarding the general principles on neutrality in times of war (*Alabama* case, 1872), the general features of territorial jurisdiction (*Island of Palmas* case, 1928), and the principle of proportionality as a limit to reactions against illegal acts (*Naulilaa* case, 1928).[36] In the *Island of Palmas* case, for example, the United States and The Netherlands appointed Max Huber as single arbitrator to settle their dispute. This prestigious professor, who later became the President of the Permanent Court of International Justice, rendered an award that is still a classical text on the acquisition of sovereignty.[37]

At the same time, arbitrators have felt the need to be consistent with the jurisprudence of the International Court of Justice, as well as that of other international tribunals in more specialized domains. Actually, they have tended to assign more weight to the Court's precedents than to arbitral precedents.[38] There is good reason for arbitrators to do so: the Court is more representative of world legal opinion, given its size and the global reach of the institutions that participate in the judicial appointments.[39] The Court is in a better position than arbitrators to speak for the international community and develop its basic norms.

So a constructive interaction has traditionally taken place between arbitrators and judges, and is likely to continue in the future. It is important to emphasize that the use of arbitration has not deprived the Court of the opportunity to clarify and develop the law through the adjudication of a sufficiently large number of relevant cases. There is no reason to believe that things will change in the years ahead.

35 See Alf Ross, *A Textbook of International Law. General Part* (London: Longmans, Green and Co., 1947), p. 87.

36 Dupuy and Kerbrat, *Droit international public*, p. 391.

37 Cornelis G. Roelofsen, "International Arbitration and Courts," in Bardo Fassbender and Anne Peters (eds.), *The Oxford Handbook of the History of International Law* (Oxford: Oxford University Press, 2012), p. 167.

38 See Gray and Kingsbury, "Inter-State Arbitration since 1945: Overview and Evaluation," p. 71.

39 The members of the ICJ are elected by the General Assembly of the United Nations and by the Security Council. See article 4 of the Statute of the ICJ. Article 9, in turn, provides that electors shall bear in mind that "in the body as a whole the representation of the main forms of civilization and of the principal legal systems of the world should be assured."

According to James Crawford, in the last quarter century, "the number of contentious cases before the Court has significantly increased, despite a number of disputes being referred to ad hoc arbitral tribunals."[40] The Court's ability to shape the general features of international law does not seem to be in jeopardy. Arbitral tribunals (and permanent courts) are being resorted to in specific areas of the law, but the Court can discharge its essential function of developing the basic principles and concepts of international law, in addition to refining the more specific rules that may apply in those areas that are not adjudicated by specialized bodies. Thus, when Rosalyn Higgins, acting as President of the Court, addressed the General Assembly of the United Nations in 2006, she explained that the different specialized courts and arbitral tribunals see "the necessity of locating themselves within the embrace of general international law." They regularly refer, often in a manner essential to their legal reasoning, to the judgments of the Court with respect to questions of international law.[41]

To a certain extent, the International Court of Justice's mission is reminiscent of that of national constitutional tribunals. The Court is there to supervise the general framework of the legal order, which is internally divided into specific branches of the law that are adjudicated by tribunals that have a narrower subject-matter jurisdiction. The Court has a view of the "universe" of international law, and not only of the "planets" occupied by specific regimes, to use the terms popularized by Bruno Simma and Dirk Pulkowski.[42]

Of course, the Court would play a still more important part than it currently performs if access to the Court were widened. In particular, proposals have been made to empower domestic judiciaries or other international tribunals to turn to the Court for preliminary rulings on issues of international law.[43] The relevant judges could thus ask questions to the Court to get guidance as to how to interpret international law to resolve particular disputes. This procedure would be similar in spirit to the procedure that national courts can employ in the context of the European Union. If a reform along these lines were implemented, the Court's docket would expand. Although the readiness of national courts to consult the Court would vary significantly depending on the country involved, the total number of cases would surely grow. This does not mean, however, that the current institutional architecture places the Court in a marginal position in jurisprudential terms.

With regard to the Court's ability to generate case law on international law, it should be noted that the Court is sometimes minimalist in its approach to legal

40 Crawford, *Brownlie's Principles of Public International Law*, p. 732.

41 Cited in Schermers and Blokker, *International Institutional Law*, p. 498.

42 Bruno Simma and Dirk Pulkowski, "Of Planets and the Universe: Self-contained Regimes in International Law," 17 *European Journal of International Law*, 483 (2006).

43 On such proposals, see Mark Weston Janis, *International Law* (New York: Wolters Kluwer, 2016), pp. 160–162.

issues. As Hersch Lauterpacht observed decades ago, the jurisprudence of the Court exhibits a clash of conflicting tendencies. On the one hand, the Court knows of its needed contribution to the evolution of international law and seems eager to offer a complete exposition of the reasons grounding its decisions. On the other hand, the Court cautiously keeps clear from elaborating general theories, since it is aware of its own fragility when confronting politically delicate issues, given the voluntary nature of its jurisdiction.[44] The Court thus practices Bickellian "passive virtues" when it faces politically sensitive questions.[45] A notorious example of the Court's reluctance in recent years to enter into controversial issues is furnished by the *Kosovo* advisory opinion.[46] The Court refused to address deep questions concerning the conditions under which secession may be justified as a matter of international law. It chose to limit itself to the narrow issue whether the unilateral declaration of independence by the provisional government in Kosovo was in breach of international law. As to whether Kosovo was entitled to secession, it said nothing.[47]

In addition, the Court has been unwilling to accept applications by third parties to intervene in judicial proceedings to protect their legal interests.[48] The Court has said that third parties are already protected by the fact that the effects of its judgments are restricted to the parties to the dispute.[49] Antonio Cassese has criticized the Court's attitude, which he considers to be reminiscent of traditional bilateral arbitral proceedings.[50] Martti Koskenniemi has observed in this connection that the Court has often preferred to "bilateralize" the law that governs a given dispute: "it has tended to base obligations rather on the specific relation between the disputing States than general rules."[51]

To the extent that the Court pursues minimalist strategies to avoid controversial issues, its capacity to produce general legal doctrines declines. This is unfortunate, particularly since arbitration can hardly compensate for this jurisprudential deficit.

44 Hersch Lauterpacht, *The Development of International Law by the International Court* (London: Stevens & Sons, 1958; reprinted by Grotius Publications, 1982), p. 155.

45 For the classic defense of the "passive virtues" of the judiciary, see Alexander M. Bickel, *The Least Dangerous Branch: The Supreme Court at the Bar of Politics* (Indianapolis: Bobbs-Merrill, 1962).

46 *Accordance with International Law of the Unilateral Declaration of Independence in Respect of Kosovo, Advisory Opinion*, I.C.J. Reports 2010, p. 403.

47 For a criticism of the Court's minimalism in its Kosovo advisory opinion, see Armin von Bogdandy and Ingo Venzke, *In Whose Name? A Public Law Theory of International Adjudication* (Oxford: Oxford University Press, 2014), pp. 187–188. For a detailed analysis of the opinion, see Pau Bossacoma Busquets, *Morality and Legality of Secession. A Theory of National Self-Determination* (London: Palgrave Macmillan, 2019), pp. 181–188.

48 Article 62 of the Statute of the ICJ allows for third-party interventions.

49 See article 59 of the Statute of the ICJ.

50 Cassese, "The International Court of Justice: It is High Time to Restyle the Respected Old Lady," pp. 242–243.

51 Martti Koskenniemi, *From Apology to Utopia. The Structure of International Legal Argument* (Cambridge: Cambridge University Press, 2005, originally published in Helsinki: Lakimiesliiton Kustannus, 1989), pp. 462–463.

11.5 ARBITRATION AND THE FAILURES OF INTERNATIONAL COURTS

We have observed, so far, that arbitration exhibits some strengths as a method to resolve legal differences between states, and that it contributes, however modestly, to the international law-making process. We should not believe, however, that arbitral tribunals are prone to succeed where international courts have failed.

Gary Born, for example, has compared two basic models of international adjudication.[52] "First-generation tribunals," as he calls them, are standing international courts with broad jurisdiction over classic-public international law disputes. The Permanent Court of International Justice, the International Court of Justice, and the International Tribunal for the Law of the Sea are prominent exemplars of this model. "Second-generation tribunals" are instead specialized bodies, usually constituted on a case-by-case basis, exercising relatively narrow jurisdiction over particular categories of international disputes. Examples include international commercial arbitration tribunals that decide controversies involving states or state-related entities; investor-state arbitral tribunals; claims settlement mechanisms, such as the Iran-United States Claims Tribunal; and the World Trade Organization dispute settlement bodies. Gary Born argues that second-generation tribunals have performed better than first-generation ones: they have decided more cases, and their decisions have generally been complied with, or have been effectively enforced.

This is an interesting contrast, but I would argue that the success or failure of these different bodies is not in a significant way a function of institutional design. Rather, it is a function of the nature of the matters to be adjudicated and the types of remedies the tribunals can shape. Second-generation tribunals have primarily operated in the areas of international investment and trade, providing relief in the form of monetary remedies and economic countermeasures. In contrast, first-generation courts were expected to deal with very politically sensitive issues for which such kind of relief would have been insufficient. It is easier to convince states to bring their trade disputes to the adjudicative bodies of the World Trade Organization, for example, and to have them comply with the decisions rendered by such bodies, than to convince states to refer a territorial dispute of vital importance to a judicial forum. It has been observed that the controversies the International Court of Justice usually resolves on the merits, through judgments that the parties tend to abide by, are border and diplomatic protection cases where the stakes are relatively low compared with the cost of conflict between two nations. When the stakes are high, in contrast, the parties are unwilling to resort to the Court.[53]

Actually, at the domestic level, history shows that securing the rule of law was a gradual process that started with private law before it extended to public law. To

[52] Gary Born, "A New Generation of International Adjudication," 61 *Duke Law Journal*, 775 (2012).

[53] See Tom Ginsburg and Richard H. McAdams, "Adjudicating in Anarchy: An Expressive Theory of International Dispute Resolution," 45 *William & Mary Law Review*, 1229 (2004).

simplify the story quite a bit, states were able at an early stage to pacify conflicts between private individuals through a legal system that included courts of compulsory jurisdiction. It took a longer period of time for the states themselves to be effectively subjected to the law. It was indeed a great challenge to construct an independent judiciary equipped with the tools to impose the law on public authorities. And even in this area, distinctions need to be drawn. Placing the bureaucratic branch of the state (the administration) under the law, and making that branch accountable before the courts, was typically a first step. A second, more difficult step, involved the establishment of constitutional constraints on the democratic branch (the government and the parliament). A successful constitutional judiciary has been hard to build. Still nowadays, avoidance techniques such as the "political questions" doctrine are sometimes invoked to bar the intervention of courts in sensitive issues. And academics disagree as to whether the judicialization of political conflicts under constitutional norms may end up unduly politicizing the constitutional judiciary.[54] The classical controversy in the 1920's between Hans Kelsen and Carl Schmitt on this issue is still alive, albeit in new forms, in contemporary constitutional democracies.[55]

It is small wonder, therefore, that some types of disputes in the international arena are more difficult to legalize and judicialize than others are. Indeed, before permanent courts were created, arbitration played a central role in the composition of differences between states, as was explained earlier. State-to-state arbitration was really "first" in generational terms. Yet, when the controversies involved politically delicate matters, states were often reluctant to resort to arbitration. A doctrine was developed that distinguished between legal and political disputes. The latter were considered to be non-justiciable. It was typical for governments and commentators to assert that controversies affecting "the independence, the honor, or the vital interests" of states were political. The underlying idea was that arbitrators (as well as courts) should only adjudicate minor matters. The important matters were to be left to international politics. ("De maximis non curat praetor.") This doctrinal construction had a weak theoretical foundation, but it served a legitimating purpose. States invoked that doctrine in order to rationalize their otherwise unacceptable decision not to bring certain differences to the pertinent arbitral forum.[56] This

54 For a critical view of judicialization, see Ran Hirschl, *Towards Juristocracy. The Origins and Consequences of the New Constitutionalism* (Cambridge, Massachusetts: Harvard University Press, 2007).

55 On this historical debate, see the texts collected by Lars Vinx, *The Guardian of the Constitution. Hans Kelsen and Carl Schmitt on the Limits of Constitutional Law* (Cambridge: Cambridge University Press, 2015). See also, David Dyzenhaus, *Legality and Legitimacy: Carl Schmitt, Hans Kelsen and Herman Heller in Weimar* (Oxford: Oxford University Press, 1997).

56 For a brilliant criticism of this doctrine, see Hersch Lauterpacht, *The Function of Law in the International Community* (Hamden, Connecticut: Archon Books, 1966; originally published by Oxford University Press, 1933), pp. 166–201.

chapter in the history of international adjudication illustrates the difficulty of subjecting to legal procedures controversies implicating the vital interests of states.

Probably Hans Morgenthau struck too pessimistic a chord when he wrote that "disputes that are most likely to lead to war cannot be settled by judicial methods."[57] But it is fair to say that when a controversy reflects the power struggles between two nations, international tribunals will face special difficulties. Arbitration can hardly succeed where permanent courts have failed.

11.6 STATE-TO-STATE ARBITRATION AND REGIONAL INTEGRATION

A final theme to consider concerns the respective roles of arbitral tribunals and regular courts when disputes break out among states that have come together to form regional organizations of a more or less supranational kind. If differences arise that are governed by the law of the regional organization, what kind of dispute resolution mechanism is relied upon?

There are many factors we need to take into account when gauging the depth of the integration achieved by the countries that have joined their efforts in a particular region. The presence or absence of a parliament directly elected by the people, for example, is a key feature to consider. In addition, whether decisions require the unanimous consent of the governments of the member states, or a qualified or simple majority is instead sufficient, is a crucial factor to bear in mind. The procedure the organization has established to resolve disputes between the member states is also an important aspect we should pay attention to. Has a permanent court been built? If so, does it enjoy exclusive jurisdiction, or are states entitled to choose other forums instead?

We can easily appreciate the relevance of these questions when we reflect upon the structures that have been designed in various places, at different historical times.

In the United States, for example, the institution of federal courts to adjudicate controversies between states in accordance with the Constitution was an important component of the stronger union that Americans decided to establish after the failure of the Confederation. While conflicts between states within the framework of the Articles of Confederation were resolved through arbitration, it was federal courts that were to settle disputes under the new federal Constitution.[58]

In the case of the European Union, the centrality of its Court of Justice is often emphasized by those who insist on the supranational character of the Union. Again,

[57] Morgenthau, *Politics Among Nations: The Struggle for Power and Peace*, p. 454.

[58] Compare article IX of the Articles of Confederation with article III of the United States Constitution. Under the Articles of Confederation, one controversy was arbitrated: it concerned a dispute that arose in 1782 between Pennsylvania and Connecticut, each claiming the same territory in the Valley of Susquehanna River. See Jackson H. Ralston, *International Arbitration from Athens to Locarno* (Stanford: Stanford University Press, 1929), p. 190.

it is a central, "federal" court that is empowered to decide controversies between member states. As we discussed in Chapter 9, a provision in the treaty explicitly defines this power as exclusive: states are prohibited from resorting to other forums to settle disputes between them, if the disputes are governed by European Union law. Consequently, states cannot resort to state-to-state arbitration to adjudicate such legal differences.[59]

The American hemisphere's landscape displays great diversity of organizations. On one extreme of the spectrum, we find organizations that exhibit a low degree of supranationalism: They are very intergovernmental in character, they do not set up any central parliament, and they resort to arbitration in order to adjudicate disputes between states. NAFTA (North American Free Trade Agreement) is an example of this.[60] The arbitral procedure that is designed to settle controversies under NAFTA, moreover, is not exclusive: the World Trade Organization dispute resolution mechanisms may instead be chosen.[61] All this is also true of the United States-Mexico-Canada Agreement (USMCA) modifying NAFTA.[62]

On the other extreme, we encounter organizations that are patterned after the European Union model, such as the Andean Community (which includes Bolivia, Colombia, Ecuador, and Peru). A regional parliament elected by the people has been created, and a central tribunal, the Court of Justice of the Andean Community seated in Quito (Ecuador), has been set up to interpret and apply regional law to the controversies between states. Judges are appointed by the states through a unanimous decision, from slates of three candidates submitted by each state. They serve for six-year terms, and can be reappointed once. The court has exclusive jurisdiction over state-to-state disputes governed by regional law.[63]

In between, we find hybrid organizations that mix features of different models. MERCOSUR (an organization comprising Argentina, Brazil, Paraguay, Uruguay, and Venezuela) is an interesting example. A regional parliament has been established whose members are appointed by national legislatures or directly elected by citizens in the respective states. A standing tribunal is in charge of adjudicating differences between MERCOSUR partners, the Permanent Review Court (*Tribunal Permanente de Revisión*), which seats in Asunción, Paraguay. The members of this tribunal are called "arbitrators." Each state designates an arbitrator, and an additional arbitrator is appointed by common agreement. All of them serve for

59 See article 344 of the Treaty on the Functioning of the European Union. Thus, in its Judgment of 30 May 2006, *Commission* v. *Ireland*, C-459/03, the Court of Justice of the European Union found that Ireland had violated European Union law when it instituted arbitral proceedings against the United Kingdom, under the United Nations Convention on the Law of the Sea, to resolve a dispute that was partially governed by European Union law.

60 See Chapter 20 of NAFTA.

61 See article 2005, Chapter 20, of NAFTA.

62 See Chapter 31 of USMCA.

63 See article 42 of the treaty establishing the Court of Justice (*Tratado de Creación del Tribunal de Justicia de la Comunidad Andina*). In addition to the judicial function it exercises with exclusivity, the Court can act as an arbitral body. See article 38 of the treaty.

very limited terms: two years, in the case of unilaterally designated arbitrators, and three years, in the case of the arbitrator chosen by common accord.[64] No principle of exclusivity applies: the states can move to other forums to settle their disagreements under MERCOSUR law.[65]

So there is a large variety of institutional possibilities, as this quick look at the European and American landscapes reveals. The advantage of founding a permanent court with exclusive jurisdiction to adjust differences among states is that adjudicative consistency and the production of rules to implement the law of the organization can be better secured. The controversies erupting among states will be placed before that court, which will have the necessary raw material to construct a comprehensive jurisprudence. The court, moreover, will be aware that any future dispute involving other member states will be brought to it, so it needs to be careful when fixing its interpretation of the relevant law in the instant case.

All things considered, there seems to be a strong correlation between the "federalist" impulse to create strong supranational institutions, on the one hand, and the formation of permanent courts, on the other. While arbitration or something close to it is typically resorted to in relatively loose intergovernmental organizations, adjudication by a standing court seems necessary to signal that the organization is of a more supranational kind, maybe pointing in a federal direction. Somehow, a supranational parliament elected by the people, whose laws are directly binding on citizens, calls for the creation of a specific permanent court that is empowered to settle differences between member states. Instead of referring cases to arbitration (or to the International Court of Justice), a supranational organization is more likely to found its own court.

As Henry Schermers and Niels Blokker explain, states generally prefer to control policy-making in international organizations as much as possible. For this reason, "parliamentary and judicial organs are an exceptional phenomenon." "States are cautious in creating such organs which escape their direct control." In Europe, the establishment of the European Parliament and the Court of Justice of the European Union is "directly linked to the scope of the powers" attributed to the Union.[66] The creation of the Court of Justice evinces the degree to which the European Union has a federalist ambition. Arbitration, in contrast, appears to be more in keeping with international organizations of an intergovernmental character, which are less supranational than the European Union is.

In sum, the passage from arbitration to adjudication by specific permanent courts seems to be connected to the degree of constitutionalization of international organizations. The constitutional arrow points away from arbitration.

64 See article 18 of *Protocolo de los Olivos*.
65 See article 1(2) of *Protocolo de los Olivos*.
66 Schermers and Blokker, *International Institutional Law*, p. 495.

11.7 CONCLUSION

Overall, arbitration as a mechanism to settle differences between states under international law displays the same potential advantages it exhibits in other spheres. Given such advantages, there is good reason for states to have been accorded the possibility of resorting to arbitration to resolve their disputes, instead of litigating in court. Even if the law to be applied includes norms of a peremptory nature, arbitration is not to be excluded from the adjudicative menu. As is true of arbitration more generally, however, state-to-state arbitration can only make a modest contribution to the production of a consistent body of rules, although arbitration played a critical role in the development of international law before permanent courts were formed in the twentieth century. Arbitration, moreover, is likely to be transcended when an organization of a supranational sort is created and differences among member states need to be adjusted. The more strongly supranational the organization turns out to be, the stronger the impulse to erect a specific permanent court to deal with such differences.

Afterword

Throughout this book, we have explored various modalities of arbitration in a number of legal domains. Important differences have been noted. We have studied forms of arbitration involving disputes of a horizontal nature (private-law arbitration and state-to-state arbitration) and other forms that relate to controversies of a vertical character (investor-state arbitration). We have also paid attention to the presence or absence of courts in the background endowed with compulsory jurisdiction. While arbitrators dealing with domestic private law or international investment law do not operate in isolation, since local courts are otherwise empowered to handle cases, no such situation arises in the international sphere when states are in dispute. International adjudication, we have noted, retains an arbitral foundation, as no court can exercise jurisdiction unless its authority flows from the consent of the contending states.

We have also observed that arbitration has deep normative roots. In the private law sphere, arbitration is linked to the value of private autonomy. A constitutional regime based on liberal principles should create some room for arbitration to flourish. Constraints, however, are warranted in the name of public interests that are sufficiently weighty. In the case of investor-state arbitration, its central justification is tied to the need to neutralize the potential vulnerability of foreigners. This justification connects investment treaty law to equality and other values underlying human rights law. The protections that investors are afforded must be read in light of other values, however, and must be accommodated in a larger scheme that encompasses protection of public health, labor rights, indigenous rights, and the environment, among other important interests. In the sphere of international law, in turn, arbitration is an expression of the autonomy of states, which are free to choose the best means to settle their disputes in a peaceful manner. Ideally they should do so under the shadow of international courts endowed with compulsory jurisdiction. The latter have yet to be built, however, as we know.

Throughout the different chapters, we have discussed the potential virtues of arbitration in diverse settings. The specialization and procedural flexibility that arbitration makes possible tend to be regarded as advantages in many different areas. Confidentiality, in contrast, is a more problematic and controversial aspect of arbitration, and it is not a universal characteristic.

Along with the strengths of arbitration, we have assessed its weaknesses and limitations. Arbitration, in particular, is not designed to produce a coherent body of case law. Permanent courts that are hierarchically organized are better equipped to generate this public good. The institutional limitation of arbitration in jurisprudential terms is not problematic if regular courts are in place to formulate the pertinent legal rules. When no such courts are available, however, or when their role is very marginal, the shortcomings of arbitration raise concerns. In addition, democratic checks on arbitral jurisprudence become necessary, if arbitration comes to occupy the central position in the adjudicative domain.

As we reflect on the role of arbitration in our world, we discern some grave imperfections in current legal regimes. The popularity of international commercial arbitration, for instance, is partly the result of the need to transcend the local favoritism that domestic courts may be prone to engage in. The existence of this potential bias, of course, is something we should be worried about. International commercial arbitration is also preferred to litigation because, as we saw, the legal infrastructure that has been set up to facilitate international private transactions does not establish a level playing field. While the New York Convention of 1958 secures the enforcement of arbitral agreements and awards in an effective way, there is no similarly successful global instrument to protect choice-of-court agreements and foreign judicial decisions.

Arbitration is an extraordinary institution to study and reflect upon. On the one hand, it challenges us to construct a refined theory to justify its role and the constraints it ought to respect in the context of liberal constitutional democracies. On the other hand, arbitration tells us a lot about the flaws of our legal world, especially as we move from the domestic domain to the international stage. Legal and political transformations in the future are likely to have an impact on arbitration, leading to new normative conceptions and institutional configurations. Arbitration thus serves as a mirror to better understand the rest of the legal landscape it is inevitably part of.

Index

www.ingramcontent.com/pod-product-compliance
Lightning Source LLC
LaVergne TN
LVHW082319171026
850499LV00004B/98
* 9 7 8 1 1 0 8 8 4 2 8 3 9 *